Betty Crocker

the big book of cookies

Houghton Mifflin Harcourt
Boston   New York

General Mills

Editorial Director: Jeff Nowak

Publishing Manager: Christine Gray

Editor: Diane Carlson

Food Editors: Andrea Bidwell,
Catherine Swanson

Recipe Development and Testing:
Betty Crocker Kitchens

Photography: General Mills Photography
Studios and Image Library

Photographers: Andy Swarbrick,
Patrick Kelley

Food Stylists: Carol Grones,
Amy Peterson, Jerry Dudycha

Publisher: Natalie Chapman

Associate Publisher: Jessica Goodman

Executive Editor: Anne Ficklen

Editor: Meaghan McDonnell

Senior Production Editor:
Marina Padakis Lowry

Cover Design: Suzanne Sunwoo

Art Director: Tai Blanche

Interior Design and Layout:
Holly Wittenberg

Manufacturing Manager: Tom Hyland

**The Betty Crocker Kitchens seal guarantees
success in your kitchen. Every recipe has
been tested in America's Most Trusted
Kitchens™ to meet our high standards of
reliability, easy preparation and great taste.**

FIND MORE GREAT IDEAS AT
BettyCrocker.com

For consistent baking
results, the Betty Crocker
Kitchens recommend
Gold Medal® Flour.

Published simultaneously in Canada

For information about permission to reproduce selections from this book,
write to Permissions, Houghton Mifflin Harcourt Publishing Company,
215 Park Avenue South, New York, New York 10003.

www.hmhbooks.com

Library of Congress Cataloging-in-Publication Data:
Betty Crocker the big book of cookies.
    p. cm.
  Includes index.
  ISBN 978-1-118-17742-6 (pbk. : acid-free paper), ISBN 978-1-118-28852-8 (ebk.),
ISBN 978-1-118-28749-1 (ebk.), ISBN 978-1-118-28750-7 (ebk.)
1. Cookies. 2. Cookbooks. I. Title: Big book of cookies.
  TX772.B545 2012
  641.86'54—dc23
                          2011043309

Manufactured in the United States of America

DOC 10 9 8 7 6
4500443602

Cover photos: (clockwise) Baby Polar Bear Shortbread Cookies (page 93),
Chocolate-Marshmallow Pillows (page 262), Sugar Cookies (page 29), Pink Peppermint
Whoopie Pies (page 82), Pretzel Brownie Bars (page 226), French Macaroons with
Bittersweet Chocolate Ganache (page 132)

Dear Friends,

Baking cookies or eating cookies—which is more fun? Baking cookies fills your home with great smells that welcome family and friends, and decorating cookies fuels your family's creativity. But eating cookies is equally fun—each treat is a bit magical, turning an ordinary day into something special, when you eat one . . . or two! What else can deliver so much joy in such a small package?

Baking perfect cookies and bars isn't rocket science. With our top tricks and tips, you too can be a cookie-baking pro! From quick and easy no-bakes to adorably decorated holiday cookies, you'll find a recipe for every occasion. Just flip through the gorgeous photos of every recipe . . . and try NOT to let your mouth water!

Homemade cookies—the perfect gift for any occasion? Yes! What other gift is guaranteed to never be returned or re-gifted? Whether a simple "thank-you," a birthday gift for that hard-to-buy-for teen or even as an anniversary present, homemade cookies will be a hit every time. Delicious, for sure—but they also give an extra touch of your love and caring that purchased gifts just can't deliver. And don't miss the creative ways included inside for wrapping your cookies for gifting, whether you give just one or an entire batch.

Here in *Betty Crocker The Big Book of Cookies* you'll find cookies, brownies and bar recipes for any time you need to "bring something to share" or . . . when your sweet tooth strikes! There are cookie-jar favorites, contest-winning recipes and even several gluten-free recipes. Just be warned—these recipes are going to make you VERY popular!

Bake a batch and wait for the smiles!

Warmly,
Betty Crocker

Contents

Cookie Baking Success Secrets

What could be better than freshly baked homemade cookies? With the tips and tricks you'll learn here, you'll be baking them up in no time.

Use the Right Ingredients

- **Flours:** Stick to bleached or unbleached all-purpose flour for cookies and bars. Whole wheat flour can also be used, but only substitute it for one-third to one-half the amount of all-purpose flour called for in your recipe to prevent the cookies from becoming too dry. Skip bread and cake flours when making cookies. Bread flour causes cookies and bars to become tough, and cake flour causes cookies to be too delicate and fragile.

- **Sweeteners:** In addition to adding sweetness to cookies and bars, sweeteners also help brown and add tenderness to baked goods. Most recipes call for granulated white sugar or brown sugar or both, but other types of sweeteners like honey or maple syrup are used in specific recipes.

- **Leavenings:** Cookies usually call for baking soda and/or baking powder. They are not interchangeable, so be sure to use what your recipe calls for.

- **Fats and Oils:** Fats add tenderness and flavor to cookies and bars. For best results, use butter or, if the recipe calls for it, shortening. If you choose to use margarine, use only products with at least 65% fat. Any other spreads or reduced-fat products contain more water, resulting in cookies that are too soft, tough and puffy.

- **Eggs:** Eggs add richness, moisture and structure to cookies and bars. All the recipes in this book have been tested with large eggs. Egg product substitutes, made of egg whites, can be substituted for whole eggs, but the baked cookies and bars may have a drier texture.

Measuring Flour and Powdered Sugar

The correct amount of flour in cookie recipes can be critical to cookie success. To accurately measure flour (and powdered sugar), stir up the flour in your container to lighten any packing that has taken place. Lightly spoon the flour into a measuring cup; level off with the straight edge of a metal spatula or knife.

Softening Butter

If the recipe calls for softened butter, it's important to soften it correctly. If the butter is too soft, the dough will be too soft and cause the cookies to spread too much. Perfectly softened butter leaves a slight indentation when touched lightly, yet still holds its shape (with no melted spots). The best way to soften butter is to leave it at room temperature 30 to 45 minutes, as it will soften evenly. To soften in the microwave, remove the foil or wax wrapper. Place in a glass bowl or measuring cup, uncovered. Microwave ½ to 1 cup butter on High 15 to 30 seconds.

- **Liquids:** Liquids like water, fruit juice, milk or cream tend to make cookies crisper by causing them to spread more. Add only as much liquid as the recipe calls for.

- **Oats:** Quick-cooking and old-fashioned oats are interchangeable unless a recipe calls for a specific type. Instant oatmeal products contain other ingredients and flavors, so they should not be used as a substitute for oats in cookie recipes.

- **Nuts, Peanuts:** When nuts are called for in a recipe, you can substitute any variety of nut or peanuts. Nuts can become rancid, giving them an unpleasant, strong flavor that can ruin the taste of cookies. Always taste these items before adding them to a recipe; if they don't taste fresh, throw them out.

Not All Cookie Sheets Are Created Equal

Choosing the right cookie sheet can make all the difference in how your cookies bake up.

- A cookie sheet is a flat pan that may be open on one to three sides. If the sheet has four sides, cookies may not brown as evenly.
- Cookie sheets come in basically three types. Here's how cookies bake on each type:
  - **Shiny Aluminum with Smooth Surface:** These are the top choice for cookie bakers. They reflect heat, allowing cookies to bake evenly and brown properly. The recipes in this book were tested using these cookie sheets.
  - **Insulated:** These sheets help prevent cookies from turning too dark on the bottom. Cookies baked on these sheets might take longer to bake; the bottoms will be light colored, and cookies may not brown as much overall. Cookies may be difficult to remove from these sheets because the bottoms of the cookies are more tender.
  - **Nonstick and Dark-Surface:** Cookies baked on these sheets may result in cookies that are smaller in diameter and more rounded. The tops and especially the bottoms will be more browned and the bottoms may be hard. Check cookies at the minimum bake time so they don't get too brown or burn. Follow the manufacturer's directions; some recommend reducing the oven temperature by 25°F.
- Choose sheets that are at least 2 inches smaller (on all sides) than the inside of your oven to allow heat to circulate.
- Have at least two cookie sheets, so while one batch is baking, you're getting the next batch ready to go into the oven.

Bake a Test Cookie

Make sure your cookies will turn out perfectly by baking one cookie as a test first, to see the shape of the cookie before you commit to baking any more. That way, you can make adjustments to the dough before baking the rest of the batch.

- If test cookie spreads too much, add 1 to 2 tablespoons of flour to the dough.

- If test cookie is too round or hard, add 1 to 2 tablespoons of milk to the dough.

To Grease or Not to Grease?

Grease cookie sheets only if the recipe calls for it. Use shortening or cooking spray. Unless the recipe directs, do not use butter, margarine or oil as the area between the cookies might burn during baking.

If you are using nonstick cookie sheets, do not grease the pans. Cookies will spread too much on these pans if they are greased.

As an alternative to greasing, cookie sheets or pans can be lined with parchment paper or use a silicone baking mat, available at cookware stores.

Storing Cookies and Bars

- **Crisp Cookies:** Store at room temperature in loosely covered containers.

- **Soft and Chewy Cookies:** Store at room temperature in resealable food-storage plastic bags or tightly covered containers.

- **Both Types of Cookies:** Keep crisp cookies from becoming soft by storing them separately from soft, chewy cookies.

- **Frosted or Decorated Cookies:** Let cookies harden before storing. Place between layers of parchment or waxed paper, plastic wrap or foil.

- **Flavored Cookies:** Use separate containers to store different flavored cookies to prevent them from picking up flavors from the other cookies.

- **Bars:** Follow directions in specific bar recipes for the correct storage. Most can be tightly covered, but some may be loosely covered or refrigerated.

- **Freezing Cookies and Bars:** Tightly wrap completely cooled cookies and bars; label. Freeze unfrosted cookies up to 1 year and frosted/decorated cookies up to 3 months. Place in single layers in freezer containers, and cover with waxed paper before adding another layer. Do not freeze meringue, custard-filled or cream-filled cookies.

Top Tips for Perfect Cookies

1 Use completely cooled cookie sheets. Cookies will spread too much on sheets that are still warm.

2 Make cookies all the same size so they bake evenly. Spring-handled cookie or ice-cream scoops make evenly portioning the dough a breeze. Measure the volume of the scoop with water first to make sure it's the size your cookie recipe says to portion the dough by.

3 Bake cookies on the middle oven rack. For even baking, it's best to bake one sheet at a time. If you do bake two sheets at once, position oven racks as close to the middle as possible and switch sheets halfway through baking.

4 Check cookies at the minimum bake time and bake longer if needed.

5 Many cookies benefit by cooling on the cookie sheet a minute or two so they firm up and are easier to remove from the sheet.

6 Remove cookies from the cookie sheet using a flat, thin metal spatula. Cool as directed.

7 If cookies were left too long on the cookie sheet and are difficult to remove, put the cookies back into the oven for 1 to 2 minutes, and then remove them from the sheet. They should come off easily.

Sugar Cookies (page 29)

chapter one

cookie jar favorites

Chocolate and Caramel Compost Cookies

PREP TIME: 45 minutes **START TO FINISH:** 45 minutes   **2 dozen cookies**

¾ cup packed brown sugar

½ cup sugar

½ cup butter or margarine, softened

½ cup shortening

2 tablespoons coffee grounds from brewed coffee

1½ teaspoons vanilla

1 egg

2 cups all-purpose flour

1 teaspoon baking soda

½ teaspoon salt

1 bag (6 oz) semisweet chocolate chips (1 cup)

1½ cups slightly crushed rippled potato chips

1½ cups Cocoa Puffs® cereal

30 round chewy caramels in milk chocolate (from 12-oz bag), unwrapped, cut into quarters

1 Heat oven to 350°F. Spray cookie sheets with cooking spray. In large bowl, beat sugars, butter and shortening with electric mixer on medium speed until light and fluffy.

2 Add coffee grounds, vanilla and egg; beat on low speed until blended.

3 Add flour, baking soda and salt; beat until soft dough forms. Stir in remaining ingredients.

4 Onto cookie sheets, drop dough by ¼-cupfuls 2 inches apart. Bake 11 to 14 minutes or until light golden brown. Cool 4 minutes; remove from cookie sheets to cooling racks. Cool completely before storing in airtight container.

1 Cookie: Calories 260; Total Fat 13g (Saturated Fat 6g; Trans Fat 1g); Cholesterol 20mg; Sodium 190mg; Total Carbohydrate 33g (Dietary Fiber 1g); Protein 2g **Exchanges:** 1 Starch, 1 Other Carbohydrate, 2½ Fat **Carbohydrate Choices:** 2

Sweet Success Tip

These are the perfect cookies to use up your leftover potato chips, cereals, candies and even coffee grounds.

Chocolate–Banana Bread Cookies

PREP TIME: 1 hour 30 minutes START TO FINISH: 1 hour 30 minutes   **2½ dozen cookies**

1 cup semisweet chocolate chips (6 oz)

½ cup butter or margarine, softened

¾ cup mashed very ripe bananas (about 2 medium)

1 egg

1 pouch Betty Crocker sugar cookie mix

1 cup chopped walnuts

1 In medium microwavable bowl, microwave chocolate chips uncovered on High 50 to 60 seconds, stirring every 30 seconds, until melted and smooth; cool 10 minutes.

2 In large bowl, beat butter, bananas and egg with electric mixer on medium speed 2 minutes. Add cooled chocolate; beat 1 minute or until blended. Add cookie mix; beat on low speed 30 seconds or until soft dough forms. Stir in walnuts. Cover and refrigerate 30 minutes or until firm.

3 Heat oven to 375°F. Onto ungreased cookie sheets, drop dough by 2 tablespoonfuls per cookie about 2 inches apart (refrigerate any remaining dough until ready to use). Bake 10 to 12 minutes or until puffed and dry on tops (centers will be very soft). Cool 2 minutes; remove from cookie sheets to cooling racks. Cool completely before storing in airtight container, using waxed paper between cookie layers.

1 Cookie: Calories 160; Total Fat 9g (Saturated Fat 3.5g; Trans Fat 0.5g); Cholesterol 15mg; Sodium 75mg; Total Carbohydrate 18g (Dietary Fiber 0g); Protein 1g **Exchanges:** ½ Starch, ½ Other Carbohydrate, 2 Fat **Carbohydrate Choices:** 1

Sweet Success Tips

For the best banana flavor, use very ripe bananas. Very ripe bananas will be slightly soft with peels that are speckled and turning dark to almost black.

The butter, bananas and egg mixture may appear curdled after first 2 minutes of beating. Don't worry, the mixture will become smooth after the chocolate and cookie mix are added.

Chocolate Sundae-Cone Cookies

PREP TIME: 1 hour 20 minutes **START TO FINISH:** 1 hour 20 minutes   **2½ dozen cookies**

1 bag (11.5 or 12 oz) semisweet chocolate chunks (2 cups), divided

½ cup butter or margarine, softened

1 egg

1 pouch Betty Crocker chocolate chip cookie mix

1 cup white vanilla baking chips (6 oz)

4 sugar cones, coarsely crushed (about 1¼ cups)

½ cup dry-roasted peanuts, coarsely chopped

1 Heat oven to 350°F. In large microwavable bowl, microwave 1 cup chocolate chunks uncovered on High 1 minute to 1 minute 30 seconds, stirring every 30 seconds, until melted and smooth. Add butter; using spoon, beat until blended. Add egg; beat until combined. Add cookie mix; stir until soft dough forms. Stir in remaining 1 cup chocolate chunks and the vanilla baking chips. Gently stir in crushed cones just until combined.

2 Onto ungreased cookie sheets, drop dough by 2 tablespoonfuls per cookie; flatten tops slightly. Sprinkle with peanuts, pressing lightly into dough. Bake 8 to 10 minutes or until puffed and dry on tops (centers will be very soft). Cool 3 minutes; remove from cookie sheets to cooling racks. Cool completely before storing in airtight container.

1 Cookie: Calories 220; Total Fat 12g (Saturated Fat 7g; Trans Fat 0g); Cholesterol 15mg; Sodium 125mg; Total Carbohydrate 26g (Dietary Fiber 1g); Protein 2g **Exchanges:** 1 Starch, ½ Other Carbohydrate, 2½ Fat **Carbohydrate Choices:** 2

Sweet Success Tips

Sugar cones add crunchy texture, so they should not be finely crushed. To keep them coarse, crush by hand into about ½- to 1-inch pieces.

Because these cookies are loaded with extra goodies, after flattening tops, you may need to gently press dough together to keep them from separating during baking.

Brown Butter Sugar Snaps

PREP TIME: 1 hour 50 minutes START TO FINISH: 1 hour 50 minutes   4½ dozen cookies

¾ **cup butter or margarine**

1½ **cups all-purpose flour**

¼ **teaspoon baking powder**

¼ **teaspoon salt**

½ **cup granulated sugar**

½ **cup packed dark brown sugar**

1 **egg**

½ **teaspoon vanilla**
   Granulated sugar

1 Heat oven to 350°F. In small saucepan, heat butter over medium heat 4 to 7 minutes, stirring frequently, until deep nutty brown (watch carefully because butter burns easily). Immediately pour browned butter into large bowl; cool 10 minutes.

2 Meanwhile, in small bowl, stir together flour, baking powder and salt until blended; set aside. Add ½ cup granulated sugar and brown sugar to cooled butter; beat with electric mixer on medium speed 2 minutes or until well blended. Add egg and vanilla; beat on low speed until combined. Add flour mixture; beat until soft crumbly dough forms. Press together to form ball; divide in half.

3 On lightly floured surface, or between 2 sheets waxed paper or cooking parchment paper, roll out each dough half to ⅛-inch thickness. Using 2-inch cookie cutters, cut out dough into desired shapes, gently pressing together and rerolling scraps as necessary. Onto ungreased cookie sheets, place cutouts about 1½ inches apart. Sprinkle with granulated sugar.

4 Bake 7 to 9 minutes or until edges are light brown. Cool 2 minutes; remove from cookie sheets to cooling racks. Cool completely before storing in airtight container.

1 Cookie: Calories 50; Total Fat 2.5g (Saturated Fat 1.5g; Trans Fat 0g); Cholesterol 10mg; Sodium 35mg; Total Carbohydrate 7g (Dietary Fiber 0g); Protein 0g **Exchanges:** ½ Other Carbohydrate, ½ Fat **Carbohydrate Choices:** ½

Sweet Success Tips

Milk solids turn nutty brown on bottom of saucepan as butter browns. Watch carefully and stir with heat-resistant spatula to avoid burning. Although milk solids can be strained out if desired, if left in they add extra flavor and interesting appearance to cookies.

For a sparkly, crunchy top, sprinkle cutouts with sparkling sugar before baking.

Pecan Roll Cookies

PREP TIME: 1 hour START TO FINISH: 1 hour   2 dozen cookies

¼ cup plus 3 tablespoons butter or margarine, softened, divided

1 egg

1 pouch Betty Crocker sugar cookie mix

6 tablespoons (¼ cup plus 2 tablespoons) packed light brown sugar

⅔ cup chopped pecans, toasted*

GLAZE, IF DESIRED

3 tablespoons butter or margarine, melted

1 cup powdered sugar

¾ teaspoon regular or clear vanilla

1 to 3 tablespoons milk

1 Heat oven to 350°F. In large bowl, beat ¼ cup butter and egg with electric mixer on medium speed until blended. Add cookie mix; beat on low speed until dough is evenly moist and crumbly.

2 On cookie sheet covered with 17-inch piece waxed paper, place dough; press to flatten slightly. Top dough with second piece waxed paper. Roll out dough into 12×11-inch rectangle. Refrigerate 10 minutes; remove top sheet waxed paper. Spread dough with 3 tablespoons butter. Sprinkle with brown sugar; top with pecans.

3 Starting with long side, carefully roll up tightly; refrigerate 30 minutes. Cut log into ½-inch slices. On ungreased cookie sheets, place slices 2 inches apart, reshaping if necessary.

4 Bake 8 to 10 minutes or until light brown on bottom. Cool 2 minutes; remove from cookie sheets to cooling racks. Cool completely. In medium bowl, stir together 3 tablespoons butter, the powdered sugar and vanilla. Stir in milk, 1 tablespoon at a time, until smooth and consistency of thick syrup. Drizzle over cookies; let stand until set. To store, place waxed paper between cookie layers. Store in airtight container.

*To toast pecans, heat oven to 350°F. Spread pecans in ungreased shallow pan. Bake uncovered 6 to 10 minutes, stirring occasionally, until light brown.

1 Cookie: Calories 170; Total Fat 8g (Saturated Fat 3g; Trans Fat 1g); Cholesterol 20mg; Sodium 100mg; Total Carbohydrate 25g (Dietary Fiber 0g); Protein 1g **Exchanges:** ½ Starch, 1 Other Carbohydrate, 1½ Fat **Carbohydrate Choices:** 1½

Chocolate Chip Cookies

PREP TIME: 10 minutes **START TO FINISH:** 55 minutes **4 dozen cookies**

¾ cup granulated sugar

¾ cup packed brown sugar

1 cup butter or margarine, softened

1 teaspoon vanilla

1 egg

2¼ cups all-purpose flour

1 teaspoon baking soda

½ teaspoon salt

1 bag (12 oz) semisweet or dark chocolate chips (2 cups)

1 cup coarsely chopped nuts, toasted* if desired

1 Heat oven to 375°F. In large bowl, beat sugars, butter, vanilla and egg with electric mixer on medium speed, or mix with spoon, until well blended. Stir in flour, baking soda and salt (dough will be stiff). Stir in chocolate chips and nuts.

2 Onto ungreased cookie sheets, drop dough by rounded tablespoonfuls about 2 inches apart.

3 Bake 8 to 10 minutes or until light brown (centers will be soft). Cool 1 to 2 minutes; remove from cookie sheets to cooling racks.

To toast nuts, heat oven to 350°F. Spread nuts in ungreased shallow pan. Bake uncovered 6 to 10 minutes, stirring occasionally, until light brown.

1 Cookie: Calories 140; Total Fat 8g (Saturated Fat 3.5g; Trans Fat 0g); Cholesterol 15mg; Sodium 80mg; Total Carbohydrate 16g (Dietary Fiber 0g); Protein 1g **Exchanges:** 1 Other Carbohydrate, 1½ Fat **Carbohydrate Choices:** 1

Chocolate Chip Bars: Press dough into ungreased 13×9-inch pan. Bake 15 to 20 minutes or until golden brown. Cool in pan on cooling rack. Makes 48 bars.

Jumbo Chocolate Chip Cookies: Onto ungreased cookie sheets, drop dough by ¼ cupfuls or #16 cookie/ice-cream scoopfuls about 3 inches apart. Bake 12 to 15 minutes or until edges are set (centers will be soft). Cool 1 to 2 minutes; remove from cookie sheets to cooling racks. Makes 1½ dozen cookies.

Sweet Success Tip

For perfectly sized and shaped cookies, use a #70 cookie scoop.

Triple Chippers

1½ cups packed brown sugar

1 cup granulated sugar

1 cup butter or margarine, softened

1 cup shortening

2 teaspoons vanilla

2 eggs

3¾ cups all-purpose flour

2 teaspoons baking soda

1 teaspoon salt

1½ cups white vanilla baking chips

1 cup semisweet chocolate chips (6 oz)

½ cup butterscotch chips

1 Heat oven to 350°F. In large bowl, mix sugars, butter, shortening, vanilla and eggs with electric mixer on medium speed until creamy, or mix with spoon. Stir in flour, baking soda and salt. Stir in white, chocolate and butterscotch chips.

2 Onto ungreased large cookie sheet, drop dough by ¼ cupfuls about 3 inches apart.

3 Bake 12 to 15 minutes or until light golden brown. Cool 4 minutes; remove from cookie sheet to cooling rack.

1 Cookie: Calories 410; Total Fat 22g (Saturated Fat 11g; Trans Fat 1.5g); Cholesterol 35mg; Sodium 280mg; Total Carbohydrate 49g (Dietary Fiber 1g); Protein 3g **Exchanges:** 1 Starch, 2 Other Carbohydrate, 4½ Fat **Carbohydrate Choices:** 3

Double-Chocolate Cherry Cookies

PREP TIME: 1 hour START TO FINISH: 1 hour 4 dozen cookies

1¼ **cups sugar**

1 **cup butter or margarine, softened**

¼ **cup milk**

¼ **teaspoon almond extract**

1 **egg**

1¾ **cups all-purpose flour**

⅓ **cup unsweetened baking cocoa**

½ **teaspoon baking soda**

1 **cup quick-cooking oats**

1 **cup semisweet chocolate chips (6 oz)**

1 **cup dried cherries**

1 Heat oven to 350°F. In large bowl, beat sugar, butter, milk, almond extract and egg with electric mixer on medium speed until smooth. Stir in flour, cocoa and baking soda. Stir in remaining ingredients.

2 Onto ungreased cookie sheets, drop dough by rounded tablespoonfuls about 2 inches apart.

3 Bake 10 to 12 minutes or until almost no indentation remains when touched in center and surface is no longer shiny. Immediately remove from cookie sheets to cooling racks.

1 Cookie: Calories 110; Total Fat 5g (Saturated Fat 3g; Trans Fat 0g); Cholesterol 15mg; Sodium 50mg; Total Carbohydrate 15g (Dietary Fiber 1g); Protein 1g **Exchanges:** 1 Other Carbohydrate, 1 Fat **Carbohydrate Choices:** 1

Sweet Success Tip

Try using 1 teaspoon vanilla instead of the almond extract.

Spiced Chocolate Chip Cookies

PREP TIME: 1 hour 15 minutes **START TO FINISH:** 1 hour 15 minutes **5 dozen cookies**

1 cup butter or margarine, softened

1½ cups packed brown sugar

1 teaspoon vanilla

1 egg

2 cups all-purpose flour

1 teaspoon baking soda

1½ teaspoons ground cinnamon

1 teaspoon ground ginger

½ teaspoon salt

1 package (12 oz) semisweet chocolate chips (2 cups)

1 cup chopped walnuts

1 Heat oven to 375°F. In large bowl, beat butter, brown sugar, vanilla and egg with electric mixer on medium speed, or mix with spoon. On low speed, beat in remaining ingredients except chocolate chips and walnuts. Stir in chocolate chips and walnuts.

2 Onto ungreased cookie sheets, drop dough by rounded teaspoonfuls about 1 inch apart.

3 Bake 7 to 9 minutes or until light brown (centers will be soft). Cool 1 to 2 minutes; remove from cookie sheets to cooling racks.

1 Cookie: Calories 110; Total Fat 6g (Saturated Fat 3g; Trans Fat 0g); Cholesterol 10mg; Sodium 65mg; Total Carbohydrate 13g (Dietary Fiber 0g); Protein 1g **Exchanges:** 1 Other Carbohydrate, 1 Fat **Carbohydrate Choices:** 1

Rolling Cookies

On lightly floured surface, shape refrigerated dough (one-half at a time) into flattened round without cracks.

Using ruler or sticks as guide, roll dough ¼ inch thick.

Using cookie cutters dipped in flour, cut desired shapes.

Using a Decorating Bag

Insert coupler inside disposable pastry bag. (Cut end if necessary so coupler will reach tip of bag.)

Attach tip with ring; open bag, pulling opening far over hand and fill with frosting.

Squeeze and twist with even pressure to pipe frosting onto cookies.

Decorating Cookies

Colored Sugar: Sprinkle cookies with decorating sugar or decors before baking.

Frosted: Frost cookies and top with nuts, decorating sugar or decors. Or frost and drizzle dots of colored frosting or gel food color on top; use a toothpick to make designs.

Painted: Make egg yolk paints and paint cookies before baking.

Sugar Cookies

PREP TIME: 55 minutes START TO FINISH: 2 hours 55 minutes   5 dozen cookies

1½   cups powdered sugar
  1   cup butter, softened
  1   teaspoon vanilla
  ½   teaspoon almond extract
  1   egg
2½   cups all-purpose flour
  1   teaspoon baking soda
  1   teaspoon cream of tartar
      Granulated sugar or
      Colored Sugar (below)

1 In large bowl, beat powdered sugar, butter, vanilla, almond extract and egg with electric mixer on medium speed, or mix with spoon, until well blended. Stir in flour, baking soda and cream of tartar. Cover and refrigerate at least 2 hours.

2 Heat oven to 375°F. Lightly grease cookie sheets with shortening or cooking spray, or line with cooking parchment paper or silicone baking mats.

3 Divide dough in half. Roll each half on lightly floured surface until ¼ inch thick. Cut into desired shapes with 2- to 2½-inch cookie cutters. Sprinkle with granulated sugar. On cookie sheets, place cutouts about 2 inches apart.

4 Bake 7 to 8 minutes or until edges are light brown. Remove from cookie sheets to cooling racks.

1 Cookie: Calories 60; Total Fat 3g (Saturated Fat 2g; Trans Fat 0g); Cholesterol 10mg; Sodium 45mg; Total Carbohydrate 8g (Dietary Fiber 0g); Protein 0g **Exchanges:** ½ Starch, ½ Fat **Carbohydrate Choices:** ½

Colored Sugar: Place ½ cup granulated sugar in resealable food-storage plastic bag. Add liquid food color to tint as desired. Seal bag. Squeeze and rub sugar in bag until it becomes evenly colored. Homemade colored sugar might clump; if it does, just break apart until clumps are gone.

Sugar Cookies with Colored Sugar, Frosted and Decorated Sugar Cookies

Frosted and Decorated Sugar Cookies: Omit granulated sugar. Frost cooled cookies with favorite vanilla frosting tinted with food color if desired. Decorate with colored sugar, small candies, candied fruit or nuts if desired.

Paintbrush Sugar Cookies: Omit granulated sugar. Cut rolled dough into desired shapes with cookie cutters. (Cut no more than 12 cookies at a time to keep them from drying out.) Mix 1 egg yolk and ¼ teaspoon water. Divide mixture among several custard cups. Tint each with a different food color to make bright colors. (If paint thickens while standing, stir in a few drops water.) Paint designs on cookies with small paintbrushes. Bake as directed in Step 4.

Salted Margarita Bites

PREP TIME: 1 hour **START TO FINISH:** 1 hour 30 minutes   **4 dozen cookies**

1 pouch Betty Crocker sugar cookie mix

1 tablespoon slightly packed grated fresh lime peel

⅓ cup butter or margarine, softened

1 egg

2 teaspoons fresh lime juice

½ teaspoon coarse (kosher or sea) salt

1 In large bowl, stir together cookie mix and lime peel until blended. Add butter, egg and lime juice. Beat with electric mixer on medium-low speed until blended and soft dough forms.

2 On 17-inch piece plastic wrap, shape dough into 12-inch log. Wrap tightly; freeze at least 30 minutes or until firm enough to slice.

3 Heat oven to 375°F. Unwrap dough; cut into ¼-inch slices. On ungreased cookie sheets, place slices 2 inches apart, reshaping if necessary; lightly sprinkle with salt.

4 Bake 8 to 10 minutes or until pale brown on bottom. Cool 1 minute; remove from cookie sheets to cooling racks. Cool completely before storing in airtight container. If desired, garnish cookies with freshly grated lime peel just before serving.

1 Cookie: Calories 50; Total Fat 2.5g (Saturated Fat 1g; Trans Fat 0g); Cholesterol 10mg; Sodium 65mg; Total Carbohydrate 8g (Dietary Fiber 0g); Protein 0g **Exchanges:** ½ Other Carbohydrate, ½ Fat **Carbohydrate Choices:** ½

Sweet Success Tips

Dough can be made up to 2 days ahead. Cover and refrigerate until ready to use.

For easier handling, make sure dough remains cold before baking. If necessary, return dough to freezer or refrigerator until chilled.

Gluten-Free Sugar Cookies

PREP TIME: 25 minutes START TO FINISH: 2 hours 25 minutes 20 cookies

- 1 cup sorghum flour
- 1 cup white rice flour
- ½ cup almond flour
- ½ cup potato starch flour
- 1 teaspoon cream of tartar
- 1 teaspoon baking soda
- 1 teaspoon gluten-free baking powder
- 1 teaspoon xanthan gum
- ½ teaspoon salt
- 1 cup granulated sugar
- ½ cup melted ghee or coconut oil
- 1 teaspoon gluten-free vanilla
- ½ teaspoon lemon oil
- 2 eggs
- 2 tablespoons coarse sugar

1 In small bowl, stir together all flours, cream of tartar, baking soda, baking powder, xanthan gum and salt; set aside.

2 In medium bowl, beat remaining ingredients except coarse sugar with electric mixer on low speed 1 minute or until well blended. Add flour mixture; beat until blended. Shape dough into a ball. Wrap in plastic wrap; refrigerate at least 2 hours.

3 Heat oven to 350°F. Spray cookie sheets and rolling pin with cooking spray without flour. On nonstick baking mat or parchment paper sprayed with cooking spray without flour, roll dough to ¼-inch thickness with rolling pin. Using 3- to 3½-inch cookie cutter, cut shapes from dough; place 1 to 1½ inches apart on cookie sheets. Sprinkle with coarse sugar.

4 Bake 10 to 15 minutes or until set and lightly browned on edges. Immediately remove from cookie sheets to cooling racks.

✱ *Cooking Gluten Free? Always read labels to make sure each recipe ingredient is gluten free. Products and ingredients sources can change.*

1 Cookie: Calories 190; Total Fat 8g (Saturated Fat 5g; Trans Fat 0g); Cholesterol 20mg; Sodium 150mg; Total Carbohydrate 28g (Dietary Fiber 1g); Protein 2g **Exchanges:** ½ Starch, 1½ Other Carbohydrate, 1½ Fat **Carbohydrate Choices:** 2

Contributed by Jean Duane, Alternative Cook { http://www.alternativecook.com }

Sweet Success Tips

The lemon oil adds a nice flavor to the sugar cookie. It is available at most kitchen or cookware stores.

Almond flour and almond meal are not the same thing. Almond flour is made from blanched and finely ground almonds. Almond meal is ground almonds. Almond flour works best in this recipe.

Peanut Butter Cookies

PREP TIME: 45 minutes **START TO FINISH:** 45 minutes **2½ dozen cookies**

½ cup granulated sugar
½ cup packed brown sugar
½ cup peanut butter
½ cup butter or margarine, softened
1 egg
1¼ cups all-purpose flour
¾ teaspoon baking soda
½ teaspoon baking powder
¼ teaspoon salt
Additional granulated sugar

1 Heat oven to 375°F. In large bowl, beat ½ cup granulated sugar, the brown sugar, peanut butter, butter and egg with electric mixer on medium speed, or mix with spoon. Stir in flour, baking soda, baking powder and salt.

2 Shape dough into 1¼-inch balls. On ungreased cookie sheets, place balls about 3 inches apart. Flatten in crisscross pattern with fork dipped in additional granulated sugar.

3 Bake 9 to 10 minutes or until light brown. Cool 5 minutes; remove from cookie sheets to cooling racks.

1 Cookie: Calories 100; Total Fat 5g (Saturated Fat 2.5g; Trans Fat 0g); Cholesterol 15mg; Sodium 105mg; Total Carbohydrate 12g (Dietary Fiber 0g); Protein 2g **Exchanges:** ½ Starch, ½ Other Carbohydrate, 1 Fat **Carbohydrate Choices:** 1

Almond Butter Cookies: Substitute creamy almond butter containing salt for the peanut butter. Continue as directed. Reduce bake time to 8 to 10 minutes. Cookies will be flatter than those made with peanut butter.

Rich Peanut Butter Cookies

PREP TIME: 45 minutes START TO FINISH: 45 minutes   2 dozen cookies

1 cup packed brown sugar
½ cup peanut butter
½ cup butter or margarine, softened
1 egg
1¼ cups all-purpose flour
¾ teaspoon baking soda
½ teaspoon baking powder
¼ teaspoon salt
1 cup peanut butter chips (6 oz)
Granulated sugar

1 Heat oven to 375°F. In large bowl, beat brown sugar, peanut butter, butter and egg with electric mixer on medium speed until creamy. On low speed, beat in flour, baking soda, baking powder and salt. Stir in peanut butter chips.

2 Shape dough into 1½-inch balls. Dip tops of balls into granulated sugar. On ungreased cookie sheets, place balls, sugared sides up, about 3 inches apart (do not flatten).

3 Bake 9 to 10 minutes or until light brown. Cool 5 minutes; remove from cookie sheets to cooling racks.

1 Cookie: Calories 180; Total Fat 9g (Saturated Fat 3.5g; Trans Fat 0g); Cholesterol 20mg; Sodium 150mg; Total Carbohydrate 21g (Dietary Fiber 0g); Protein 3g **Exchanges:** 1 Starch, ½ Other Carbohydrate, 1½ Fat **Carbohydrate Choices:** 1½

PB&J Sandwich Cookies

PREP TIME: 45 minutes START TO FINISH: 1 hour 15 minutes   1½ dozen sandwich cookies

1 **pouch Betty Crocker peanut butter cookie mix**

   Vegetable oil and egg called for on cookie mix package

⅓ **cup Betty Crocker Rich & Creamy vanilla frosting**

2 **tablespoons creamy peanut butter**

⅓ **cup favorite jelly, jam or preserves**

1 Heat oven to 375°F. Make cookies as directed on pouch, using oil and egg. Cool completely, about 30 minutes.

2 In small bowl, stir frosting and peanut butter until smooth.

3 For each sandwich cookie, spread heaping teaspoon peanut butter mixture on bottom of 1 cookie; spread slightly less than 1 teaspoon jelly over peanut butter mixture. Top with another cookie.

1 Sandwich Cookie: Calories 130; Total Fat 6g (Saturated Fat 1.5g; Trans Fat 0g); Cholesterol 15mg; Sodium 100mg; Total Carbohydrate 17g (Dietary Fiber 0g); Protein 1g **Exchanges:** 1 Other Carbohydrate, 1 Fat **Carbohydrate Choices:** 1

Triple PB&J Sandwich Cookies: Make cookies as directed. In microwavable bowl, microwave 1 bag (10 oz) peanut butter chips and 2 teaspoons shortening uncovered on High about 1 minute or until almost melted; stir until smooth. If necessary, microwave at additional 5-second intervals. Dip half of each sandwich cookie into mixture. Immediately roll outside of frosted edge in chopped peanuts. Lay flat to dry.

Sweet Success Tip

You can make sandwich cookies with Betty Crocker oatmeal, chocolate chip or sugar cookie mixes, too.

PB and Banana Cake Cookies

PREP TIME: 40 minutes START TO FINISH: 40 minutes   1½ dozen cookies

½   cup butter, softened

¼   cup creamy peanut butter

½   cup packed brown sugar

1   egg

1   ripe medium banana, mashed

½   teaspoon vanilla

1¼ cups all-purpose flour

1   teaspoon baking powder

½   teaspoon baking soda

¼   teaspoon salt

Melted chocolate frosting, if desired

Chopped roasted peanuts, if desired

1 Heat oven to 350°F. In large bowl, beat butter, peanut butter and brown sugar with electric mixer on medium speed 2 minutes or until creamy. Beat in egg. On low speed, beat in banana and vanilla until smooth.

2 In small bowl, mix flour, baking powder, baking soda and salt. On low speed, beat flour mixture into peanut butter mixture.

3 Onto ungreased cookie sheet, drop dough by rounded tablespoonfuls about 1 inch apart.

4 Bake 12 minutes or until golden brown. Cool 2 minutes; remove from cookie sheet to cooling rack. Drizzle cookies with melted frosting and sprinkle with peanuts.

1 Cookie: Calories 132; Total Fat 7g (Saturated Fat 4g); Sodium 153g; Total Carbohydrate 15g (Dietary Fiber 1g); Protein 2g **Exchanges:** ½ Starch, ½ Other Carbohydrate, 1½ Fat **Carbohydrate Choices:** 1

Maple-Nut Chocolate Chunk Cookies

PREP TIME: 1 hour 25 minutes **START TO FINISH:** 1 hour 25 minutes **2½ dozen cookies**

COOKIES

- 1¼ cups all-purpose flour
- ½ teaspoon baking powder
- ¼ teaspoon salt
- ⅛ teaspoon ground allspice
- ½ cup butter or margarine, melted
- ½ cup packed light brown sugar
- ⅓ cup granulated sugar
- 1 egg
- 1 teaspoon maple flavoring
- ¾ cup coarsely chopped salted mixed nuts
- ¾ cup semisweet chocolate chunks

FROSTING

- 2 tablespoons half-and-half or milk
- 2 tablespoons butter or margarine, softened
- 1½ teaspoons light corn syrup
- 1 teaspoon maple flavoring
- 1¾ to 2 cups powdered sugar

1 Heat oven to 350°F. In medium bowl, stir together flour, baking powder, salt and allspice until blended; set aside. In large bowl, beat melted butter, brown sugar and granulated sugar with electric mixer on medium speed 2 minutes or until light and creamy. Add egg and 1 teaspoon maple flavoring; beat on low speed until blended. Add flour mixture; beat until soft dough forms. Stir in nuts and chocolate chunks.

2 Onto ungreased cookie sheets, drop dough by rounded tablespoonfuls 1 inch apart. Bake 9 to 11 minutes or until edges are light brown. Cool 1 minute; remove from cookie sheets to cooling racks.

3 In medium bowl, stir together half-and-half, 2 tablespoons butter, the corn syrup, 1 teaspoon maple flavoring and ¼ cup powdered sugar until blended and smooth. Slowly stir in 1½ cups powdered sugar until blended. If necessary, stir in remaining ¼ cup powdered sugar, 1 tablespoon at a time, until smooth and desired spreading consistency. For each cookie, spread about 1½ teaspoons frosting almost to edge; let stand until set. Store in airtight container.

1 Cookie: Calories 150; Total Fat 7g (Saturated Fat 3.5g; Trans Fat 0g); Cholesterol 20mg; Sodium 80mg; Total Carbohydrate 21g (Dietary Fiber 0g); Protein 1g **Exchanges:** ½ Starch, 1 Other Carbohydrate, 1½ Fat **Carbohydrate Choices:** 1½

Sweet Success Tips

It's best to chop nuts by hand, keeping them in large coarse pieces to give cookies a crunchy texture. Don't be tempted to chop nuts in a food processor. Even if watched carefully, a food processor chops nuts too finely.

Chocolate chips can be substituted for chocolate chunks.

Jean's Gluten-Free Snickerdoodles

PREP TIME: 45 minutes **START TO FINISH:** 45 minutes **1½ dozen cookies**

COOKIES

½	**cup white rice flour**
½	**cup finely ground tapioca flour**
½	**cup sweet white sorghum flour**
½	**cup potato starch flour**
2	**teaspoons xanthan gum**
1	**teaspoon cream of tartar**
¼	**teaspoon gluten-free baking powder**
¼	**teaspoon salt**
2	**eggs**
½	**cup melted ghee**
¾	**cup sugar**
2	**teaspoons gluten-free vanilla**
1	**teaspoon gluten-free vanilla bean paste, if desired**

TOPPING

2	**tablespoons sugar**
1	**teaspoon ground cinnamon**

Sweet Success Tips

Vanilla bean paste is made from ground vanilla beans mixed with vanilla extract. Adding it to these cookies boosts the vanilla flavor, but if you can't find it, they'll still taste great.

Ghee (clarified butter) is a butter substitute that does not contain the protein casein found in butter. It can be substituted one-for-one with oil, but not with butter. Butter contains water, which will throw off the ratios if used instead of oil or melted ghee. Ghee is found in the dairy section or baking aisle.

1 Heat oven to 350°F. Line cookie sheet with cooking parchment paper; spray paper with cooking spray (without flour).

2 In small bowl, mix flours, xanthan gum, cream of tartar, baking powder and salt with whisk; set aside. In medium bowl, beat eggs, ghee, ¾ cup sugar, the vanilla and vanilla bean paste. Gradually add flour mixture, beating until well blended.

3 In small bowl, mix 2 tablespoons sugar and the cinnamon. Drop dough by tablespoonfuls into topping and roll to coat. On cookie sheet, place balls about 2 inches apart; flatten slightly.

4 Bake 19 to 21 minutes or until golden brown. Cool 5 minutes; remove from cookie sheet to cooling rack.

★ *Cooking Gluten Free? Always read labels to make sure each recipe ingredient is gluten free. Products and ingredients sources can change.*

1 Cookie: Calories 160; Total Fat 6g (Saturated Fat 3.5g; Trans Fat 0g); Cholesterol 40mg; Sodium 50mg; Total Carbohydrate 23g (Dietary Fiber 1g); Protein 1g **Exchanges:** 1 Starch, ½ Other Carbohydrate, 1 Fat **Carbohydrate Choices:** 1½

Contributed by Jean Duane, Alternative Cook { http://www.alternativecook.com }

Cinnamon-Raisin Oatmeal Cookies

PREP TIME: 1 hour **START TO FINISH:** 1 hour **2½ dozen cookies**

1 cup packed brown sugar

1 cup butter or margarine, softened

2 teaspoons vanilla

2 eggs

1¾ cups all-purpose flour

1 teaspoon baking soda

1 teaspoon ground cinnamon

¼ teaspoon salt

1 cup old-fashioned oats

1 cup Fiber One® original bran cereal

½ cup raisins

1 Heat oven to 350°F. In large bowl, beat brown sugar and butter with electric mixer on medium speed until creamy. On low speed, beat in vanilla and eggs until well blended. Beat in flour, baking soda, cinnamon and salt until well blended. With spoon, stir in oats, cereal and raisins.

2 Onto ungreased cookie sheets, drop dough by heaping tablespoonfuls about 2 inches apart.

3 Bake 12 to 15 minutes or until set and golden brown. Immediately remove from cookie sheets to cooling racks.

1 Cookie: Calories 140; Total Fat 7g (Saturated Fat 4g; Trans Fat 0g); Cholesterol 30mg; Sodium 130mg; Total Carbohydrate 18g (Dietary Fiber 1g); Protein 1g **Exchanges:** ½ Starch, ½ Other Carbohydrate, 1½ Fat **Carbohydrate Choices:** 1

Apple-Oat Cookies

PREP TIME: 40 minutes **START TO FINISH:** 1 hour 40 minutes   **3 dozen cookies**

¾ **cup butter or margarine, softened**

1 **cup granulated sugar**

½ **cup packed brown sugar**

1 **teaspoon vanilla**

2 **eggs**

1¾ **cups all-purpose flour**

1 **teaspoon baking soda**

1½ **teaspoons ground cinnamon**

½ **teaspoon salt**

2 **cups old-fashioned or quick-cooking oats**

1 **medium apple, peeled, shredded (about 1 cup shredded)**

1 **cup powdered sugar**

2 **to 3 tablespoons apple juice or milk**

1 Heat oven to 375°F. Spray cookie sheets with cooking spray. In large bowl, beat butter, granulated sugar and brown sugar with electric mixer on medium speed until creamy. Beat in vanilla and eggs, scraping sides occasionally, until blended.

2 In medium bowl, mix flour, baking soda, cinnamon and salt. Gradually beat flour mixture into sugar mixture. Stir in oats and apple. Onto cookie sheets, drop dough by rounded tablespoonfuls 2 inches apart.

3 Bake about 10 minutes or until edges are light golden brown. Cool 1 minute; remove from cookie sheets to cooling racks. Cool completely, about 15 minutes.

4 In medium bowl, beat powdered sugar and apple juice until smooth, using whisk or fork. Drizzle over cooled cookies on cooling racks. Let stand about 1 hour or until glaze is set.

1 Cookie: Calories 130; Total Fat 4.5g (Saturated Fat 2.5g; Trans Fat 0g); Cholesterol 20mg; Sodium 100mg; Total Carbohydrate 20g (Dietary Fiber 0g); Protein 1g **Exchanges:** 1½ Other Carbohydrate, 1 Fat **Carbohydrate Choices:** 1

Sweet Success Tips

For easy cleanup when glazing cookies, place waxed paper or paper towels under the cooling rack.

For fuller cookies and less spread while baking, refrigerate dough between baking batches.

Apricot Spice Cookies

PREP TIME: 1 hour 20 minutes **START TO FINISH:** 1 hour 20 minutes **6 dozen cookies**

⅔ cup granulated sugar

⅔ cup packed brown sugar

½ cup butter or margarine, softened

½ cup shortening

1 teaspoon baking soda

1 teaspoon ground cinnamon or cardamom

1 teaspoon vanilla

½ teaspoon baking powder

½ teaspoon salt

2 eggs

3 cups quick-cooking oats

1 cup all-purpose flour

¾ cup chopped dried apricots

½ cup finely chopped pecans

1 Heat oven to 375°F. In large bowl, beat all ingredients except oats, flour, apricots and pecans with electric mixer on medium speed until creamy, or mix with spoon. Stir in remaining ingredients.

2 Onto ungreased cookie sheets, drop dough by rounded teaspoonfuls about 2 inches apart.

3 Bake 8 to 10 minutes or until edges are brown and centers are soft. Cool 1 to 2 minutes; remove from cookie sheets to cooling racks.

1 Cookie: Calories 70; Total Fat 3.5g (Saturated Fat 1.5g; Trans Fat 0g); Cholesterol 10mg; Sodium 50mg; Total Carbohydrate 8g (Dietary Fiber 0g); Protein 1g **Exchanges:** ½ Starch, ½ Fat **Carbohydrate Choices:** ½

Sweet Success Tip

To make drop cookies uniform in size, use a spring-handled cookie scoop available in a variety of sizes at most grocery and discount stores.

On-the-Trail Cookies

PREP TIME: 55 minutes **START TO FINISH:** 55 minutes   **3 dozen cookies**

- **1** cup granulated sugar
- **1** cup packed brown sugar
- **1** cup peanut butter
- **½** cup butter or margarine, softened
- **½** cup butter-flavor or regular shortening
- **2** teaspoons vanilla
- **2** eggs
- **1½** cups quick-cooking or old-fashioned oats
- **2** cups all-purpose flour
- **1** teaspoon baking powder
- **1** teaspoon baking soda
- **2** cups candy-coated chocolate candies
- **1** cup peanuts
- **¾** cup raisins

1 Heat oven to 375°F. In large bowl, beat sugars, peanut butter, butter, shortening, vanilla and eggs with electric mixer on medium speed until smooth, or mix with spoon. Stir in oats. Stir in flour, baking powder and baking soda thoroughly. Stir in candies, peanuts and raisins.

2 Onto ungreased cookie sheets, drop dough by rounded tablespoonfuls about 2 inches apart. Flatten slightly with bottom of glass.

3 Bake 8 to 10 minutes or until edges are brown and centers are soft. Cool 1 to 2 minutes; remove from cookie sheets to cooling racks.

1 Cookie: Calories 270; Total Fat 14g (Saturated Fat 5g; Trans Fat 0.5g); Cholesterol 20mg; Sodium 115mg; Total Carbohydrate 32g (Dietary Fiber 2g); Protein 5g **Exchanges:** ½ Starch, 1½ Other Carbohydrate, ½ High-Fat Meat, 2 Fat **Carbohydrate Choices:** 2

Sweet Success Tip

For monster-size cookies, drop dough by slightly less than ¼ cupfuls, and flatten slightly. Bake 12 to 14 minutes.

Monster-Style Cookies

PREP TIME: 45 minutes START TO FINISH: 45 minutes   1½ dozen cookies

¾   cup creamy peanut butter

½   cup butter or margarine, softened

¾   cup packed brown sugar

½   cup granulated sugar

1   teaspoon vanilla

2   eggs

1¼   cups all-purpose flour

1   teaspoon baking soda

2½   cups quick-cooking or old-fashioned oats

½   cup white vanilla baking chips

½   cup sweetened dried cranberries

1 Heat oven to 375°F. In large bowl, beat peanut butter and butter with electric mixer on medium speed until creamy. Add sugars; beat until fluffy. Beat in vanilla and eggs until well mixed. On low speed, beat in flour and baking soda. Stir in oats, baking chips and cranberries.

2 Onto ungreased cookie sheets, drop dough by ¼ cupfuls about 3 inches apart.

3 Bake 11 to 15 minutes or until edges are golden brown. Cool 1 minute; remove from cookie sheets to cooling racks.

1 Cookie: Calories 310; Total Fat 14g (Saturated Fat 6g; Trans Fat 0g); Cholesterol 40mg; Sodium 220mg; Total Carbohydrate 38g (Dietary Fiber 2g); Protein 6g **Exchanges:** 1 Starch, 1½ Other Carbohydrate, ½ High-Fat Meat, 2 Fat **Carbohydrate Choices:** 2½

Sweet Success Tips

To make 3½ dozen smaller cookies, drop dough by tablespoonfuls (about 2 inches apart) instead of ¼ cupfuls. Bake 8 to 10 minutes.

Have semisweet chocolate chips on hand? Go ahead and use them instead of the white vanilla baking chips.

Apple-Date Swirl Cookies

PREP TIME: 35 minutes START TO FINISH: 3 hours 20 minutes   5 dozen cookies

FILLING

- **1 cup chopped dates**
- **¾ cup finely chopped peeled apple**
- **¼ cup granulated sugar**
- **1 teaspoon grated orange peel**
- **¼ cup orange juice**

COOKIES

- **½ cup granulated sugar**
- **½ cup packed brown sugar**
- **½ cup butter or margarine, softened**
- **½ teaspoon vanilla**
- **1 egg**
- **1⅔ cups all-purpose flour**
- **½ teaspoon baking soda**
- **¼ teaspoon salt**
- **¼ teaspoon ground cinnamon**

1 In 1-quart saucepan, mix filling ingredients. Cook over medium-high heat, stirring constantly, until mixture boils and thickens. Boil and stir 5 minutes. Cool.

2 In large bowl, beat ½ cup granulated sugar, the brown sugar, butter, vanilla and egg with electric mixer on medium speed, or mix with spoon, until well blended. Stir in flour, baking soda, salt and cinnamon.

3 Between sheets of waxed paper or plastic wrap, roll or pat dough into 16×8-inch rectangle. Remove top paper. Spread cooled filling over dough. Roll up dough with filling inside, starting with 16-inch side and using waxed paper to lift and roll. Wrap tightly. Refrigerate 2 to 3 hours or until firm.

4 Heat oven to 375°F. Cut roll with sharp knife into ¼-inch slices, occasionally cleaning off knife. On ungreased cookie sheets, place slices about 1 inch apart. Bake 8 to 11 minutes or until lightly browned. Remove from cookie sheets to cooling racks.

1 Cookie: Calories 60; Total Fat 1.5g (Saturated Fat 1g; Trans Fat 0g); Cholesterol 10mg; Sodium 35mg; Total Carbohydrate 10g (Dietary Fiber 0g); Protein 0g **Exchanges:** ½ Other Carbohydrate, ½ Fat **Carbohydrate Choices:** ½

Sweet Success Tips

Shape up your cookies! Rotate the roll slightly with each cut so the roll stays rounded.

Use a kitchen scissors to make quick work of chopping the dates.

Ginger Crinkles

PREP TIME: 40 minutes START TO FINISH: 40 minutes   **3 dozen cookies**

1   cup sugar

¾   cup butter or margarine, softened

¼   cup molasses

1   egg

2   cups all-purpose flour

1   tablespoon ground ginger

2   teaspoons baking soda

1   teaspoon ground cinnamon

¼   teaspoon ground cloves

¼   teaspoon salt

3   tablespoons sugar

1 Heat oven to 375°F. In large bowl, beat 1 cup sugar and the butter with electric mixer on medium speed until soft and fluffy, or mix with spoon. Beat in molasses and egg. Stir in remaining ingredients except 3 tablespoons sugar until well blended.

2 In small bowl, place 3 tablespoons sugar. Shape dough by tablespoonfuls into balls; roll in sugar. On ungreased cookie sheets, place balls 2 inches apart.

3 Bake 6 to 8 minutes or until golden brown. Remove from cookie sheets to cooling racks.

1 Cookie: Calories 100; Total Fat 4g (Saturated Fat 2.5g; Trans Fat 0g); Cholesterol 15mg; Sodium 115mg; Total Carbohydrate 14g (Dietary Fiber 0g); Protein 1g **Exchanges:** 1 Starch, ½ Fat **Carbohydrate Choices:** 1

Soft Molasses Cookies

PREP TIME: 55 minutes **START TO FINISH:** 55 minutes   **4 dozen cookies**

1   cup sugar

¾   cup sour cream

½   cup butter or margarine, softened

½   cup shortening

½   cup molasses

1   egg

3   cups all-purpose flour

1½ teaspoons baking soda

1   teaspoon ground cinnamon

1   teaspoon ground ginger

½   teaspoon salt

Additional sugar

1 Heat oven to 375°F. In large bowl, beat 1 cup sugar, the sour cream, butter, shortening, molasses and egg with electric mixer on medium speed, or mix with spoon. Stir in remaining ingredients.

2 Onto ungreased cookie sheets, drop dough by rounded tablespoonfuls about 2 inches apart.

3 Bake 9 to 11 minutes or until almost no indentation remains when touched in center. Cool 1 to 2 minutes; remove from cookie sheets to cooling racks. Sprinkle with additional sugar while warm.

1 Cookie: Calories 100; Total Fat 5g (Saturated Fat 2g; Trans Fat 0g); Cholesterol 10mg; Sodium 85mg; Total Carbohydrate 13g (Dietary Fiber 0g); Protein 1g **Exchanges:** ½ Starch, ½ Other Carbohydrate, 1 Fat **Carbohydrate Choices:** 1

Soft Molasses Cookies with Vanilla Frosting: Bake and cool cookies as directed in step 3, except omit sprinkling with sugar. In large bowl, stir 3 cups powdered sugar, ⅓ cup butter or margarine, softened, 1½ teaspoons vanilla and 2 to 3 tablespoons milk until smooth and spreadable. Frost cookies.

Soft Molasses Cookies and Soft Molasses Cookies with Vanilla Frosting

Chocolate Crinkles

PREP TIME: 1 hour **START TO FINISH:** 4 hours   **6 dozen cookies**

2 cups granulated sugar

½ cup vegetable oil

2 teaspoons vanilla

4 oz unsweetened baking chocolate, melted, cooled

4 eggs

2 cups all-purpose flour

2 teaspoons baking powder

½ teaspoon salt

1 cup powdered sugar

1 In large bowl, stir granulated sugar, oil, vanilla and chocolate until well mixed. Stir in eggs, one at a time. Stir in flour, baking powder and salt. Cover and refrigerate at least 3 hours.

2 Heat oven to 350°F. Grease cookie sheets with shortening or cooking spray, or line with cooking parchment paper or silicone baking mats.

3 In small bowl, place powdered sugar. Drop dough by rounded teaspoonfuls into powdered sugar; roll around to coat. Shape into balls. On cookie sheets, place balls about 2 inches apart.

4 Bake 10 to 12 minutes or until almost no indentation remains when touched in center. Immediately remove from cookie sheets to cooling racks.

1 Cookie: Calories 70; Total Fat 2.5g (Saturated Fat 1g; Trans Fat 0g); Cholesterol 10mg; Sodium 35mg; Total Carbohydrate 10g (Dietary Fiber 0g); Protein 1g **Exchanges:** ½ Starch, ½ Fat **Carbohydrate Choices:** ½

Clockwise: Citrus–Brown Sugar Refrigerator
Cookies, Brown Sugar Refrigerator Cookies,
Toasted Coconut–Brown Sugar Refrigerator Cookies

Brown Sugar Refrigerator Cookies

PREP TIME: 55 minutes START TO FINISH: 2 hours 55 minutes   **6 dozen cookies**

1 cup packed brown sugar

1 cup butter or margarine, softened

1 teaspoon vanilla

1 egg

3 cups all-purpose flour

1½ teaspoons ground cinnamon

½ teaspoon baking soda

½ teaspoon salt

⅓ cup finely chopped nuts

1 In large bowl, beat brown sugar, butter, vanilla and egg with electric mixer on medium speed, or mix with spoon. Stir in remaining ingredients except nuts. Stir in nuts.

2 On plastic wrap, shape dough into 10×3-inch rectangle. Wrap and refrigerate about 2 hours or until firm, but no longer than 24 hours.

3 Heat oven to 375°F. Cut rectangle into ⅛-inch slices. On ungreased cookie sheets, place slices 2 inches apart.

4 Bake 6 to 8 minutes or until light brown. Cool 1 to 2 minutes; remove from cookie sheets to cooling racks.

1 Cookie: Calories 60; Total Fat 3g (Saturated Fat 1.5g; Trans Fat 0g); Cholesterol 10mg; Sodium 50mg; Total Carbohydrate 7g (Dietary Fiber 0g); Protein 0g **Exchanges:** ½ Other Carbohydrate, ½ Fat **Carbohydrate Choices:** ½

Citrus–Brown Sugar Refrigerator Cookies: Add 1 tablespoon grated lemon or orange peel with the flour. Frost cookies with Vanilla Glaze. For glaze, mix 2 cups powdered sugar, ⅓ cup melted butter and 1 teaspoon vanilla. Stir in 2 to 4 tablespoons hot water, 1 tablespoon at a time, until glaze is smooth and has the consistency of thick syrup. Drizzle over cookies; sprinkle with grated lemon peel.

Maple–Brown Sugar Refrigerator Cookies: Substitute 2 teaspoons maple flavor for the vanilla.

Toasted Coconut–Brown Sugar Refrigerator Cookies: Add 1 cup toasted coconut with the flour. Frost cookies with Vanilla Glaze (see above) and sprinkle with additional toasted coconut.

Sweet Success Tip

Freeze the tightly wrapped cookie dough for up to 2 months, then slice and bake when you want. Just add 1 or 2 minutes to the bake time when the dough comes straight from the freezer.

Banana–Chocolate Chip Biscotti

PREP TIME: 35 minutes **START TO FINISH:** 1 hour 35 minutes **40 cookies**

1 cup sugar

½ cup butter or margarine, softened

½ cup mashed very ripe banana (1 medium)

1 teaspoon vanilla

2 eggs

3 cups all-purpose flour

3 teaspoons baking powder

¼ teaspoon salt

½ cup miniature semisweet chocolate chips

1 Heat oven to 350°F. Grease large cookie sheet with shortening or cooking spray, or line with cooking parchment paper or silicone baking mat.

2 In large bowl, beat sugar and butter with electric mixer on medium speed, or mix with spoon. Beat in banana, vanilla and eggs until smooth. Stir in flour, baking powder and salt. Stir in chocolate chips.

3 Divide dough in half. On cookie sheet, shape each half into 10×3-inch rectangle with greased hands (dough will be sticky).

4 Bake about 25 minutes or until toothpick inserted in center comes out clean. Cool on cookie sheet 15 minutes; move to cutting board. Using sharp knife, cut crosswise into ½-inch slices.

5 Place slices, cut side down, on cookie sheets. Bake 10 to 12 minutes or until golden brown and dry on top. Turn cookies. Bake about 10 minutes longer or until golden brown. Remove from cookie sheets to cooling racks.

1 Cookie: Calories 90; Total Fat 3.5g (Saturated Fat 2g; Trans Fat 0g); Cholesterol 15mg; Sodium 70mg; Total Carbohydrate 14g (Dietary Fiber 0g); Protein 1g **Exchanges:** ½ Starch, ½ Other Carbohydrate, ½ Fat **Carbohydrate Choices:** 1

Hazelnut Biscotti

PREP TIME: 25 minutes START TO FINISH: 1 hour 40 minutes   40 cookies

1 cup hazelnuts (filberts), coarsely chopped
1 cup sugar
½ cup butter or margarine, softened
1 teaspoon almond extract
1 teaspoon vanilla
2 eggs
3½ cups all-purpose flour
1 teaspoon baking powder
½ teaspoon baking soda

1 Heat oven to 350°F. Spread hazelnuts in ungreased shallow pan. Bake uncovered about 10 minutes, stirring occasionally, until golden brown; cool.

2 Meanwhile, in large bowl, beat sugar, butter, almond extract, vanilla and eggs with electric mixer on medium speed, or mix with spoon. Stir in flour, baking powder and baking soda. Stir in hazelnuts. Place dough on lightly floured surface. Gently knead 2 to 3 minutes or until dough holds together and hazelnuts are evenly distributed.

3 Divide dough in half. On large ungreased cookie sheet, shape each half into 10×3-inch rectangle, rounding edges slightly.

4 Bake about 25 minutes or until center is firm to the touch. Cool on cookie sheet 15 minutes; move to cutting board. Using sharp knife, cut each rectangle crosswise into ½-inch slices.

5 Place 20 slices, cut side down, on ungreased cookie sheet. Bake about 15 minutes or until crisp and light brown. Immediately remove from cookie sheet to cooling rack; cool. Cool cookie sheet 5 minutes; repeat with remaining slices.

1 Cookie: Calories 100; Total Fat 4.5g (Saturated Fat 1.5g; Trans Fat 0g); Cholesterol 15mg; Sodium 50mg; Total Carbohydrate 14g (Dietary Fiber 0g); Protein 2g **Exchanges:** ½ Starch, ½ Other Carbohydrate, 1 Fat **Carbohydrate Choices:** 1

Almond Biscotti: Substitute 1 cup slivered almonds for the hazelnuts.

Lime Christmas Wreaths (page 94)

holiday cookies

Cute Witch Cookies

PREP TIME: 1 hour **START TO FINISH:** 1 hour **10 cookies**

COOKIES

- **1 pouch Betty Crocker sugar cookie mix**
- **1 egg**
- **⅓ cup butter or margarine, softened**
- **1 tablespoon all-purpose flour**

DECORATIONS

- **12 (7-inch) chocolate licorice twists (from 12-oz bag)**
- **½ cup Betty Crocker Rich & Creamy chocolate frosting (from 16-oz container), divided**
- **3 tablespoons chocolate candy sprinkles**
- **1 cup Betty Crocker Rich & Creamy creamy white frosting (from 16-oz container) Green gel food color**
- **1 pouch (7 oz) Betty Crocker Cookie Icing white icing**
- **20 brown mini candy-coated milk chocolate candies**
- **20 small green gumdrops, cut in half vertically**
- **10 green mini candy-coated milk chocolate candies**
- **5 candy corn, cut in half vertically**

Sweet Success Tip

To ensure that the hat and face don't break apart, wait at least 1 hour for frosting to harden before transferring cookies to storage container.

1 Heat oven to 350°F. Make cookie dough as directed on pouch for Cutout Cookies—except cover and refrigerate dough 20 minutes. On lightly floured surface, roll out dough to ¼-inch thickness. Using 3¼-inch round cookie cutter and knife, cut out 10 circles and 10 (3-inch) triangles, gently pressing together and rerolling dough scraps as necessary.

2 For each cookie, arrange 1 dough triangle and 1 dough circle, sides touching, on ungreased cookie sheets, leaving 3 inches between cookies. Bake 8 to 9 minutes or until edges are light golden brown. Cool 1 minute; carefully remove from cookie sheets to cooling racks. Cool completely before decorating.

3 Meanwhile, cut 5 pieces licorice in half, making 10 (3½-inch) pieces for brim of hat; set aside. Cut remaining licorice into 20 (2-inch) pieces, saving 1-inch scraps. For each 2-inch piece, cut 3 (1½-inch) slits, creating "hair" strands; set aside. Using scraps, cut licorice crosswise into 20 (⅛-inch) rings. For each ring, cut through just to center; open up to form strip for eyebrows; set aside.

4 In snack-size resealable food-storage plastic bag, place 2 tablespoons chocolate frosting; seal bag. Cut ⅛-inch opening diagonally across bottom corner of bag; set aside. Frost cooled triangles (hats) with remaining chocolate frosting. Using 3½-inch licorice pieces, press into frosting at bottom of triangles to create brims; sprinkle hats with chocolate sprinkles.

5 In small bowl, place 1 cup vanilla frosting. Stir in green gel to desired color. In snack-size resealable food-storage plastic bag, place 1 tablespoon green frosting; seal bag. Cut ⅛-inch opening diagonally across bottom corner of bag; set aside. Frost circles (faces) with remaining green frosting.

6 To Decorate Cookies: For each cookie, using white icing, pipe two small round-shaped dollops onto green frosting for eyes; press 1 brown milk chocolate candy on each. To create nose, use 4 green gumdrop halves, pressing flat sides into frosting. Using green frosting in plastic bag, pipe small dollop on side gumdrop; press 1 green milk chocolate candy on dollop for wart.

7 To create hair and eyebrows, press remaining licorice pieces on frosting (see photo). To create lower lip, using chocolate frosting in plastic bag, pipe thin line frosting. Press 1 candy corn half, flat side down, on frosting, overlapping bottom lip for tooth. Connecting both sides, pipe thin line frosting over top edge of candy corn to finish mouth. Store in airtight container.

1 Cookie: Calories 540; Total Fat 19g (Saturated Fat 8g; Trans Fat 4.5g); Cholesterol 40mg; Sodium 330mg; Total Carbohydrate 88g (Dietary Fiber 0g); Protein 3g **Exchanges:** 1 Starch, 5 Other Carbohydrate, 3½ Fat **Carbohydrate Choices:** 6

Halloween Cat Cookies

PREP TIME: 45 minutes START TO FINISH: 45 minutes   20 cookies

COOKIES

1¾   cups all-purpose flour

¾   teaspoon baking soda

½   teaspoon salt

1   package (3 oz) orange-flavored gelatin

½   cup butter or margarine, softened

½   cup sugar

1   egg

½   cup buttermilk

1   teaspoon grated orange peel

DECORATIONS

¾   cup Betty Crocker Rich & Creamy dark chocolate frosting (from 16-oz container)

40   green mini candy-coated milk chocolate candies

10   orange mini candy-coated milk chocolate candies, cut in half

About 2 tablespoons shredded coconut (120 shreds)

1   pouch (7 oz) Betty Crocker Cookie Icing red icing

1 Heat oven to 350°F. Line cookie sheets with cooking parchment paper. In medium bowl, stir together flour, baking soda, salt and gelatin; set aside. In separate medium bowl, beat butter and sugar with electric mixer on medium speed until light and fluffy. Add egg; beat until blended. Beat in flour mixture alternately with buttermilk on low speed, half of each at a time, until soft dough forms. Stir in orange peel.

2 Onto lined cookie sheets, drop dough by rounded tablespoonfuls 2 inches apart. Bake 10 to 12 minutes or until bottoms are golden brown. Cool 1 to 2 minutes; remove from cookie sheets to cooling racks. Cool completely before decorating.

3 To Decorate Cookies: Into 1-pint resealable food-storage plastic bag, add chocolate frosting; reseal bag. Cut ⅛-inch opening diagonally across bottom corner of bag. Pipe cat face onto center of cookies (see photo), smoothing out frosting with small spatula as necessary. For each cookie, press into frosting 2 green milk chocolate candies for eyes, 1 orange milk chocolate candy half for nose and 6 coconut shreds for whiskers. Using chocolate frosting, pipe thin line down center of green candies, creating pupils for eyes. Using red icing, pipe on mouth. Store in airtight container.

1 Cookie: Calories 180; Total Fat 7g (Saturated Fat 4g; Trans Fat 1g); Cholesterol 25mg; Sodium 200mg; Total Carbohydrate 26g (Dietary Fiber 0g); Protein 2g **Exchanges:** ½ Starch, 1 Other Carbohydrate, 1½ Fat **Carbohydrate Choices:** 2

Sweet Success Tips

To ensure that cookies are done, carefully peek at underside, making sure bottoms are golden brown.

Resealable food-storage plastic bags are great substitutes for decorating bags. Depending on the ingredient, small squeeze bottles can also work well. Kids find both very easy to use, and cleanup is a breeze!

Candy Corn Roll-Up Cookies

PREP TIME: 1 hour 10 minutes START TO FINISH: 3 hours 5 minutes   3½ dozen cookies

1 cup butter or margarine, softened

1½ cups powdered sugar

1 egg

Grated peel of 1 medium orange (1 to 2 tablespoons)

2½ cups all-purpose flour

1 teaspoon baking soda

1 teaspoon cream of tartar

⅛ teaspoon orange gel food color

⅛ teaspoon yellow gel food color

Coarse sugar, if desired

1 In large bowl, beat butter, powdered sugar, egg and orange peel with electric mixer on medium speed, or mix with spoon. Stir in flour, baking soda and cream of tartar.

2 Divide dough into thirds. Tint one portion orange and one portion yellow; leave remaining portion plain. Flatten each portion into a round. Wrap in plastic wrap; refrigerate 20 minutes.

3 On separate sheets of lightly floured waxed paper, roll each portion of dough into 12×9-inch rectangle. Place orange rectangle on top of yellow rectangle, using waxed paper ends to help flip dough over. Top with plain dough rectangle. Starting on a long side, and using waxed paper as an aid, roll dough into a log. Wrap in plastic; refrigerate 1 hour.

4 Heat oven to 375°F. Cut dough into ¼-inch slices. On ungreased cookie sheets, place slices about 1 inch apart. Sprinkle with coarse sugar.

5 Bake 7 to 8 minutes or until edges are set. Cool 1 minute; remove from cookie sheets to cooling racks.

1 Cookie: Calories 90; Total Fat 4.5g (Saturated Fat 3g; Trans Fat 0g); Cholesterol 15mg; Sodium 65mg; Total Carbohydrate 10g (Dietary Fiber 0g); Protein 1g **Exchanges:** ½ Starch, 1 Fat **Carbohydrate Choices:** ½

Sweet Success Tips

For a fun look, turn these into lollipop cookies. Before baking, place paper lollipop sticks on cookie sheet, and lay bottom of each dough slice on top of a stick. Bake as directed in recipe.

When grating the orange, be careful to avoid the pith—the soft white layer between the peel and the fruit—as it can be bitter.

Chocolate Bat Cookies

PREP TIME: 55 minutes **START TO FINISH:** 2 hours 5 minutes   **4 dozen cookies**

¾ **cup butter, softened**

1⅓ **cups granulated sugar**

1 **egg**

1 **teaspoon vanilla**

1½ **cups all-purpose flour**

¾ **cup unsweetened baking cocoa**

⅛ **teaspoon salt**

2 **tablespoons red cinnamon candies (96 candies)**

Black decorator sugar crystals

1 In large bowl, beat butter, granulated sugar, egg and vanilla with electric mixer on medium speed, or mix with spoon. Stir in flour, cocoa and salt. Divide dough in half. Flatten each portion into a round. Wrap in plastic wrap; refrigerate 1 hour.

2 Heat oven to 375°F. On lightly floured surface, roll one portion of dough at a time ⅛ inch thick. (Keep remaining dough in refrigerator until ready to roll.) Cut with 4½×½-inch bat-shaped cookie cutter. (If dough becomes too sticky to cut, refrigerate 10 minutes before rerolling.) Place 2 red cinnamon candies on each cookie for eyes. Sprinkle with sugar crystals. On ungreased cookie sheets, place cookies about 1 inch apart.

3 Bake 8 to 10 minutes or until edges are set. Cool 1 minute; remove from cookie sheets to cooling racks.

1 Cookie: Calories 70; Total Fat 3.5g (Saturated Fat 2g; Trans Fat 0g); Cholesterol 10mg; Sodium 30mg; Total Carbohydrate 10g (Dietary Fiber 0g); Protein 1g **Exchanges:** ½ Other Carbohydrate, ½ Fat **Carbohydrate Choices:** ½

Sweet Success Tips

Outline the edges of the bat with black decorating gel for more detail.

When shopping for black decorator sugar crystals, you might find it labeled as black sanding sugar.

Scary Cat Cookies

PREP TIME: 30 minutes **START TO FINISH:** 1 hour 15 minutes   **15 cookies**

3 oz semisweet baking chocolate

1 cup butter, softened (do not use margarine)

½ cup sugar

2¼ cups all-purpose flour

1 teaspoon vanilla

1 egg
Yellow candy sprinkles

15 yellow mini candy-coated milk chocolate candies

1 package pull-apart yellow licorice twists, cut into 1-inch pieces

1 package pull-apart pink licorice twists, cut into bits

1 Heat oven to 350°F. Grease cookie sheets with shortening.

2 In 1-quart saucepan, melt chocolate over low heat, stirring constantly. In large bowl, beat butter and sugar with electric mixer on medium speed, or mix with spoon. Stir in melted chocolate, flour, vanilla and egg.

3 Shape dough into 30 (1-inch) balls. Pull a little bit of dough from each of 15 balls to make tails; set aside. Cut about ¼-inch slit in same balls, using scissors. Separate dough at slit for cat's ears. Place balls about 2 inches apart on cookie sheets.

4 Place remaining balls below each cat head on cookie sheets for body. Shape small pieces of dough into 15 (2½-inch-long) ropes. Place end of rope under each body for tail.

5 Bake 12 to 14 minutes or until set. Remove from cookie sheets to cooling racks. Cool 30 minutes.

6 Use sprinkles to make eyes and baking bits to make noses. Add yellow licorice pieces for whiskers. Add pink licorice for tongues.

1 Cookie: Calories 310; Total Fat 16g (Saturated Fat 10g; Trans Fat 0.5g); Cholesterol 45mg; Sodium 140mg; Total Carbohydrate 38g (Dietary Fiber 1g); Protein 3g **Exchanges:** 1 Starch, 1½ Other Carbohydrate, 3 Fat **Carbohydrate Choices:** 2½

Sweet Success Tips

Use a small dab of chocolate frosting, peanut butter or melted chocolate to adhere the candy to the cat's faces.

You can substitute any small colorful candy for the miniature candy-coated baking bits.

Peanut Butter Spider Cookies

PREP TIME: 1 hour **START TO FINISH:** 1 hour   **3 dozen cookies**

1 pouch Betty Crocker peanut butter cookie mix

3 tablespoons vegetable oil

1 tablespoon water

1 egg

36 round chewy caramels in milk chocolate (from 12-oz bag), unwrapped

Black or red string licorice

72 mini candy-coated milk chocolate candies

1 tube (0.68 oz) Betty Crocker black decorating gel

1 Heat oven to 375°F. In medium bowl, stir cookie mix, oil, water and egg until dough forms.

2 Shape dough into 36 (1-inch) balls. Place balls 2 inches apart on ungreased cookie sheets.

3 Bake 8 to 10 minutes or until light golden brown. Immediately press 1 chewy caramel in center of each cookie. Cool 2 minutes; remove from cookie sheets to cooling racks.

4 Cut licorice into 8 (2-inch) pieces for each spider. Attach legs by sticking into chewy caramel. Use baking bits for eyes and black gel to make pupils of eyes. Store in single layer in tightly covered container.

1 Cookie: Calories 120; Total Fat 4.5g (Saturated Fat 1g; Trans Fat 0g); Cholesterol 5mg; Sodium 95mg; Total Carbohydrate 18g (Dietary Fiber 0g); Protein 1g **Exchanges:** 1 Other Carbohydrate, 1 Fat **Carbohydrate Choices:** 1

Glowing Spiced Pumpkins

PREP TIME: 2 hours 15 minutes **START TO FINISH:** 4 hours 35 minutes   **32 cookies**

1 pouch Betty Crocker sugar cookie mix

⅓ cup butter, melted

1 egg

1 tablespoon all-purpose flour

2 teaspoons pumpkin pie spice

1¼ teaspoons ground nutmeg

1 teaspoon vanilla

8 hard round butterscotch candies, unwrapped, crushed

8 hard round cinnamon candies, unwrapped, crushed

1 In medium bowl, mix all ingredients except candies with spoon. Cover; refrigerate 1 hour.

2 Heat oven to 350°F. Line cookie sheet with cooking parchment paper. On floured surface, roll dough ⅛ inch thick. Cut with 3½-inch pumpkin-shaped cookie cutter. Place cutouts about 2 inches apart on cookie sheets. With small cookie cutters or paring knife, cut out eyes, nose and mouth in jack-o'-lantern style.

3 Using ¼-teaspoon measure, place butterscotch candies in cutouts for eyes and cinnamon candies in cutouts for nose and mouth. Fill each cutout as full as possible, making sure candies touch dough on all sides of each hole.

4 Bake 8 to 9 minutes or until candy is melted and cookies are set. Cool until candies harden, about 4 minutes. Remove from cookie sheets to cooling racks; cool completely, about 30 minutes.

1 Cookie: Calories 100; Total Fat 3.5g (Saturated Fat 1.5g; Trans Fat 0.5g); Cholesterol 10mg; Sodium 70mg; Total Carbohydrate 15g (Dietary Fiber 0g); Protein 0g **Exchanges:** ½ Starch, ½ Other Carbohydrate, ½ Fat **Carbohydrate Choices:** 1

Sweet Success Tips

Use a mini food processor to easily crush the hard candies. Or place candies in a small resealable freezer plastic bag; smash with a rolling pin or the flat side of a meat mallet until finely crushed.

Use any other color or flavor of hard candy as desired. Orange hard candies work well.

Giant Witch Cookies

PREP TIME: 40 minutes START TO FINISH: 1 hour 20 minutes   **10 cookies**

1   cup sugar

1   cup butter or margarine, softened

1   egg

1   teaspoon vanilla

3   cups all-purpose flour

½   teaspoon baking powder

½   teaspoon salt

1   container Betty Crocker Rich & Creamy vanilla frosting

3   or 4 drops green food color

3   or 4 drops yellow food color

1   container Betty Crocker Rich & Creamy chocolate frosting

Assorted candies for decorating, as desired

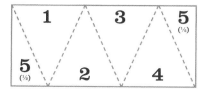

1 In large bowl, beat sugar and butter with electric mixer on medium speed until creamy. Beat in egg and vanilla. Stir in flour, baking powder and salt. Divide dough in half; wrap in plastic wrap. Refrigerate 1 hour for easier handling.

2 Heat oven to 375°F. Line cookie sheets with cooking parchment paper. Shape half of dough into 10 (1½-inch) balls. On parchment-lined cookie sheets, pat each ball of dough into 4-inch circle, using floured fingers if necessary. Place 2 or 3 circles on each cookie sheet, about 9 inches apart.

3 On floured surface, divide remaining half of dough into 2 portions. Roll each portion into 9×6-inch rectangle. Cut each rectangle into 4 whole triangles and 2 half triangles (see diagram). Press 2 half triangles together to form fifth whole triangle. Cut ½-inch strip from top edge of each dough circle on cookie sheet; set aside. Place triangle over each cut edge of circle, covering ¼ inch of cut edge; press to seal, aligning edge of triangle with edge of circle. Slightly bend point of "hat" if desired. Roll each ½-inch strip into 2 (1-inch) ropes; attach to either side of "hat" for brim.

4 Bake 7 to 11 minutes or until edges of cookies are golden and surfaces look dry. With broad metal pancake turner, remove cookies from cookie sheets to cooling racks. Cool completely, about 30 minutes.

5 Tint vanilla frosting green with green and yellow food colors. Spread on circles for witches' faces. Spread chocolate frosting on hats. Make faces using candies.

1 Cookie: Calories 730; Total Fat 32g (Saturated Fat 15g; Trans Fat 6g); Cholesterol 70mg; Sodium 490mg; Total Carbohydrate 106g (Dietary Fiber 1g); Protein 4g **Exchanges:** 1½ Starch, 5½ Other Carbohydrate, 6 Fat **Carbohydrate Choices:** 7

Sweet Success Tips

To color the frosting a more intense green, use electric green gel paste instead of liquid food color.

To make licorice more pliable, warm it in the microwave 3 to 5 seconds.

Witches' Brooms

PREP TIME: 35 minutes START TO FINISH: 1 hour 5 minutes   20 cookies

½ cup packed brown sugar

½ cup butter or margarine, softened

2 tablespoons water

1 teaspoon vanilla

1½ cups all-purpose flour

⅛ teaspoon salt

10 pretzel rods (about 8½ inches long), cut in half crosswise

2 teaspoons shortening

⅔ cup semisweet chocolate chips

⅓ cup butterscotch chips

½ teaspoon shortening

1 Heat oven to 350°F. In medium bowl, beat brown sugar, butter, water and vanilla with electric mixer on medium speed until blended. Stir in flour and salt. Shape dough into 20 (1¼-inch) balls.

2 Place pretzel rod halves on ungreased cookie sheets. Press ball of dough onto cut end of each pretzel rod. Press dough with fork to look like bristles of broom. Bake about 12 minutes or until set but not brown. Remove from cookie sheets to cooling racks. Cool completely.

3 Cover cookie sheets with waxed paper. Place brooms on waxed paper. In 1-quart saucepan, melt 2 teaspoons shortening and the chocolate chips over low heat, stirring occasionally, until smooth. Remove from heat. Spoon melted chocolate over brooms, leaving about 1 inch at top of pretzel handle and bottom halves of cookie bristles uncovered.

4 In small microwavable bowl, microwave butterscotch chips and ½ teaspoon shortening uncovered on Medium-High (70%) 30 to 50 seconds, stirring after 30 seconds, until chips can be stirred smooth. Pour mixture into resealable food-storage plastic bag, snip off bottom corner and drizzle over chocolate. Let stand until chocolate is firm before storing.

1 Cookie: Calories 180; Total Fat 8g (Saturated Fat 5g; Trans Fat 0g); Cholesterol 10mg; Sodium 160mg; Total Carbohydrate 24g (Dietary Fiber 1g); Protein 2g **Exchanges:** ½ Starch, 1 Other Carbohydrate, 1½ Fat **Carbohydrate Choices:** 1½

Sweet Success Tip

Cookie dough can be covered and refrigerated up to 24 hours before baking. If it's too firm to shape, let it stand at room temperature 30 minutes.

Cookie Bones

PREP TIME: 2 hours 45 minutes **START TO FINISH:** 3 hours 15 minutes   **4 dozen cookies**

1   pouch Betty Crocker sugar
    cookie mix
⅓   cup butter or margarine,
    softened
2   tablespoons all-purpose
    flour
1   egg
24 pretzel rods, broken in half
3   cups white vanilla baking
    chips (18 oz)

1 Heat oven to 350°F. In medium bowl, stir cookie mix, butter, flour and egg until soft dough forms. Place dough in refrigerator to chill slightly, about 30 minutes.

2 Roll dough into 96 half-tablespoon-size balls. Press and roll 1 dough ball around both ends of each pretzel to from bone shape; repeat with remaining dough and pretzels. Place 1 inch apart on ungreased cookie sheets. Bake 6 to 8 minutes or until edges of cookie are light golden brown. Cool completely on cooling racks, about 15 minutes.

3 In small microwavable bowl, microwave baking chips uncovered on High in 30-second increments until melted when stirred. Dip each cookie into coating. Place on cooling racks until set, about 15 minutes.

1 Cookie: Calories 140; Total Fat 5g (Saturated Fat 3g; Trans Fat 0g); Cholesterol 10mg; Sodium 160mg; Total Carbohydrate 20g (Dietary Fiber 0g); Protein 2g **Exchanges:** ½ Starch, 1 Other Carbohydrate, 1 Fat **Carbohydrate Choices:** 1

Sweet Success Tip

Use vanilla-flavored candy coating (almond bark) for the white vanilla baking chips.

Pumpkin Cookies
with Browned Butter Frosting

PREP TIME: 55 minutes START TO FINISH: 1 hour 40 minutes   2½ dozen cookies

COOKIES

- ⅔ **cup granulated sugar**
- ⅔ **cup packed brown sugar**
- ¾ **cup butter, softened**
- 1 **teaspoon vanilla**
- ½ **cup (from 15-oz can) pumpkin (not pumpkin pie mix)**
- 2 **eggs**
- 2¼ **cups all-purpose flour**
- 1 **teaspoon baking soda**
- 1 **teaspoon ground cinnamon**
- ½ **teaspoon salt**

BROWNED BUTTER FROSTING

- 3 **cups powdered sugar**
- 1 **teaspoon vanilla**
- 3 **to 4 tablespoons milk**
- ⅓ **cup butter★**

1 Heat oven to 375°F. In large bowl, beat granulated sugar, brown sugar, ¾ cup butter and 1 teaspoon vanilla with electric mixer on medium speed, scraping bowl occasionally, until well blended. Beat in pumpkin and eggs until well mixed. On low speed, beat in flour, baking soda, cinnamon and salt.

2 On ungreased cookie sheets, drop dough by heaping tablespoonfuls about 2 inches apart.

3 Bake 10 to 12 minutes or until almost no indentation remains when touched in center. Immediately remove from cookie sheets to cooling racks. Cool completely, about 45 minutes.

4 In medium bowl, place powdered sugar, 1 teaspoon vanilla and 3 tablespoons milk. In 1-quart saucepan, heat ⅓ cup butter over medium heat, stirring constantly, just until light brown.

5 Pour browned butter over powdered sugar mixture. Beat on low speed about 1 minute or until smooth. Gradually add just enough of the remaining 1 tablespoon milk to make frosting creamy and spreadable. Generously frost cooled cookies. Store in tightly covered container.

★*Do not use margarine or vegetable oil spreads in the frosting; it will burn.*

1 Cookie: Calories 190; Total Fat 7g (Saturated Fat 4.5g; Trans Fat 0g); Cholesterol 30mg; Sodium 135mg; Total Carbohydrate 29g (Dietary Fiber 0g); Protein 2g **Exchanges:** ½ Starch, 1½ Other Carbohydrate, 1½ Fat **Carbohydrate Choices:** 2

Spicy Pumpkin Cookies with Browned Butter Frosting: Add ⅛ teaspoon each ground cloves and ground ginger with the flour.

Pumpkin Whoopie Pies: Omit Browned Butter Frosting. In medium bowl, beat 1½ cups powdered sugar, ½ jar (7 oz) marshmallow creme and 6 tablespoons butter or margarine, softened, about 2 minutes or until light and fluffy. Place flat sides of 2 cookies together with 2 tablespoons filling, sandwich-style. Makes 15 sandwich cookies. Store in tightly covered container.

Halloween Goody Bars

PREP TIME: 35 minutes **START TO FINISH:** 3 hours 30 minutes **32 bars**

1½ cups quick-cooking oats

1½ cups all-purpose flour

1 cup packed brown sugar

¾ teaspoon salt

1 cup butter, melted

1 cup chopped pecans

1 can (14 oz) sweetened condensed milk (not evaporated)

1 cup semisweet chocolate chips (6 oz)

2 tablespoons butter, softened

¾ cup orange and brown candy-coated chocolate candies

1 Heat oven to 350°F. Spray 13×9-inch pan with cooking spray.

2 In large bowl, mix oats, flour, brown sugar, salt and 1 cup butter with spoon. Stir in pecans. Remove 1 cup; reserve for topping. Press remaining mixture into pan.

3 In 2-quart saucepan, cook condensed milk, chocolate chips and 2 tablespoons butter over medium heat, stirring constantly, until chips are melted and mixture is smooth. Spread chocolate mixture over crust. Sprinkle with candies and reserved oat mixture; press into chocolate mixture.

4 Bake 23 to 25 minutes or until set. Cool completely, about 2½ hours. Cut into 8 rows by 4 rows.

1 Bar: Calories 240; Total Fat 13g (Saturated Fat 7g; Trans Fat 0g); Cholesterol 20mg; Sodium 140mg; Total Carbohydrate 28g (Dietary Fiber 1g); Protein 3g **Exchanges:** ½ Starch, 1½ Other Carbohydrate, 2½ Fat **Carbohydrate Choices:** 2

Sweet Success Tip

Make these bars year-round, using different colors of chocolate candies to match the season.

Whoopie Pies

PREP TIME: 45 minutes **START TO FINISH:** 1 hour 25 minutes   1½ **dozen sandwich cookies**

COOKIES

- 1 cup granulated sugar
- ½ cup butter, softened
- ½ cup buttermilk
- 2 teaspoons vanilla
- 1 egg
- 2 oz unsweetened baking chocolate, melted, cooled
- 1¾ cups all-purpose flour
- ½ teaspoon baking soda
- ½ teaspoon salt

CREAMY MARSHMALLOW FILLING

- 3 cups powdered sugar
- 1 jar (7 oz) marshmallow creme
- ¾ cup butter, softened
- 6 to 7 teaspoons milk

1 Heat oven to 400°F. Grease cookie sheets with shortening or cooking spray, or line with cooking parchment paper or silicone baking mat.

2 In large bowl, beat granulated sugar, ½ cup butter, the buttermilk, vanilla, egg and chocolate with electric mixer on medium speed, or mix with spoon. Stir in flour, baking soda and salt. Onto cookie sheets, drop dough by rounded tablespoonfuls about 2 inches apart.

3 Bake 8 to 10 minutes or until almost no indentation remains when touched in center. Immediately remove from cookie sheets to cooling racks. Cool completely, about 30 minutes.

4 In large bowl, beat filling ingredients on medium speed about 2 minutes or until light and fluffy. Place flat sides of 2 cookies together with slightly less than 3 tablespoons filling, sandwich-style. Store in tightly covered container.

1 Sandwich Cookie: Calories 350; Total Fat 15g (Saturated Fat 9g; Trans Fat 0.5g); Cholesterol 45mg; Sodium 210mg; Total Carbohydrate 50g (Dietary Fiber 1g); Protein 2g **Exchanges:** 1 Starch, 2½ Other Carbohydrate, 3 Fat **Carbohydrate Choices:** 3

Chocolate Chip Whoopie Pies: Fold ½ cup miniature semisweet chocolate chips into the filling.

Pink Peppermint Whoopie Pies: Add 6 drops red food color to filling ingredients. Once cookies are assembled, sprinkle edges of filling with crushed peppermint candies or candy canes.

Toffee Whoopie Pies: Fold ½ cup chocolate-covered toffee bits into the filling.

Pink Peppermint Whoopie Pies
and Whoopie Pies

Cute Turkey Cookies

PREP TIME: 15 minutes **START TO FINISH:** 2 hours   **8 cookies**

½ **cup miniature semisweet chocolate chips**

8 **fudge-striped shortbread cookies**

8 **fudge-covered graham crackers**

8 **miniature chocolate-covered peanut butter cup candies, unwrapped**

1 **roll (1.7 oz) round chewy caramels in milk chocolate, unwrapped**

24 **pieces candy corn**

1 **tube (0.68 oz) Betty Crocker black decorating gel**

1 In small resealable freezer plastic bag, place chocolate chips; seal bag. Microwave on High about 1 minute or until softened. Gently squeeze bag until chocolate is smooth; cut off tiny bottom corner of bag. On work surface, lay shortbread cookies flat, with stripes vertical, in a row. Squeeze bag to pipe a line of melted chocolate across bottom of each cookie, crosswise over fudge stripes. Center longer side of 1 graham cracker on chocolate line; hold until chocolate begins to set. Repeat with remaining cookies and graham crackers. Allow to set up, about 30 minutes.

2 If necessary, reheat chocolate in microwave on High 10 to 30 seconds; gently squeeze bag until chocolate is smooth. Pipe about ½ teaspoon melted chocolate on wider end of 1 peanut butter cup; place over hole on 1 shortbread cookie, resting against graham cracker. Repeat with remaining peanut butter cups.

3 Pipe about ½ teaspoon melted chocolate on bottom of 1 round caramel; place on 1 peanut butter cup (for turkey body). Repeat with remaining round caramels. Allow to set up, about 15 minutes.

4 Turn cookies so graham crackers are flat on work surface and you are looking at the shortbread cookies (turkey feathers). Pipe small amount of chocolate on one side of 1 candy corn piece; center on round caramel and peanut butter cup for beak. Hold in position until chocolate begins to set, 1 to 2 minutes. Repeat with remaining 7 candy corn pieces.

5 Pipe small amount of chocolate on one side of 1 candy corn piece; place 1 candy corn piece on chocolate graham crackers against body, on either side, for turkey legs. Repeat with remaining candy corn pieces. Using black gel, add eyes on each candy corn beak. Let stand until set, about 1 hour.

1 Cookie: Calories 190; Total Fat 9g (Saturated Fat 3.5g; Trans Fat 0.5g); Cholesterol 0mg; Sodium 60mg; Total Carbohydrate 27g (Dietary Fiber 1g); Protein 1g **Exchanges:** 2 Other Carbohydrate, 2 Fat **Carbohydrate Choices:** 2

Chocolate Reindeer Cookies

PREP TIME: 1 hour 40 minutes **START TO FINISH:** 2 hours **32 cookies**

COOKIES

- **2 cups all-purpose flour**
- **1 teaspoon baking soda**
- **¼ teaspoon salt**
- **½ cup semisweet chocolate chips (3 oz)**
- **½ cup butter or margarine, softened**
- **½ cup packed light brown sugar**
- **1 cup granulated sugar**
- **2 eggs**

DECORATIONS

- **16 caramels, unwrapped**
- **16 chocolate licorice twists (7 inch)**
- **1 pouch (7 oz) Betty Crocker Cookie Icing chocolate icing**
- **1 pouch (7 oz) Betty Crocker Cookie Icing white icing**
- **1 pouch (7 oz) Betty Crocker Cookie Icing red icing**
- **32 bite-size chocolate-covered caramels (from 10-oz box)**
- **64 brown mini candy-coated milk chocolate candies**

1 Heat oven to 350°F. Spray 2 cookie sheets with cooking spray or line with cooking parchment paper. In medium bowl, stir together flour, baking soda and salt; set aside. In small microwavable cup, microwave chocolate chips uncovered on High 30 to 45 seconds, stirring after 30 seconds, until melted and smooth; set aside.

2 In large bowl, beat butter and sugars with electric mixer on medium speed until fluffy. Add eggs, one at a time, beating until combined. Add melted chocolate; beat until blended. Add flour mixture; beat until soft dough forms. Refrigerate dough 20 minutes.

3 Shape dough into 64 (1-inch) and 32 (¾-inch) balls. For each cookie, arrange 1 (¾-inch) and 2 (1-inch) balls, edges touching, on ungreased cookie sheets, leaving 2 inches between cookies. Bake 9 to 10 minutes or until golden brown. Cool 1 minute; remove from cookie sheets to cooling racks. Cool completely before decorating.

4 Meanwhile, to make ears, cut caramels in half horizontally. Cut each half into quarters, making 64 thin squares. Using fingers, slightly press together opposite corners of squares, forming leaf shapes (see photo); set aside.

5 To make antlers, cut each licorice twist into 4 (1¾-inch) pieces. Cut 2 (1-inch) slits in each piece, creating 3 sections; cut off half of each outer section (see photo).

6 To Make Reindeer: Pipe 4 small dollops chocolate icing onto smaller portion of cooled cookie; press on ears and antlers. For eyes, pipe white icing onto cookie in 2 small oval-shaped dollops; press 1 milk chocolate candy on each. For nose, pipe small dollop of chocolate icing onto cookie; press on 1 chocolate-covered caramel. Using red icing, pipe mouth onto cookie.

1 Cookie: Calories 110; Total Fat 4g (Saturated Fat 2.5g; Trans Fat 0g); Cholesterol 20mg; Sodium 85mg; Total Carbohydrate 17g (Dietary Fiber 0g); Protein 1g **Exchanges:** ½ Starch, ½ Other Carbohydrate, 1 Fat **Carbohydrate Choices:** 1

Ginger Elf Cookies

PREP TIME: 40 minutes START TO FINISH: 40 minutes   **26 cookies**

COOKIES

- 1¼ **cups all-purpose flour**
- 1 **teaspoon baking soda**
- ¼ **teaspoon salt**
- 1½ **teaspoons ground ginger**
- 1 **teaspoon ground cinnamon**
- ½ **cup butter or margarine, softened**
- ½ **cup packed dark brown sugar**
- ¼ **cup granulated sugar**
- 2 **eggs**

DECORATIONS

- 1 **pouch (7 oz) Betty Crocker Cookie Icing chocolate icing**
- 1 **pouch (7 oz) Betty Crocker Cookie Icing white icing**
- 1 **pouch (7 oz) Betty Crocker Cookie Icing red icing**
- 13 **green or red Betty Crocker Fruit Roll-Ups® (from two 5-oz boxes), unwrapped**
- 52 **brown mini candy-coated milk chocolate candies**
- 52 **red and green mini candy-coated milk chocolate candies**

1 Heat oven to 350°F. In medium bowl, stir together flour, baking soda, salt and spices; set aside. In large bowl, beat butter and sugars with electric mixer on medium speed until light and fluffy. Add eggs, one at a time, beating until blended. Gradually beat in flour mixture until soft dough forms.

2 Onto ungreased cookie sheets, drop dough by rounded tablespoonfuls 2 inches apart. Bake 9 to 11 minutes or until golden brown. Cool 1 to 2 minutes; remove from cookie sheets to cooling racks. Cool completely before decorating.

3 To Decorate Cookies: Using chocolate icing, pipe hair. Using white icing, pipe two small dollops for eyes; press 1 brown milk chocolate candy on each. Using red icing, pipe pea-sized dot for nose; press on 1 red milk chocolate candy. Pipe on ears and mouth. To make hats, cut fruit snacks in half vertically into rectangles. Fold rectangles in half, creating squares. Fold squares in half diagonally to create triangles. To create hat brims, slightly roll up 1 edge of each triangle. If necessary, gently pull and stretch hat to fit cookie. Fold hat tip down, at an angle, to meet brim (see photo). Using white icing, pipe small dot where tip of hat meets brim; press 1 red milk chocolate candy on dot. Let stand until frosting is set. Store in airtight container, using waxed paper between cookie layers.

1 Cookie: Calories 80; Total Fat 4g (Saturated Fat 2.5g; Trans Fat 0g); Cholesterol 25mg; Sodium 100mg; Total Carbohydrate 11g (Dietary Fiber 0g); Protein 1g **Exchanges:** ½ Starch, 1 Fat **Carbohydrate Choices:** 1

Sweet Success Tip

Ice cream scoops come in a variety of sizes and are a great way to make uniform-sized cookies. They also come in handy when dealing with "sticky" cookie dough.

Holiday Penguin Cookies

PREP TIME: 1 hour 10 minutes **START TO FINISH:** 1 hour 30 minutes   **12 cookies**

COOKIES

- 1 **pouch Betty Crocker sugar cookie mix**
- 1 **egg**
- ⅓ **cup butter or margarine, softened**
- 1 **tablespoon flour**

DECORATIONS

- 1 **container (12 oz) Betty Crocker Whipped fluffy white frosting**
- 2 **tablespoons coarse white sparkling sugar**
- ¼ **cup coarse black sparkling sugar**
- 1 **pouch (7 oz) Betty Crocker Cookie Icing white icing**
- 24 **brown mini candy-coated milk chocolate candies**
- 6 **candy corn, cut in half vertically**
- 24 **black jelly beans**

1 Heat oven to 350°F. Make cookie dough as directed on pouch for Cutout Cookies. On lightly floured surface, roll out dough to ¼-inch thickness. Using table knife, cut out 12 ovals (3½×2½ inches) and 12 small circles, slightly larger than a quarter, gently pressing together and rerolling dough scraps as necessary.

2 For each cookie, arrange 1 oval and 1 circle, edges touching, on ungreased cookie sheets, leaving 2 inches between cookies. Bake 7 to 9 minutes until edges are light golden brown. Cool 1 minute; carefully remove from cookie sheets to cooling racks. Cool completely before frosting.

3 Spread frosting evenly over cooled cookies. For each cookie, using teaspoon, carefully sprinkle white sugar in center of frosted oval, creating belly. Carefully sprinkle black sugar over remainder of frosted cookie. Using white icing, pipe small dollops for eyes; press 1 milk chocolate candy on each. Press into frosting 1 candy corn, flat side down, for nose and 2 jelly beans for feet.

1 Cookie: Calories 410; Total Fat 16g (Saturated Fat 6g; Trans Fat 3.5g); Cholesterol 30mg; Sodium 200mg; Total Carbohydrate 64g (Dietary Fiber 0g); Protein 2g **Exchanges:** 1 Starch, 3½ Other Carbohydrate, 3 Fat **Carbohydrate Choices:** 4

Sweet Success Tips

To make dough easier to handle when rolling, cover with plastic wrap and refrigerate 15 minutes.

A 3-inch plastic or paper cup squeezed into oval shape works well as a cookie cutter for the penguin body.

Baby Polar Bear Shortbread Cookies

PREP TIME: 1 hour 15 minutes **START TO FINISH:** 1 hour 15 minutes **38 cookies**

COOKIES

- 1 **cup butter, softened**
- ¾ **cup granulated sugar**
- ½ **teaspoon vanilla**
- ½ **teaspoon salt**
- 2¼ **cups all-purpose flour**

ICING

- 1 **cup powdered sugar**
- 3 **to 5 teaspoons milk**
- ¼ **teaspoon vanilla**

DECORATIONS

- ¾ **cup grated white chocolate baking bar (about 1 oz from 4-oz package)**
- 76 **white vanilla baking chips, tips cut off (about ¼ cup)**
- 76 **mini semisweet chocolate chips (about 2 teaspoons)**
- 19 **small round chocolate-covered creamy mints, cut in half**
- 1 **pouch (7 oz) Betty Crocker Cookie Icing chocolate icing**

1 Heat oven to 350°F. In large bowl, beat butter and granulated sugar with electric mixer on medium speed until light and fluffy. Add vanilla and salt; beat until blended. Beat in flour gradually on low speed until soft dough forms. Shape dough into ball.

2 On lightly floured surface, roll out dough to ¼-inch thickness. Using 2-inch round cookie cutter, cut out 38 circles, gently pressing together and rerolling scraps as necessary. On ungreased cookie sheets, place circles 2 inches apart.

3 Bake 10 to 12 minutes until edges are just beginning to brown. Immediately remove from cookie sheets to cooling racks. Cool completely before decorating.

4 In small bowl, stir together powdered sugar, 3 teaspoons milk and ¼ teaspoon vanilla until blended. If necessary, stir in additional milk, 1 teaspoon at a time, until smooth and desired consistency.

5 To Decorate Cookies: Using knife, spread icing over cookies in thin layer. For each cookie, immediately sprinkle about ¾ teaspoon white chocolate evenly over icing. Press into icing 2 vanilla baking chips, cut side down, for ears, 2 chocolate chips for eyes and 1 mint, cut side down, for nose. Using chocolate icing, pipe mouth.

1 Cookie: Calories 120; Total Fat 6g (Saturated Fat 4g; Trans Fat 0g); Cholesterol 15mg; Sodium 70mg; Total Carbohydrate 16g (Dietary Fiber 0g); Protein 1g **Exchanges:** ½ Starch, ½ Other Carbohydrate, 1 Fat **Carbohydrate Choices:** 1

Sweet Success Tip

Shortbread dough gets its flakiness from butter, so using it to make this recipe is recommended.

Lime Christmas Wreaths

PREP TIME: 1 hour 10 minutes START TO FINISH: 2 hours 45 minutes   2½ dozen cookies

½ cup butter, softened
¼ cup sour cream
¾ cup granulated sugar
1 egg
2 tablespoons grated lime peel
1 tablespoon lime juice
1 teaspoon vanilla
2½ cups all-purpose flour
½ teaspoon baking soda
¼ teaspoon salt
1 cup powdered sugar
2 to 3 tablespoons lime juice
   Colored sugars, if desired
   White or colored sprinkles, if desired

1 In large bowl, beat butter, sour cream and granulated sugar with electric mixer on medium speed until creamy. Add egg, lime peel, lime juice and vanilla; beat until smooth. On low speed, beat in flour, baking soda and salt until dough forms. Gather dough into ball; divide in half. Shape each half into a round; wrap in plastic wrap. Refrigerate 1 hour.

2 Heat oven to 375°F. Place pastry cloth on work surface; sprinkle with flour. With floured cloth-covered rolling pin, roll 1 round of dough ⅛ inch thick. Cut with floured 3-inch fluted cutter. With 1-inch scalloped or fluted canapé cutter, cut out center of each round. On ungreased cookie sheets, place wreath cutouts 1 inch apart. Cut each small cutout in half; brush backs of small cutouts with water and place on wreaths for bows. Repeat with second round of dough.

3 Bake 6 to 8 minutes or until edges start to brown. Remove from cookie sheets to cooling racks; cool completely.

4 In small bowl, mix powdered sugar and 2 tablespoons of the lime juice with whisk. Stir in remaining 1 tablespoon lime juice, 1 teaspoon at a time, until glaze is thin. Working with a few cookies at a time, brush glaze over cookies and immediately decorate with sugars and sprinkles. Let stand until set. Store in layers with waxed paper between in tightly covered container.

1 Cookie: Calories 110; Total Fat 3.5g (Saturated Fat 2g; Trans Fat 0g); Cholesterol 15mg; Sodium 65mg; Total Carbohydrate 17g (Dietary Fiber 0g); Protein 1g **Exchanges:** ½ Starch, ½ Other Carbohydrate, ½ Fat **Carbohydrate Choices:** 1

Sweet Success Tips

If you prefer, you can skip the glaze, and sprinkle the unbaked cookies with colored sugar before baking. Some sprinkles will melt during baking, so do some experimenting before sprinkling all of the cookies.

Silicone brushes work very well for brushing the glaze onto the cookies. They can be purchased in most kitchen stores or kitchen sections of department stores.

Snowflake Mittens

PREP TIME: 1 hour **START TO FINISH:** 1 hour 45 minutes **21 cookies**

1 pouch Betty Crocker sugar cookie mix

1 tablespoon all-purpose flour

⅓ cup butter, softened

1 egg

1 tablespoon grated lemon peel

1 container Betty Crocker Rich & Creamy creamy white frosting

3 drops blue food color

1 can (6.4 oz) Betty Crocker Easy Flow white decorating icing

White snowflake sprinkles or other white sprinkles, if desired

1 Heat oven to 375°F. In large bowl, stir cookie mix, flour, butter, egg and lemon peel until dough forms; gather into ball. Divide dough in half; shape into 2 rounds. Wrap 1 round in plastic wrap.

2 On floured surface, roll unwrapped round ¼ inch thick. Cut with 3½-inch mitten-shaped cookie cutter. On ungreased large cookie sheets, place cutouts 1 inch apart. Repeat with second round. Reroll scraps and cut out additional cookies.

3 Bake 8 to 10 minutes or until edges are light golden brown. Cool 1 minute before removing from cookie sheets to cooling racks; cool completely.

4 Using ½ cup of the creamy white frosting, frost cuffs of mittens. Stir food color into remaining white frosting. Frost remaining portion of mittens with blue frosting. With decorating icing and small round tip, pipe small snowflake onto each mitten. Decorate with snowflake sprinkles. With star tip, decorate cuffs of mittens with decorating icing, if desired. Let dry.

1 Cookie: Calories 130; Total Fat 5g (Saturated Fat 2.5g; Trans Fat 1g); Cholesterol 20mg; Sodium 90mg; Total Carbohydrate 18g (Dietary Fiber 0g); Protein 1g **Exchanges:** ½ Starch, ½ Other Carbohydrate, 1 Fat **Carbohydrate Choices:** 1

Sweet Success Tips

Spoon some of the blue frosting into a small resealable food-storage plastic bag; cut off a tiny corner of bag and pipe each child's name across the cuff of a mitten.

Bake the cookies a day ahead and store them in an airtight container. Get the frosting and decorating items ready, and let the kids help decorate.

Crispy Ginger Men

PREP TIME: 50 minutes **START TO FINISH:** 50 minutes   **10 cookies**

- 3 cups Cheerios® cereal
- 2 cups coarsely chopped gingersnap cookies (about 30 cookies)
- ¼ cup butter
- 1 bag (10.5 oz) miniature marshmallows (5½ cups)
- ½ cup white vanilla baking chips
- 1 teaspoon vegetable oil
  Assorted decorating candies, if desired
  Betty Crocker Fruit by the Foot® chewy fruit snack rolls (any flavor), if desired

1 In large bowl, mix cereal and chopped cookies. In 2-quart nonstick saucepan, melt butter. Add marshmallows; cook and stir over medium-low heat until marshmallows are completely melted. Pour over cereal mixture; mix until coated.

2 Line cookie sheet with waxed paper; spray paper with cooking spray. Spray 3¾-inch open gingerbread man cookie cutter with cooking spray; place on cookie sheet. Spray hands well with cooking spray. Firmly pack cereal mixture evenly into cookie cutter, filling cutter completely; push out of cutter. Repeat until all mixture is used. Let stand until set.

3 In small resealable freezer plastic bag, place baking chips and oil; seal bag. Microwave on High about 1 minute or until softened. Gently squeeze bag until mixture is smooth. Refrigerate about 2 minutes or until slightly set. Cut off tiny corner of bag; squeeze bag to pipe melted chips over cookies as desired to decorate, using small dots to attach candy. When decorations are set, cut strips of fruit snack and tie around necks for scarves.

1 Cookie: Calories 350; Total Fat 11g (Saturated Fat 6g; Trans Fat 0g); Cholesterol 10mg; Sodium 300mg; Total Carbohydrate 57g (Dietary Fiber 2g); Protein 4g **Exchanges:** 2 Starch, 2 Other Carbohydrate, 2 Fat **Carbohydrate Choices:** 4

Sweet Success Tips

The marshmallow mixture is sticky. Letting it stand for a few minutes decreases the stickiness. It is also helpful to spray a rubber spatula with cooking spray for mixing the marshmallows into the cereal. Also, spray your hands very well to press the mixture into the cookie cutters.

Chop the cookies by hand as you would onions, or crumble them and pulse in a food processor until they are about ¼-inch pieces. Do not overprocess.

Gingerbread Cookies

PREP TIME: 1 hour 40 minutes START TO FINISH: 3 hours 40 minutes   5 dozen cookies

COOKIES

- ½ **cup packed brown sugar**
- ½ **cup butter, softened**
- ½ **cup molasses**
- ⅓ **cup cold water**
- 3½ **cups all-purpose flour**
- 2 **teaspoons baking soda**
- 2 **teaspoons ground ginger**
- ½ **teaspoon ground allspice**
- ½ **teaspoon ground cinnamon**
- ¼ **teaspoon ground cloves**
- ¼ **teaspoon salt**

DECORATOR'S FROSTING

- 2 **cups powdered sugar**
- 2 **tablespoons water or milk**
- ½ **teaspoon vanilla**
   Food color, colored sugars and small candies, if desired

1 In large bowl, beat brown sugar, butter, molasses and water with electric mixer on medium speed, or mix with spoon, until well blended. Stir in remaining cookie ingredients until mixed. Cover; refrigerate at least 2 hours.

2 Heat oven to 350°F. Grease cookie sheets with shortening or cooking spray, or line with cooking parchment paper or silicone baking mats.

3 Divide dough in half. Roll each half on lightly floured surface until ¼ inch thick. Cut with floured gingerbread boy or girl cookie cutter or other shaped cutter. On cookie sheets, place cutouts about 2 inches apart. After cutting as many cookies as possible, lightly press scraps of dough together; reroll dough and cut additional cookies.

4 Bake 10 to 12 minutes or until no indentation remains when touched in center. Immediately remove from cookie sheets to cooling racks. Cool cookie sheets 10 minutes between batches. Let cookies stand about 30 minutes until completely cooled.

5 Meanwhile, in medium bowl, mix powdered sugar, water and vanilla with spoon until smooth and spreadable. Stir in food color, one drop at a time, until frosting is desired color. (For intense, vivid color, use paste food color. You would have to use too much liquid food color to get a vivid color, and the frosting will begin to separate and look curdled.) Cover and set aside.

6 When ready to decorate, place frosting in small resealable food-storage plastic bag. Seal bag; push frosting down in one corner. With scissors, cut off one corner of bag. Squeeze bag to pipe frosting onto cookies and make desired design. Or spread over cookies with a small metal spatula. Decorate as desired with colored sugars and candies.

1 Cookie: Calories 60; Total Fat 1.5g (Saturated Fat 1g; Trans Fat 0g); Cholesterol 0mg; Sodium 65mg; Total Carbohydrate 10g (Dietary Fiber 0g); Protein 0g **Exchanges:** ½ Other Carbohydrate, ½ Fat **Carbohydrate Choices:** ½

Sweet Success Tip

Roll dough between two sheets of waxed paper or cooking parchment paper rather than on a floured surface. Carefully peel off the top sheet of waxed paper before cutting the cookie shapes.

Peppermint Candy Canes

PREP TIME: 1 hour 10 minutes **START TO FINISH:** 1 hour 40 minutes   **5½ dozen cookies**

⅓ cup butter, softened

¼ cup shortening

½ cup sugar

1 egg

1¼ cups all-purpose flour

¼ teaspoon baking powder

¼ teaspoon salt

1 teaspoon peppermint extract

5 drops red food color

3½ oz vanilla-flavored candy coating (almond bark)

1 Heat oven to 375°F. In large bowl, beat butter, shortening and sugar with electric mixer on medium speed until light and fluffy. Beat in egg. Stir in flour, baking powder, salt, peppermint extract and food color until mixed.

2 Place dough in cookie press. Fit ½-inch star template in press. Onto ungreased large cookie sheets, press 15-inch lines of dough 3 inches apart. Score at 3-inch intervals. Pull top of dough into a curve, forming candy cane.

3 Bake 5 to 7 minutes or until edges just start to brown. Immediately and carefully remove from cookie sheets to cooling racks; cool completely.

4 Place waxed paper under cooling racks. In small resealable freezer plastic bag, place candy coating; seal bag. Microwave on High 1 minute or until softened. Gently squeeze bag until coating is smooth; cut off tiny corner of bag. Squeeze bag to pipe coating diagonally over each candy cane for striped effect. Move position of cookie before coating sets completely so coating doesn't adhere to cooling rack.

1 Cookie: Calories 40; Total Fat 2.5g (Saturated Fat 1g; Trans Fat 0g); Cholesterol 5mg; Sodium 20mg; Total Carbohydrate 4g (Dietary Fiber 0g); Protein 0g **Exchanges:** ½ Fat **Carbohydrate Choices:** 0

Sweet Success Tips

The cookies are very fragile when they are warm, but are quite sturdy once they are cooled. To remove them from the cookie sheet, slide the spatula under the curved end first.

Once the cookies are cooled, they can be stacked in containers; they won't stick together or break easily.

Oatmeal Shortbread Santas

PREP TIME: 55 minutes **START TO FINISH:** 1 hour 40 minutes   **1 dozen cookies**

⅔ cup butter or margarine, softened

½ cup packed brown sugar

1 teaspoon vanilla

1 cup all-purpose flour

¾ cup quick-cooking oats

¼ teaspoon baking powder

2 cans (6.4 oz each) Betty Crocker Easy Flow white decorating icing

6 miniature marshmallows, cut in half

1 tablespoon red decorating sugar

24 blue mini candy-coated milk chocolate candies

12 red mini candy-coated milk chocolate candies

1 In large bowl, beat butter, brown sugar and vanilla with electric mixer on medium speed until creamy. Stir in flour, oats and baking powder. Gather dough into ball. Wrap in plastic wrap; refrigerate 30 minutes.

2 Heat oven to 350°F. On well-floured surface, roll dough ¼ inch thick. Cut with 3- to 3½-inch heart-shaped cookie cutter. On ungreased cookie sheet, place cutouts 2 inches apart.

3 Bake 8 to 10 minutes or until edges are light golden brown. Cool 1 minute; remove from cookie sheet to cooling rack. Cool completely.

4 Turn cookies so pointed ends are up. Using desired tip, pipe frosting on upper one-third of cookie for hat. Place 1 marshmallow half at tip of each hat; sprinkle with red sugar. Using small dots of frosting, attach 2 blue candies on each cookie for eyes. Pipe small frosting mustache below eyes; place red candy in center for mouth. Pipe frosting on lower one-third of each cookie for beard. Store in single layer, loosely covered.

1 Cookie: Calories 190; Total Fat 11g (Saturated Fat 7g; Trans Fat 0g); Cholesterol 25mg; Sodium 85mg; Total Carbohydrate 20g (Dietary Fiber 0g); Protein 2g **Exchanges:** 1 Starch, ½ Other Carbohydrate, 2 Fat **Carbohydrate Choices:** 1

Sweet Success Tip

These cookies are fragile when they are hot but are very sturdy once they have cooled.

Thumbprint Cookies

PREP TIME: 50 minutes **START TO FINISH:** 50 minutes **3 dozen cookies**

¼ cup packed brown sugar
¼ cup shortening
¼ cup butter, softened
½ teaspoon vanilla
1 egg, separated
1 cup all-purpose flour
¼ teaspoon salt
1 cup finely chopped nuts
About 6 tablespoons jelly or jam (any flavor)

1 Heat oven to 350°F. In medium bowl, beat brown sugar, shortening, butter, vanilla and egg yolk with electric mixer on medium speed, or mix with spoon. Stir in flour and salt.

2 Shape dough into 1-inch balls. In small bowl, beat egg white slightly with fork. Place nuts in another small bowl. Dip each ball into egg white, roll in nuts. On ungreased cookie sheets, place balls about 1 inch apart. Press thumb into center of each cookie to make indentation, but do not press all the way to the cookie sheet.

3 Bake 8 to 10 minutes or until light brown. Quickly remake indentations with end of wooden spoon if necessary. Immediately remove from cookie sheets to cooling racks. Fill each with about ½ teaspoon of the jelly.

1 Cookie: Calories 70; Total Fat 4.5g (Saturated Fat 1g; Trans Fat 0g); Cholesterol 10mg; Sodium 30mg; Total Carbohydrate 7g (Dietary Fiber 0g); Protein 0g **Exchanges:** ½ Starch, ½ Fat **Carbohydrate Choices:** ½

Hazelnut-Chocolate Thumbprint Cookies: Roll balls of dough in finely chopped hazelnuts (filberts). Instead of jelly, fill indentations with hazelnut spread with cocoa.

Lemon-Almond Thumbprint Cookies: Roll balls of dough into finely chopped slivered almonds. Instead of jelly, fill indentations with lemon curd.

Peanut-Fudge Thumbprint Cookies: Roll balls of dough in finely chopped dry-roasted peanuts. Instead of jelly, fill indentations with hot fudge topping (look for the thick topping, not the pourable or syrup variety).

Left to right: Lemon-Almond Thumbprint Cookies, Thumbprint Cookies, Hazelnut-Chocolate Thumbprint Cookies

Spiced Hazelnut Thumbprints

PREP TIME: 1 hour START TO FINISH: 1 hour   **2½ dozen cookies**

½ **cup butter or margarine, softened**

6 **tablespoons sugar**

1 **teaspoon vanilla**

1 **egg yolk**

1 **cup all-purpose flour**

½ **cup hazelnuts (filberts), toasted, skins removed and nuts ground (6 tablespoons)**

½ **teaspoon ground cinnamon**

¼ **teaspoon ground cloves**

¼ **teaspoon salt**

⅓ **cup strawberry or raspberry preserves**

1 Heat oven to 350°F. In large bowl, beat butter and sugar with electric mixer on medium speed until light and fluffy. Beat in vanilla and egg yolk until blended. On low speed, beat in flour, hazelnuts, cinnamon, cloves and salt.

2 Shape dough into 1-inch balls. On ungreased cookie sheets, place balls 2 inches apart.

3 Bake 10 minutes. Using end of handle of wooden spoon, press a well into center of each cookie. Fill each well with ½ teaspoon preserves. Bake about 10 minutes longer or until edges are light golden. Cool 2 minutes; remove from cookie sheets to cooling racks.

1 Cookie: Calories 70; Total Fat 4g (Saturated Fat 2g; Trans Fat 0g); Cholesterol 15mg; Sodium 45mg; Total Carbohydrate 8g (Dietary Fiber 0g); Protein 0g **Exchanges:** ½ Other Carbohydrate, 1 Fat **Carbohydrate Choices:** ½

Sweet Success Tip

Any other nut may be used in place of the hazelnuts.

Cherry-Topped Chocolate Tassies

PREP TIME: 25 minutes **START TO FINISH:** 1 hour 10 minutes   **2 dozen cookies**

½ cup butter, softened

1 package (3 oz) cream cheese, softened

1 cup all-purpose flour

⅛ teaspoon salt

1 cup miniature semisweet chocolate chips

24 large maraschino cherries, drained

1 Heat oven to 350°F. Spray 24 mini muffin cups with cooking spray.

2 In medium bowl, beat butter and cream cheese with electric mixer on medium speed until well mixed. On low speed, beat in flour and salt until dough forms.

3 Shape dough into 24 (1¼-inch) balls. Press 1 ball in bottom and up side of each muffin cup. Fill each cup with about 2 teaspoons chocolate chips. Top each with a cherry.

4 Bake 13 to 16 minutes or until edges of cups are golden brown. Cool in pan on cooling rack 10 minutes. Remove from muffin cups to cooling racks; cool completely.

1 Cookie: Calories 110; Total Fat 7g (Saturated Fat 4.5g; Trans Fat 0g); Cholesterol 15mg; Sodium 50mg; Total Carbohydrate 10g (Dietary Fiber 0g); Protein 1g **Exchanges:** ½ Other Carbohydrate, 1½ Fat **Carbohydrate Choices:** ½

Sweet Success Tips

Sprinkle cookie edges while they are still hot with powdered sugar or red decorating sugar.

These tassies are fragile when they're hot, so it's important to let them cool 10 minutes before removing from the muffin cups. They set up once they are cooled.

Cherry-Chocolate Cookie Cups

PREP TIME: 45 minutes **START TO FINISH:** 1 hour 30 minutes **4 dozen cookies**

1 pouch Betty Crocker sugar cookie mix

⅓ cup unsweetened baking cocoa

½ cup butter or margarine, softened

2 tablespoons water

1 egg

1 bag (12 oz) white vanilla baking chips

¼ cup whipping cream

¼ cup amaretto

½ cup finely chopped candied cherries

Red decorating sugar crystals or 8 candied cherries, each cut into 6 pieces

1 Heat oven to 350°F. Lightly spray 48 mini muffin cups with cooking spray. In medium bowl, stir cookie mix and cocoa until well mixed. Stir in butter, water and egg until soft dough forms.

2 Shape dough into 48 (1-inch) balls. (If dough is sticky, use moistened fingers.) Press 1 ball in bottom and up side of each muffin cup.

3 Bake 8 to 9 minutes or until edges are set. Gently press end of handle of wooden spoon into bottom and against side of each cookie cup to flatten, being careful not to make holes in dough. Bake 2 to 3 minutes longer or until bottom is set. Cool in pan on cooling rack 20 to 30 minutes.

4 Meanwhile, in medium microwavable bowl, mix baking chips and cream. Microwave on High 30 seconds; stir. Microwave 20 to 30 seconds longer or until mixture is smooth and chips are melted. Stir in amaretto and chopped cherries. Let stand 10 to 15 minutes until slightly thickened; stir.

5 Using tip of knife or metal spatula, lift cookie cups out of pan, gently twisting and lifting up; place on cooling racks. Repress centers with spoon if necessary. Spoon about 1½ teaspoons cherry mixture into each cup. Sprinkle with red sugar or top with cherry piece.

1 Cookie: Calories 110; Total Fat 5g (Saturated Fat 3g; Trans Fat 0g); Cholesterol 10mg; Sodium 60mg; Total Carbohydrate 14g (Dietary Fiber 0g); Protein 1g **Exchanges:** 1 Other Carbohydrate, 1 Fat **Carbohydrate Choices:** 1

Sweet Success Tip

Don't like amaretto? Orange-flavored liqueur also tastes great. Try your favorite flavor of liqueur, or just omit it.

White Chocolate–Dipped Cherry Thins

PREP TIME: 1 hour 15 minutes **START TO FINISH:** 4 hours 30 minutes **6 dozen cookies**

1 cup sugar

1 cup butter or margarine, softened

1 teaspoon vanilla

1 teaspoon almond extract

1 egg

3 cups all-purpose flour

½ teaspoon baking soda

½ teaspoon salt

1 container (8 oz) red candied cherries, finely chopped (about 1 cup)

¼ cup chopped walnuts

1 package (20 oz) vanilla-flavored candy coating (almond bark)

Edible glitter, if desired

1 In large bowl, beat sugar, butter, vanilla, almond extract and egg with electric mixer on medium speed until well blended. On low speed, beat in flour, baking soda and salt. Stir in cherries and walnuts.

2 Divide dough into 2 (8-inch) logs. Wrap in plastic wrap. Refrigerate at least 2 hours or until firm.

3 Heat oven to 375°F. Cut rolls into ⅛-inch slices. On ungreased cookie sheets, place slices 2 inches apart. Bake 6 to 8 minutes or until light brown. Cool slightly; remove from cookie sheets to cooling racks. Cool completely, about 15 minutes.

4 Meanwhile, in medium microwavable bowl, microwave candy coating as directed on package until melted and smooth. Dip about one-third of each cookie at an angle into coating, allowing excess coating to drip back into bowl. Place on waxed paper; sprinkle with glitter. Let stand about 1 hour or until coating is set.

1 Cookie: Calories 100; Total Fat 5g (Saturated Fat 3g; Trans Fat 0g); Cholesterol 10mg; Sodium 50mg; Total Carbohydrate 12g (Dietary Fiber 0g); Protein 1g **Exchanges:** 1 Other Carbohydrate, 1 Fat **Carbohydrate Choices:** 1

Sweet Success Tips

Keep a roll or two of this cookie dough on hand ready to bake. Cookie dough can be covered and refrigerated up to 24 hours before baking. Dough can also be frozen in an airtight container up to 2 months. Thaw just until soft enough to slice.

Candy coating may set up while you are dipping the cookies. Just heat again in the microwave on High in 10-second intervals.

Cherry-Almond Refrigerator Cookies

PREP TIME: 1 hour 15 minutes **START TO FINISH:** 3 hours 30 minutes   **5 to 6 dozen cookies**

½ cup slivered almonds

1 cup butter or margarine, softened

1 cup granulated sugar

½ cup packed brown sugar

1 egg

1 teaspoon almond extract

2½ cups all-purpose flour

1½ teaspoons baking powder

½ teaspoon salt

1 cup chopped red candied cherries

1 Sprinkle almonds in ungreased heavy skillet. Cook over medium heat 5 to 7 minutes, stirring frequently until nuts begin to brown, then stirring constantly until nuts are light brown. Cool 10 minutes. In food processor, process almonds until finely chopped; set aside.

2 In large bowl, beat butter, granulated sugar and brown sugar with electric mixer on medium speed until smooth and creamy. Add egg and almond extract; beat on medium speed until smooth. On low speed, beat in flour, baking powder and salt until dough forms. Stir in cherries and chopped almonds.

3 Form dough into 2 (8-inch) logs. Wrap in plastic wrap or waxed paper. Refrigerate at least 2 hours or until firm.

4 Heat oven to 375°F. Cut dough into ⅛- to ¼-inch slices. On ungreased cookie sheets, place slices 2 inches apart.

5 Bake 7 to 9 minutes or until edges start to turn golden brown. Cool 1 minute; remove from cookie sheets to cooling racks.

1 Cookie: Calories 80; Total Fat 3.5g (Saturated Fat 2g; Trans Fat 0g); Cholesterol 10mg; Sodium 60mg; Total Carbohydrate 12g (Dietary Fiber 0g); Protein 1g **Exchanges:** ½ Starch, ½ Other Carbohydrate, ½ Fat **Carbohydrate Choices:** 1

Sweet Success Tips

These are ideal holiday cookies. You can keep the logs of dough in the refrigerator up to 2 weeks and bake them as you need fresh cookies. Or double-wrap them and freeze up to 2 months.

Add an elegant look to these cookies by piping with powdered sugar drizzle. It is quick and easy if you line up rows of cookies so you can just pipe along a long row. Separate the cookies slightly as they set so they don't stick together.

Shortbread Cookies

PREP TIME: 20 minutes **START TO FINISH:** 40 minutes   **2 dozen cookies**

¾ **cup butter, softened**
5 **tablespoons sugar**
2 **cups all-purpose flour**

1 Heat oven to 350°F. In large bowl, stir butter and 4 tablespoons of the sugar until well mixed. Stir in flour. (If dough is crumbly, mix in 1 to 2 tablespoons more softened butter.)

2 Roll out dough ½ inch thick on lightly floured surface; sprinkle with remaining 1 tablespoon sugar. Cut into small shapes with knife or use cookie cutters. On ungreased cookie sheets, place shapes ½ inch apart.

3 Bake about 20 minutes or until set. Immediately remove from cookie sheets to cooling racks.

1 Cookie: Calories 100; Total Fat 6g (Saturated Fat 3.5g; Trans Fat 0g); Cholesterol 15mg; Sodium 40mg; Total Carbohydrate 11g (Dietary Fiber 0g); Protein 1g **Exchanges:** ½ Starch, 1 Fat **Carbohydrate Choices:** 1

Cherry-Shortbread Cookie Wedges: Make dough as directed, stirring in ½ cup chopped dried cherries, cranberries or blueberries with the flour. On ungreased cookie sheet, pat dough into 8-inch round. Sprinkle with 1 tablespoon sugar. Bake 20 to 24 minutes or until set. Cool 10 minutes on cookie sheet on cooling rack. Using sharp knife, cut into 24 wedges.

Chocolate-Dipped Shortbread Cookies: Make cookies as directed. Heat 1 cup semisweet chocolate chips and 1 teaspoon oil until mixture can be stirred smooth. Dip cookies in chocolate; wipe excess on edge of bowl. Place on waxed paper to set.

Ginger-Shortbread Cookies: Stir in 3 tablespoons chopped crystallized ginger with the flour.

Toffee-Shortbread Cookies: Stir in ½ cup toffee bits with the flour.

Sweet Success Tip

Serve these meltingly tender, buttery cookies plain, or dip the edges in melted chocolate and then in chopped nuts.

Cherry-Shortbread Cookie Wedges,
Chocolate-Dipped Shortbread Cookies

Spritz

PREP TIME: 45 minutes START TO FINISH: 45 minutes   **5 dozen cookies**

1   cup butter, softened*
½   cup sugar
2¼   cups all-purpose flour
1   egg
1   teaspoon almond extract
     or vanilla
½   teaspoon salt
     **Colored decorating sugars,
     if desired**

1 Heat oven to 400°F. In large bowl, beat butter and sugar with electric mixer on medium speed, or mix with spoon. Stir in remaining ingredients.

2 Place dough in cookie press. On ungreased cookie sheets, form desired shapes. Sprinkle with colored sugars, if desired.

3 Bake 6 to 9 minutes or until set but not brown. Immediately remove from cookie sheets to cooling racks.

Do not use margarine or vegetable oil spreads in this recipe.

1 Cookie: Calories 50; Total Fat 3g (Saturated Fat 1.5g; Trans Fat 0g); Cholesterol 10mg; Sodium 40mg; Total Carbohydrate 5g (Dietary Fiber 0g); Protein 0g **Exchanges:** ½ Other Carbohydrate, ½ Fat **Carbohydrate Choices:** ½

Chocolate Buttery Spritz: Stir 2 oz unsweetened baking chocolate, melted and cooled, into butter-sugar mixture.

Lemon Butter Flutes

PREP TIME: 1 hour 15 minutes **START TO FINISH:** 1 hour 15 minutes   **4 dozen cookies**

COOKIES

1¼	cups powdered sugar
1	cup butter or margarine, softened
1	tablespoon grated lemon peel
1	tablespoon lemon juice
1	egg
2½	cups all-purpose or unbleached flour
¼	teaspoon salt

GLAZE

1	cup powdered sugar
4	to 5 teaspoons lemon juice
2	teaspoons powdered sugar

1 Heat oven to 400°F. In large bowl, beat 1¼ cups powdered sugar and the butter with electric mixer on medium speed until light and fluffy. Add lemon peel, 1 tablespoon lemon juice and the egg; blend well. Stir in flour and salt until well mixed. Fill cookie press with dough. Using the cookie press and bar plate, press a long ribbon of dough onto ungreased cookie sheet. Score the cookie dough at 2¼-inch intervals.

2 Bake 5 to 8 minutes or until set but not brown. Cut cookies at score lines with sharp knife. Immediately remove from cookie sheets to cooling racks. Cool completely.

3 In small bowl, mix 1 cup powdered sugar and enough lemon juice for desired drizzling consistency. Drizzle over cookies; let stand until set. Sprinkle with 2 teaspoons powdered sugar.

1 Cookie: Calories 80; Total Fat 4g (Saturated Fat 2.5g; Trans Fat 0g); Cholesterol 15mg; Sodium 40mg; Total Carbohydrate 11g (Dietary Fiber 0g); Protein 0g **Exchanges:** ½ Other Carbohydrate, 1 Fat **Carbohydrate Choices:** 1

Sweet Success Tips

Substitute lime peel and lime juice for the lemon peel and juice.

The lemon glaze can be replaced with a chocolate drizzle. Melt milk chocolate chips and drizzle over cookies. Let stand until chocolate is set.

Stuffed Hazelnut Cookies

PREP TIME: 1 hour **START TO FINISH:** 1 hour   **2 dozen cookies**

FILLING

- ½ **cup hazelnut spread with cocoa**
- ½ **cup powdered sugar**
- ¼ **cup chopped hazelnuts (filberts)**

COOKIES

- 1 **cup granulated sugar**
- ½ **cup hazelnut spread with cocoa**
- ½ **cup butter, softened**
- 1 **egg**
- 1½ **cups all-purpose flour**
- ¾ **teaspoon baking soda**
- ½ **teaspoon baking powder**
- ¼ **teaspoon salt**
   Additional granulated sugar

GLAZE

- 1 **cup dark chocolate chips**
- 2 **teaspoons shortening**
- 6 **teaspoons finely chopped hazelnuts (filberts), if desired**

1 Heat oven to 375°F. In small bowl, mix ½ cup hazelnut spread, the powdered sugar and ¼ cup chopped hazelnuts. Shape into 24 (1-inch) balls.

2 In large bowl, beat 1 cup granulated sugar, ½ cup hazelnut spread, the butter and egg with electric mixer on medium speed, or mix with spoon. Stir in flour, baking soda, baking powder and salt.

3 Divide dough into 24 (1½-inch) balls. Flatten each ball into 2½-inch round. Shape 1 cookie dough round around 1 hazelnut ball, covering completely. Repeat with remaining dough and hazelnut balls. On ungreased cookie sheets, place filled dough rounds about 3 inches apart.

4 Bake 9 to 10 minutes or until edges are set. Cool 5 minutes; remove from cookie sheets to cooling racks.

5 In small microwavable bowl, heat chocolate chips and shortening in microwave on High 30 seconds; stir. Microwave about 30 seconds longer or until mixture can be stirred smooth. Drizzle over cooled cookies; sprinkle each with ¼ teaspoon finely chopped hazelnuts. Let cookies stand until glaze sets.

1 Cookie: Calories 220; Total Fat 11g (Saturated Fat 4.5g; Trans Fat 0g); Cholesterol 20mg; Sodium 110mg; Total Carbohydrate 29g (Dietary Fiber 1g); Protein 2g **Exchanges:** ½ Starch, 1½ Other Carbohydrate, 2 Fat **Carbohydrate Choices:** 2

Chocolate-Mint Layered Cookie Slices

PREP TIME: 1 hour 10 minutes **START TO FINISH:** 4 hours 40 minutes   **3½ dozen cookies**

¾ cup butter or margarine, softened
¾ cup sugar
1 egg
1 teaspoon vanilla
2¼ cups all-purpose flour
¼ teaspoon baking powder
¼ teaspoon salt
1½ cups semisweet chocolate chips (9 oz)
1 tablespoon all-purpose flour
9 drops green food color
1 teaspoon mint extract
1 teaspoon shortening

1 In large bowl, beat butter and sugar with electric mixer on medium speed until creamy. Beat in egg and vanilla. On low speed, beat in 2¼ cups flour, the baking powder and salt until dough forms. Divide dough in half (about 1¼ cups each); place 1 portion in medium bowl.

2 In small microwavable bowl, microwave ½ cup of the chocolate chips uncovered on High 30 to 60 seconds or until melted, stirring twice. Stir until smooth; cool. Add melted chocolate to dough in medium bowl; knead until combined. To remaining dough, add 1 tablespoon flour, the food color and mint extract; mix until blended. Wrap each portion of dough in waxed paper; refrigerate 30 minutes.

3 Pat chocolate dough into rectangle shape. Place between sheets of waxed paper. Roll out dough to 10×6-inch rectangle, patting into shape with fingers as needed to retain rectangle shape. Repeat with green dough; remove top sheet of waxed paper. Remove top sheet of waxed paper from chocolate dough. Turn upside down over green dough, pressing firmly; remove waxed paper. With sharp knife or pizza cutter, cut lengthwise into 3 equal strips. Stack strips so you have 1 long rectangle, about 1½ inches high and 2 inches wide, pressing firmly. Wrap in plastic wrap; refrigerate 1 hour.

4 Heat oven to 350°F. Trim edges of dough log, if desired. Cut into ¼-inch slices. On ungreased cookie sheets, place slices 2 inches apart. Bake 10 to 12 minutes or until edges start to brown. Remove from cookie sheets to cooling racks; cool completely.

5 In small microwavable bowl, microwave remaining 1 cup chocolate chips and the shortening uncovered on High 60 to 90 seconds or until melted, stirring twice. Stir until melted. Dip one edge of each cookie in chocolate. Place on waxed paper; let stand until set, about 1 hour 30 minutes to 2 hours.

1 Cookie: Calories 100; Total Fat 5g (Saturated Fat 3g; Trans Fat 0g); Cholesterol 15mg; Sodium 45mg; Total Carbohydrate 13g (Dietary Fiber 0g); Protein 1g **Exchanges:** 1 Other Carbohydrate, 1 Fat **Carbohydrate Choices:** 1

Sweet Success Tips

To speed up the setting of chocolate-dipped cookies, place on waxed paper–lined cookie sheets and refrigerate 20 minutes.

As with most refrigerator cookies, you can keep the dough in the refrigerator up to 2 weeks. Just bake part of the log, wrap up the rest and keep it for when you want fresh cookies. The dough can also be frozen up to 2 months.

Cinnamon-Chocolate Chip Butterballs

PREP TIME: 35 minutes **START TO FINISH:** 1 hour 25 minutes   **3 dozen cookies**

1¾ cups all-purpose flour

1 cup powdered sugar

2½ teaspoons ground cinnamon

½ teaspoon salt

1 cup cold butter

1 cup miniature semisweet chocolate chips

1 teaspoon vanilla

1 Heat oven to 400°F. In large bowl, mix flour, ½ cup of the powdered sugar, 1½ teaspoons of the cinnamon and the salt. Cut in butter, using pastry blender or fork, until mixture looks like coarse crumbs. Stir in chocolate chips and vanilla (mixture will be crumbly).

2 Using hands, shape dough into 1-inch balls. On ungreased cookie sheets, place balls 1 inch apart.

3 Bake 6 to 8 minutes or until set but not brown. Immediately remove from cookie sheets to cooling racks. Cool slightly, about 20 minutes.

4 In small bowl, stir together remaining ½ cup powdered sugar and remaining 1 teaspoon cinnamon. Roll cookies in sugar mixture, shaking off excess back into bowl. Cool completely, about 30 minutes.

1 Cookie: Calories 110; Total Fat 7g (Saturated Fat 4g; Trans Fat 0g); Cholesterol 15mg; Sodium 70mg; Total Carbohydrate 11g (Dietary Fiber 0g); Protein 1g **Exchanges:** ½ Other Carbohydrate, 1½ Fat **Carbohydrate Choices:** 1

Baked Cinnamon Churros

PREP TIME: 45 minutes **START TO FINISH:** 45 minutes   **3 dozen churros**

CINNAMON-SUGAR

  2 tablespoons sugar

  1 teaspoon ground cinnamon

CHURROS

  2 cups all-purpose flour

1½ teaspoons ground cinnamon

  ¼ teaspoon salt

  ¾ cup butter or margarine, softened

  1 package (3 oz) cream cheese, softened

  1 cup sugar

  1 egg yolk

1 Heat oven to 375°F. In small cup, stir together ingredients for cinnamon-sugar; set aside.

2 In small bowl, stir together flour, 1½ teaspoons cinnamon and the salt; set aside. In large bowl, beat butter and cream cheese with electric mixer on medium speed until blended. Add 1 cup sugar; beat 2 minutes or until light and fluffy. Add egg yolk; beat on low speed just until combined. Add flour mixture; beat until soft dough forms.

3 Place dough in decorating bag fitted with ½-inch star tip. Onto ungreased cookie sheets, pipe dough into strips about 2½ inches long. Sprinkle with cinnamon-sugar.

4 Bake 7 to 9 minutes or until light brown on top and golden brown on bottom. Cool 2 minutes; remove from cookie sheets to cooling racks. Cool completely before storing in airtight container.

1 Churro: Calories 90; Total Fat 5g (Saturated Fat 3g; Trans Fat 0g); Cholesterol 20mg; Sodium 50mg; Total Carbohydrate 12g (Dietary Fiber 0g); Protein 1g **Exchanges:** 1 Other Carbohydrate, 1 Fat **Carbohydrate Choices:** 1

Sweet Success Tips

This recipe is a variation of the traditional Mexican fried cookie that is similar to a doughnut. Our version is made in the churro shape, sprinkled with the traditional cinnamon-sugar but baked instead of fried.

If you don't have a pastry bag, you can use a freezer plastic bag, cutting a ½-inch slit diagonally across one corner, or use a cookie press with a star template.

Using parchment paper–lined cookie sheets makes cleanup a breeze, especially when cookies are topped with sugar.

Mini Almond Butter Tea Cakes

PREP TIME: 35 minutes START TO FINISH: 2 hours 35 minutes   **24 tea cakes**

½ **cup butter (do not use margarine)**

½ **cup slivered almonds**

1 **cup powdered sugar**

½ **cup all-purpose flour**

¼ **teaspoon salt**

1 **teaspoon vanilla**

¼ **teaspoon almond extract**

4 **egg whites**

½ **cup sliced almonds**

2 **teaspoons white decorating sugar**

1 Heat oven to 375°F. Line 8-inch square pan with foil; spray foil with cooking spray. In 2-quart saucepan, heat butter over medium-high heat about 5 minutes, stirring frequently, until a rich hazelnut-brown color. Remove from heat; cool 5 minutes.

2 Meanwhile, in food processor, process slivered almonds until finely ground. In large bowl, stir together ground almonds, powdered sugar, flour and salt. Add vanilla, almond extract and egg whites; beat about 1 minute or until blended.

3 On medium speed, beat in browned butter until smooth, about 1 minute. Pour batter into pan. Sprinkle sliced almonds evenly over top of batter; sprinkle sugar crystals evenly over almonds.

4 Bake 20 to 25 minutes or until golden brown. Cool completely in pan on cooling rack, about 1 hour. Using foil, lift cake from pan; remove foil from cake. Cut into 6 rows by 4 rows.

1 Tea Cake: Calories 130; Total Fat 8g (Saturated Fat 3.5g; Trans Fat 0g); Cholesterol 15mg; Sodium 85mg; Total Carbohydrate 11g (Dietary Fiber 0g); Protein 2g **Exchanges:** 1 Other Carbohydrate, 1½ Fat **Carbohydrate Choices:** 1

Sweet Success Tip

For a deeper almond flavor, toast the almonds before grinding them. Place them in a single layer on a cookie sheet, then bake in a 375°F oven 5 to 8 minutes or until they're golden brown.

Chewy Triple-Ginger Cookies

PREP TIME: 3 hours **START TO FINISH:** 3 hours   **4 dozen cookies**

COOKIES

- 2 **cups all-purpose flour**
- 1 **teaspoon ground ginger**
- 1 **teaspoon ground cinnamon**
- ½ **teaspoon baking soda**
- ½ **teaspoon allspice**
- ⅛ **teaspoon ground cloves**
- ½ **cup butter or margarine, softened**
- 1 **cup packed light brown sugar**
- 2 **tablespoons light molasses**
- 1 **tablespoon grated gingerroot**
- 1 **egg**

TOPPING

- 2 **tablespoons finely chopped crystallized ginger**
- 2 **tablespoons granulated sugar**

1 In medium bowl, stir together flour, ground ginger, cinnamon, baking soda, allspice and cloves; set aside. In large bowl, beat butter and brown sugar on medium speed 3 minutes or until light and fluffy. Add molasses, gingerroot and egg; beat on low speed until blended. Add flour mixture; beat until soft dough forms.

2 Divide dough in half; shape each half into 12-inch log. Cover with plastic wrap and refrigerate 2 hours or freeze 30 minutes until firm.

3 Heat oven to 350°F. In small cup, combine crystallized ginger and granulated sugar; set aside. Cut logs into ½-inch slices. On ungreased cookie sheets, place slices 1½-inches apart. Sprinkle with ginger-sugar mixture, pressing lightly into dough.

4 Bake 8 to 10 minutes or until puffed and light brown on bottom. Cool 3 minutes; remove from cookie sheets to cooling racks. Cool completely before storing in airtight container.

1 Cookie: Calories 60; Total Fat 2g (Saturated Fat 1.5g; Trans Fat 0g); Cholesterol 10mg; Sodium 30mg; Total Carbohydrate 10g (Dietary Fiber 0g); Protein 0g **Exchanges:** ½ Other Carbohydrate, ½ Fat ˜ **Carbohydrate Choices:** ½

Sweet Success Tips

Chopping crystallized ginger with granulated sugar prevents it from clumping or sticking to knife.

If desired, roll dough logs into granulated sugar before chilling and slicing.

Cardamom Sugar Thins

PREP TIME: 2 hours 10 minutes **START TO FINISH:** 2 hours 10 minutes **5 dozen cookies**

2 cups all-purpose flour

1 teaspoon ground cardamom

½ teaspoon baking powder

¼ teaspoon salt

½ cup butter or margarine, softened

1 cup granulated sugar

1 egg

1 egg yolk

1 teaspoon vanilla

Powdered sugar

1 In medium bowl, stir together flour, cardamom, baking powder and salt until blended; set aside. In large bowl, beat butter and 1 cup granulated sugar with electric mixer on medium speed 3 minutes or until light and fluffy. Add egg, egg yolk and vanilla; beat on low speed until combined. Add flour mixture; beat until soft dough forms. Cover and refrigerate 5 to 10 minutes or until firm.

2 Heat oven to 350°F. On lightly floured surface, or between 2 sheets of waxed paper or cooking parchment paper, roll half of dough at a time to ⅛-inch thickness. Using 2-inch scalloped cookie cutter, cut out shapes, gently pressing together and rerolling scraps as necessary. Onto ungreased cookie sheets, place shapes about 1½ inches apart.

3 Bake 8 to 10 minutes or until edges are light brown. Cool 2 minutes; remove from cookie sheets to cooling racks. Sprinkle with powdered sugar. Cool completely before storing in airtight container.

1 Cookie: Calories 45; Total Fat 1.5g (Saturated Fat 1g; Trans Fat 0g); Cholesterol 10mg; Sodium 25mg; Total Carbohydrate 7g (Dietary Fiber 0g); Protein 0g **Exchanges:** ½ Other Carbohydrate, ½ Fat **Carbohydrate Choices:** ½

Sweet Success Tip

To form diamond shapes, use knife instead of cookie cutter. Cut dough into 2-inch strips then cut strips diagonally. To get ruffled edge, use pastry wheel instead of knife.

French Macaroons
with Bittersweet Chocolate Ganache

PREP TIME: 1 hour 40 minutes **START TO FINISH:** 3 hours 10 minutes   **20 sandwich cookies**

COOKIES

- **3 egg whites**
- **1¼ cups blanched whole almonds (about 7 oz)**
- **1½ cups powdered sugar**
- **¼ teaspoon salt**
- **½ teaspoon red paste or gel food color**
- **3 tablespoons granulated sugar**

GANACHE

- **¼ cup whipping cream**
- **1 teaspoon light corn syrup**
- **2 oz bittersweet or semisweet baking chocolate, finely chopped**
- **1 tablespoon butter, softened**

Sweet Success Tip

In France, these popular cookies are known as "macarons" and are sold in patisseries in a wide variety of colors and flavors.

1 Fill small bowl half full with hot water. Place egg whites in custard cup or another small bowl; place in bowl of water, making sure water doesn't get into egg whites. Let stand about 3 minutes or until egg whites reach 75°F. Line 2 cookie sheets with cooking parchment paper or silicone baking mats.

2 In blender, place almonds and ¼ cup of the powdered sugar. Cover; blend on high speed 1 to 2 minutes, scraping sides occasionally, or until almonds are very finely ground. Place strainer over medium bowl. Using rubber spatula, press almond mixture through strainer into bowl. Return any almonds left in strainer to blender; add ¼ cup of the remaining powdered sugar. Cover; blend on high speed 1 to 2 minutes, scraping sides occasionally, or until almonds are very finely ground. Press almond mixture and remaining 1 cup powdered sugar through strainer into bowl; set aside. Discard any remaining large almond pieces.

3 In another medium bowl, beat egg whites, salt and food color with electric mixer on high speed just until foamy. Gradually add granulated sugar, 1 tablespoon at a time, beating on high speed 1 to 2 minutes or until soft peaks form. Using rubber spatula, fold about half of the almond mixture into egg white mixture until completely incorporated. Fold in remaining almond mixture.

4 Spoon batter into decorating bag fitted with ½-inch plain tip. Pipe batter in 20 (1½-inch) circles onto each cookie sheet about 1½ inches apart. If tops have a peak, wet fingertips lightly on damp paper towel and press down to flatten. Tap bottom of cookie sheet on counter a few times to flatten cookies. Let stand uncovered at room temperature 30 minutes to allow a light crust to form on tops.

5 Heat oven to 300°F. Bake one pan at a time 17 to 18 minutes or until tops look set. Cool on cookie sheets on cooling racks at least 10 minutes. With metal pancake turner, remove cookies to cooling racks.

6 In 2-cup glass measuring cup, microwave cream and corn syrup uncovered on High 1 minute. Stir in chocolate and butter until chocolate is melted. Let stand about 30 minutes. Cover; refrigerate about 30 minutes or until spreading consistency.

7 For each sandwich cookie, spread about 1 teaspoon ganache on bottom edge of 1 cookie. Top with a second cookie. Store tightly covered.

1 Sandwich Cookie: Calories 140; Total Fat 7g (Saturated Fat 2g; Trans Fat 0g); Cholesterol 0mg; Sodium 45mg; Total Carbohydrate 15g (Dietary Fiber 1g); Protein 3g **Exchanges:** 1 Other Carbohydrate, ½ High-Fat Meat, ½ Fat **Carbohydrate Choices:** 1

Snowman Sugar Cookies (page 151)

gift-giving cookies

Espresso Brownie Cookies

PREP TIME: 1 hour 30 minutes **START TO FINISH:** 1 hour 30 minutes **16 cookies**

10 oz semisweet baking chocolate, chopped

6 tablespoons butter or margarine, cut-up

¾ cup all-purpose flour

½ teaspoon baking powder

½ teaspoon salt

1 cup packed light brown sugar

2 eggs

2 tablespoons instant espresso powder or granules

1 teaspoon vanilla

1 bag (12 oz) semisweet chocolate chips (2 cups)

1 In medium microwavable bowl, microwave chocolate and butter uncovered on High 1 minute to 1 minute 30 seconds, stirring every 30 seconds, until melted and smooth. Cool 10 minutes.

2 Meanwhile, in small bowl, stir together flour, baking powder and salt; set aside. In large bowl, beat brown sugar, eggs, espresso powder and vanilla with electric mixer on medium speed 3 minutes. Add cooled chocolate mixture; beat on low speed until blended. Add flour mixture; beat until soft dough forms. Stir in chocolate chips. Refrigerate dough 30 minutes or until firm enough to handle.

3 Heat oven to 350°F. Shape dough into 2-inch balls. On ungreased cookie sheets, place balls 2 inches apart. Bake 10 to 12 minutes or until tops are cracked and dry (cookies will still be soft). Cool 3 minutes; remove from cookie sheets to cooling racks. Cool completely before storing in airtight container.

1 Cookie: Calories 300; Total Fat 16g (Saturated Fat 10g; Trans Fat 0g); Cholesterol 40mg; Sodium 135mg; Total Carbohydrate 35g (Dietary Fiber 3g); Protein 3g **Exchanges:** 1 Starch, 1½ Other Carbohydrate, 3 Fat **Carbohydrate Choices:** 2

Sweet Success Tips

Instant coffee granules can be substituted for instant espresso.

When forming dough balls, use a cookie or ice cream scoop for uniform size.

Espresso Brownie Cookies

Chocolate Toffee Crinkle Cookies

PREP TIME: 1 hour **START TO FINISH:** 1 hour   **2 dozen cookies**

8 oz semisweet baking chocolate, chopped

¼ cup butter or margarine, cut up

1¼ cups all-purpose flour

¼ cup unsweetened baking cocoa

½ teaspoon baking soda

¼ teaspoon salt

1 cup sugar

2 eggs

1 teaspoon vanilla

1 bag (8 oz) toffee bits

Sugar

1 In 1-quart saucepan, heat chocolate and butter over medium-low heat, stirring frequently, until chocolate is melted and mixture is smooth; cool.

2 Heat oven to 350°F. Grease cookie sheets or line with cooking parchment paper. In medium bowl, stir together flour, cocoa, baking soda and salt; set aside. In large bowl, beat 1 cup sugar, the eggs and vanilla with electric mixer on medium speed 2 minutes or until well blended. Add cooled chocolate mixture; beat on low speed until combined. Slowly beat in flour mixture until soft dough forms. Stir in toffee bits.

3 Shape dough into 1¼-inch balls. On ungreased cookie sheets, place balls 2 inches apart. With bottom of glass dipped in sugar, flatten slightly.

4 Bake 8 to 10 minutes or until tops are dry (cookies will be soft in center). Cool 3 minutes; remove from cookie sheets to cooling racks. Cool completely before storing in airtight container.

1 Cookie: Calories 170; Total Fat 8g (Saturated Fat 4.5g; Trans Fat 0g); Cholesterol 25mg; Sodium 70mg; Total Carbohydrate 21g (Dietary Fiber 1g); Protein 2g **Exchanges:** ½ Starch, 1 Other Carbohydrate, 1½ Fat **Carbohydrate Choices:** 1½

Sweet Success Tips

Instead of dipping glass in sugar, sprinkle dough lightly with coarse sea salt before baking.

Flattening dough balls slightly before baking helps cookies bake more evenly.

Peanut Butter–Stuffed Chocolate Cookies

PREP TIME: 1 hour 30 minutes START TO FINISH: 1 hour 30 minutes   2½ dozen cookies

COOKIES

½	**cup butter or margarine, cut up**
1	**cup semisweet chocolate chips (6 oz)**
2	**tablespoons peanut butter**
1	**pouch Betty Crocker chocolate chip cookie mix**
1	**egg**
30	**mini peanut butter crackers**

DRIZZLE

1	**cup peanut butter chips (6 oz)**
1	**to 2 teaspoons vegetable oil**

1 In large microwavable bowl, microwave butter, chocolate chips and peanut butter uncovered on High 1 minute to 1 minute 30 seconds, stirring every 30 seconds, until melted and smooth. Stir in cookie mix and egg until well blended. Refrigerate dough 30 minutes or until firm enough to scoop.

2 Heat oven to 375°F. For each rounded tablespoon dough, place 1 peanut butter cracker in center, forming dough into ball around cracker. On ungreased cookie sheets, place dough balls 2 inches apart.

3 Bake 9 to 11 minutes or until tops are dry (cookies will still be soft). Cool 1 minute; remove from cookie sheets to cooling racks.

4 In 1-pint resealable food-storage plastic bag, add peanut butter chips and oil; seal bag. Microwave on High 1 minute, kneading bag after 30 seconds, until melted and smooth. Cut ⅛-inch slit diagonally across bottom corner of bag. Squeeze drizzle over cooled cookies. Let stand until set. Store in airtight container.

1 Cookie: Calories 180; Total Fat 10g (Saturated Fat 4.5g; Trans Fat 0g); Cholesterol 15mg; Sodium 130mg; Total Carbohydrate 21g (Dietary Fiber 0g); Protein 2g **Exchanges:** ½ Starch, 1 Other Carbohydrate, 2 Fat **Carbohydrate Choices:** 1½

Sweet Success Tips

For extra peanut flavor, add ¼ cup finely chopped peanuts to cookie dough.

If dough gets sticky while forming cookies, return to refrigerator 10 to 15 minutes or until firm enough to handle.

Either crunchy or creamy peanut butter works well in this recipe.

Raspberry Poinsettia Blossoms

PREP TIME: 25 minutes **START TO FINISH:** 1 hour 50 minutes   **3 dozen cookies**

¾ **cup butter or margarine, softened**

½ **cup sugar**

1 **teaspoon vanilla**

1 **box (4-serving size) raspberry-flavored gelatin**

1 **egg**

2 **cups all-purpose flour**

2 **tablespoons yellow candy sprinkles**

1 In large bowl, beat butter, sugar, vanilla, gelatin and egg with electric mixer on medium speed, or mix with spoon. On low speed, beat in flour.

2 Shape dough into 1¼-inch balls. Cover and refrigerate 1 hour.

3 Heat oven to 375°F. On ungreased cookie sheets, place balls about 2 inches apart. With sharp knife, make 6 cuts in top of each ball about three-fourths of the way through to make 6 wedges. Spread wedges apart slightly to form flower petals (cookies will separate and flatten as they bake). Sprinkle about ⅛ teaspoon yellow candy sprinkles into center of each cookie.

4 Bake 9 to 11 minutes or until set and edges begin to brown. Cool 2 to 3 minutes. Remove from cookie sheets to cooling racks. Cool completely, about 15 minutes.

1 Cookie: Calories 90; Total Fat 4g (Saturated Fat 2.5g; Trans Fat 0g); Cholesterol 15mg; Sodium 40mg; Total Carbohydrate 11g (Dietary Fiber 0g); Protein 1g **Exchanges:** 1 Other Carbohydrate, 1 Fat **Carbohydrate Choices:** 1

Sweet Success Tips

During the holidays, time can be the greatest gift. Why not get together with a few friends and host a cookie exchange? This is a great recipe to share.

For a flavor twist, use strawberry-, cranberry- or cherry-flavored gelatin instead of the raspberry.

Cinnamon Cardinal Cookies

PREP TIME: 1 hour START TO FINISH: 1 hour 50 minutes   4 dozen cookies

½ cup butter, softened

½ cup packed light brown sugar

1 teaspoon vanilla

2 cups all-purpose flour

¼ teaspoon baking soda

1½ teaspoons ground cinnamon or cardamom

⅓ cup whipping cream

48 miniature chocolate chips

Red, black and yellow decorating sugar crystals

1 In large bowl, beat butter and brown sugar with electric mixer on medium speed until light and fluffy; stir in vanilla. In small bowl, stir together flour, soda and cinnamon. On low speed, beat flour mixture into butter mixture alternately with cream. Divide dough in half. Wrap halves in plastic wrap. Refrigerate until firm, about 30 minutes.

2 Heat oven to 350°F. Lightly spray or grease 2 large cookie sheets. On lightly floured surface, roll half of dough at a time about ⅛ inch thick. Using 3-inch lightly floured cardinal-shaped cookie cutter, cut out cookies and place on cookie sheets about 2 inches apart.

3 Place miniature chocolate chip on each for eye. Sprinkle top of back, crown, tail and wing of each bird with red sugar crystals, neck and eye with black sugar crystals, and beak with yellow sugar crystals. Leave bottom breast of bird without sugar.

4 Bake 6 to 8 minutes or until light brown and set.

1 Cookie: Calories 50; Total Fat 2.5g (Saturated Fat 1.5g; Trans Fat 0g); Cholesterol 5mg; Sodium 20mg; Total Carbohydrate 6g (Dietary Fiber 0g); Protein 0g **Exchanges:** ½ Other Carbohydrate, ½ Fat **Carbohydrate Choices:** ½

Sweet Success Tip

If you don't have a cardinal-shaped cookie cutter, trace the outline of a cardinal from a coloring book or bird book, or find one online and cut it out. Use a small paring knife in the dough to cut around outline to form the bird.

Mocha Latte Logs

PREP TIME: 1 hour 30 minutes **START TO FINISH:** 2 hours   **4 dozen cookies**

COOKIES

1	**cup butter, softened**
¾	**cup granulated sugar**
¼	**cup packed brown sugar**
2	**oz unsweetened baking chocolate, melted, cooled slightly**
1	**teaspoon vanilla**
1	**egg**
1	**tablespoon instant espresso coffee powder**
2½	**cups all-purpose flour**

GLAZE

2	**tablespoons whipping cream or milk**
2	**teaspoons instant espresso coffee powder**
1	**cup powdered sugar**

1 Heat oven to 350°F. In large bowl, beat butter with electric mixer on medium speed until fluffy. Beat in sugars until well blended. Beat in melted chocolate, vanilla, egg and 1 tablespoon coffee powder. Gradually beat flour into butter mixture until well blended.

2 Roll dough into ball; flatten ball slightly. Cut dough into 8 equal wedges; roll each into 18-inch long rope. Cut each rope into 6 (3-inch) pieces. On ungreased cookie sheets, place pieces 2 inches apart. Using tines of fork, make lines along each log by pulling gently down length of each piece.

3 Bake 10 to 12 minutes or until firm but not browned. Remove from cookie sheets to cooling racks. Cool completely, about 10 minutes.

4 Place waxed paper on counter under cooling rack. In small, deep microwavable bowl or measuring cup, microwave cream uncovered on High about 15 seconds or until warm. Stir in 2 teaspoons coffee powder until dissolved. Using whisk, beat in powdered sugar until no lumps remain. Dip one end of each log into glaze. Place on cooling racks, allowing glaze to drip through rack, until glaze is dry, about 30 minutes.

1 Cookie: Calories 100; Total Fat 5g (Saturated Fat 3g; Trans Fat 0g); Cholesterol 15mg; Sodium 30mg; Total Carbohydrate 12g (Dietary Fiber 0g); Protein 1g **Exchanges:** 1 Other Carbohydrate, 1 Fat **Carbohydrate Choices:** 1

Sweet Success Tip

To melt baking chocolate in microwave, cut chocolate into 4 pieces; place in small microwavable bowl. Microwave uncovered on High 1 minute; stir. If needed, microwave an additional 10 seconds at a time and stirring after each time, just until chocolate is melted.

Chocolate-Peppermint Shortbread

PREP TIME: 15 minutes START TO FINISH: 1 hour 10 minutes   32 cookies

SHORTBREAD

- **1 cup butter or margarine, softened**
- **½ cup granulated sugar**
- **4 oz bittersweet baking chocolate, melted, cooled**
- **½ teaspoon peppermint extract**
- **2¼ cups all-purpose flour**
- **⅓ cup unsweetened baking cocoa**

GLAZE AND TOPPING

- **½ cup powdered sugar**
- **2 tablespoons unsweetened baking cocoa**
- **1 to 2 tablespoons milk**
- **2 tablespoons chopped miniature peppermint candy canes**

1 Heat oven to 325°F. Spray 2 (9-inch) glass pie plates with cooking spray.

2 In large bowl, beat butter, granulated sugar, chocolate and peppermint extract with electric mixer on medium speed until light and fluffy. On low speed, beat in flour and ⅓ cup cocoa. Divide dough in half. With lightly floured hands, press dough evenly in pie plates.

3 Bake 22 to 24 minutes or until edges just begin to pull away from sides of pie plates. Cool in pie plates 5 minutes. Carefully cut each round into 16 wedges. Cool completely in pie plates on cooling rack, about 30 minutes.

4 In small bowl, mix powdered sugar, 2 tablespoons cocoa and enough of the milk until glaze is smooth and thin enough to drizzle. Drizzle glaze over wedges; sprinkle with candies.

1 Cookie: Calories 140; Total Fat 8g (Saturated Fat 5g; Trans Fat 0g); Cholesterol 15mg; Sodium 45mg; Total Carbohydrate 15g (Dietary Fiber 1g); Protein 1g **Exchanges:** 1 Other Carbohydrate, 1½ Fat **Carbohydrate Choices:** 1

Sweet Success Tips

Cut the rounds into wedges while they are warm, but do not remove them from the pie plates until they are completely cool so they won't break.

For the best red color, look for candy canes that have bright red striping. The round peppermint candies have a larger proportion of white candy to the red color.

Maple-Walnut Shortbread Cookies

PREP TIME: 1 hour 40 minutes **START TO FINISH:** 1 hour 40 minutes   **4 dozen cookies**

1 cup butter, softened

⅓ cup sugar

1½ cups finely chopped toasted walnuts*

1 egg yolk

2 cups all-purpose flour

1 teaspoon baking powder

¼ teaspoon salt

1 teaspoon maple flavor

1 cup semisweet chocolate chips

1 In large bowl, beat butter and sugar with electric mixer on medium speed about 30 seconds or until smooth. Add ½ cup of the walnuts and the egg yolk; beat until blended. Add flour, baking powder, salt and maple flavor. On low speed, beat until stiff cookie dough forms. Shape dough into a ball. Wrap in plastic wrap; refrigerate 45 minutes.

2 Heat oven to 350°F. Divide dough into 8 equal parts. On lightly floured surface, shape each part into a rope 12 inches long and ¾ inch thick. Cut into 2-inch lengths; place about 2 inches apart on ungreased cookie sheets. Flatten cookies slightly.

3 Bake 15 to 17 minutes or until edges begin to brown. Cool 2 minutes; remove from cookie sheets to cooling racks. Cool completely, about 30 minutes.

4 In small microwavable bowl, microwave chocolate chips uncovered on High 1 minute 30 seconds, stirring every 30 seconds, until chips can be stirred smooth. In another small bowl, place remaining 1 cup walnuts.

5 For each cookie, dip ½ inch of 1 long side into chocolate, then coat chocolate edge with walnuts. Place on sheets of waxed paper; let stand about 2 hours or until chocolate is set.

*To toast walnuts, spread in ungreased shallow pan; bake at 350°F 5 to 8 minutes, stirring occasionally, until aromatic. Finely chop when cooled.

1 Cookie: Calories 100; Total Fat 7g (Saturated Fat 3.5g; Trans Fat 0g); Cholesterol 15mg; Sodium 50mg; Total Carbohydrate 8g (Dietary Fiber 0g); Protein 1g **Exchanges:** ½ Starch, 1½ Fat **Carbohydrate Choices:** ½

Sweet Success Tip

Dipping tender shortbread cookies in chocolate and coating with nuts adds sweetness and crunch.

Brown Sugar Snowflakes

PREP TIME: 1 hour 30 minutes **START TO FINISH:** 3 hours 30 minutes **2½ dozen cookies**

COOKIES

¾	cup butter, softened
¾	cup packed brown sugar
1	egg
2¼	cups all-purpose flour
½	teaspoon baking soda
¼	teaspoon salt

FROSTING

1½	teaspoons meringue powder
1	tablespoon cold water
½	cup powdered sugar
	Granulated sugar, if desired

1 In large bowl, beat butter and brown sugar with electric mixer on medium-high speed until light and fluffy. Beat in egg until blended. On low speed, beat in flour, baking soda and salt.

2 Divide dough into 4 parts; shape each part into a flat round. Wrap each round separately in plastic wrap. Refrigerate at least 2 hours until completely chilled.

3 Heat oven to 350°F. Line cookie sheets with cooking parchment paper. On floured surface, roll out 1 round at a time to ¼-inch thickness (keep remaining dough refrigerated). Cut with snowflake cutters; place about 1 inch apart on cookie sheets. Reroll scraps once, chilling dough again before cutting.

4 Bake 8 to 11 minutes or until light golden. Cool 2 minutes; remove from cookie sheets to cooling racks. Cool completely, about 30 minutes.

5 In medium bowl, beat meringue powder and cold water with electric mixer on medium speed until peaks form. Gradually beat in powdered sugar until soft peaks form, about 1 minute. Spoon frosting into decorating bag fitted with medium round tip; pipe frosting onto cookies. Sprinkle with granulated sugar. Let stand about 5 minutes or until frosting is set.

1 Cookie: Calories 110; Total Fat 5g (Saturated Fat 3g; Trans Fat 0g); Cholesterol 20mg; Sodium 80mg; Total Carbohydrate 15g (Dietary Fiber 0g); Protein 1g **Exchanges:** 1 Other Carbohydrate, 1 Fat **Carbohydrate Choices:** 1

Sweet Success Tips

Roll dough between sheets of parchment paper to keep it from sticking to the counter.

Use dark brown sugar for a little more molasses flavor.

Snowman Sugar Cookies

PREP TIME: 1 hour 20 minutes START TO FINISH: 3 hours 20 minutes   **6 dozen cookies**

- 1   **cup butter or margarine, softened**
- 1   **package (3 oz) cream cheese, softened**
- ¾   **cup sugar**
- 1   **teaspoon vanilla**
- 1   **egg**
- 3   **cups all-purpose flour**
- ⅛   **teaspoon salt**
- 1   **pouch (7 oz) Betty Crocker Cookie Icing white icing**
- 1   **pouch (7 oz) Betty Crocker Cookie Icing blue icing**
-     **Decorating sugar crystals**
-     **Orange string licorice**
-     **Miniature semisweet chocolate chips**

1 In large bowl, beat butter, cream cheese, sugar, vanilla and egg with electric mixer on medium speed until light and fluffy. Stir in flour and salt until blended. Cover and refrigerate dough at least 2 hours but no longer than 24 hours.

2 Heat oven to 375°F. On lightly floured cloth-covered surface, roll out one-fourth of dough at a time to ⅛-inch thickness. (Keep remaining dough refrigerated until ready to roll.) Cut dough with snowmen cookie cutters; place about 1 inch apart on ungreased cookie sheets.

3 Bake 7 to 10 minutes or until light brown. Immediately remove from cookie sheets to cooling racks. Cool completely. Frost cookies with white icing. Decorate snowmen using blue icing for hat and scarf; sprinkle with sugar crystals. Add orange licorice for nose and chocolate chips for eyes.

1 Cookie: Calories 60; Total Fat 3g (Saturated Fat 2g; Trans Fat 0g); Cholesterol 10mg; Sodium 25mg; Total Carbohydrate 6g (Dietary Fiber 0g); Protein 0g **Exchanges:** ½ Other Carbohydrate, ½ Fat **Carbohydrate Choices:** ½

Santa Sugar Cookies: Use Santa cookie cutter. Frost cookies with red icing; sprinkle with red sugar crystals. Decorate as desired using white icing, red gumdrops and cinnamon candy. Go to *BettyCrocker.com* for decorating tips.

Sweet Success Tip

To freeze cookies, place unfrosted cookies in airtight freezer container and label. Freeze for up to 2 months. Cookies will thaw while you decorate them.

Almond Tree Cookies

PREP TIME: 2 hours **START TO FINISH:** 2 hours   **4 dozen cookies**

COOKIES

- **1 cup butter or margarine, softened**
- **½ cup granulated sugar**
- **½ teaspoon almond extract**
- **2 cups all-purpose flour**

FROSTING

- **1 cup powdered sugar**
- **2 tablespoons butter or margarine, softened**
- **1 to 2 tablespoons milk**
- **8 or 10 drops green food color**

1 Heat oven to 350°F. In medium bowl, beat 1 cup butter, the granulated sugar and almond extract with electric mixer on medium speed until smooth. On low speed, beat in flour.

2 Shape dough into 1-inch balls; place 2 inches apart on ungreased cookie sheets.

3 Bake 12 to 15 minutes or until firm to the touch. Cool 1 minute; remove from cookie sheets to cooling racks. Cool completely, about 30 minutes.

4 In small bowl, beat powdered sugar, 2 tablespoons butter and the milk on medium speed until smooth and spreadable. Stir in green food color until uniform color.

5 Spoon frosting into resealable food-storage plastic bag. Seal bag; cut off tiny corner of bag. Squeeze bag to pipe tree shape in zigzag pattern on each cookie with frosting.

1 Cookie: Calories 80; Total Fat 4.5g (Saturated Fat 2.5g; Trans Fat 0g); Cholesterol 10mg; Sodium 30mg; Total Carbohydrate 9g (Dietary Fiber 0g); Protein 0g **Exchanges:** ½ Other Carbohydrate, 1 Fat **Carbohydrate Choices:** ½

Sweet Success Tip

Add ornaments to the cookie trees by sprinkling with yellow, red and green holiday candy decors.

Almond Angel Cookies

PREP TIME: 1 hour START TO FINISH: 3 hours 45 minutes   **4 dozen cookies**

- 1 **cup butter or margarine, softened**
- 1 **cup sugar**
- 2 **tablespoons milk**
- 1 **teaspoon vanilla**
- ½ **teaspoon almond extract**
- ¼ **teaspoon salt**
- 2½ **cups all-purpose flour**
- 2 **tablespoons yellow decorating sugar**
- 2 **tablespoons blue decorating sugar**
- 96 **small pretzel twists**
- 2 **tablespoons sliced almonds**
- 1 **tube (4.25 oz) Betty Crocker Decorating Icing yellow icing**
- 1 **tube (4.25 oz) Betty Crocker Decorating Icing pink icing**

1 In large bowl, beat butter with electric mixer on medium-high speed until light and fluffy. Add sugar; beat until creamy, scraping bowl frequently. Stir in milk, vanilla, almond extract and salt. Stir in flour until well mixed.

2 Measure ½ cup of dough into resealable food-storage plastic bag; refrigerate. Divide remaining dough in half; roll each into a 6-inch log. Roll 1 log in yellow sugar; roll other log in blue sugar. Wrap logs separately in plastic wrap or waxed paper. Chill until firm, at least 2 hours.

3 Heat oven to 350°F. For each cookie, place 2 pretzels with flat sides touching on ungreased large cookie sheets, 3 inches apart. Cut dough into 48 (¼-inch) slices. (If dough cracks, allow to sit at room temperature a few minutes.) To make angel body, fold in opposite sides at top of each slice to make triangular-shaped body; place each slice on top of 2 pretzels, so double loops of pretzels form angel wings at each side. Press lightly into pretzels. Using reserved dough from plastic bag, roll ½ teaspoon dough into ball; place on top for head of each angel. Press 2 sliced almonds into dough to make song book. Repeat to make 48 cookies.

4 Bake 11 to 14 minutes or until edges are firm and just begin to brown. Cool 2 to 3 minutes. Remove from cookie sheets to cooling racks. Cool completely, about 15 minutes.

5 Pipe yellow icing on cooled cookies to make eyes and hair. Use pink to draw mouths. Let stand until frosting is set.

1 Cookie: Calories 100; Total Fat 4g (Saturated Fat 2.5g; Trans Fat 0g); Cholesterol 10mg; Sodium 70mg; Total Carbohydrate 14g (Dietary Fiber 0g); Protein 1g **Exchanges:** 1 Other Carbohydrate, 1 Fat **Carbohydrate Choices:** 1

Peanut Butter Reindeer Cookies

PREP TIME: 50 minutes **START TO FINISH:** 50 minutes **2 dozen cookies**

1 pouch Betty Crocker peanut butter cookie mix

3 tablespoons vegetable oil

1 tablespoon water

1 egg

2 tablespoons granulated sugar

72 semisweet chocolate chips (about 3 tablespoons)

12 star-shaped Christmas pretzels or pretzel sticks

1 Heat oven to 375°F. In medium bowl, mix cookies as directed on package, using oil, water and egg.

2 Shape dough into 1¼-inch balls. On ungreased cookie sheets, place balls 2 inches apart. Dip bottom of drinking glass in sugar; press each ball until about ½ inch thick.

3 Pinch bottom edge of each cookie to form a longer point. At point of each cookie, place 1 chocolate chip for nose; press down slightly. Place 2 chocolate chips on each cookie for eyes; press down slightly. With small sharp knife, cut star points from Christmas pretzels to form 48 small V-shaped pretzels (if using pretzel sticks, cut into quarters). Press 2 pretzel pieces into top of each cookie for antlers.

4 Bake 9 to 11 minutes or until edges begin to brown. Remove from cookie sheets to cooling racks.

1 Cookie: Calories 120; Total Fat 5g (Saturated Fat 1.5g; Trans Fat 0g); Cholesterol 10mg; Sodium 115mg; Total Carbohydrate 16g (Dietary Fiber 0g); Protein 2g **Exchanges:** ½ Starch, ½ Other Carbohydrate, 1 Fat **Carbohydrate Choices:** 1

Sweet Success Tips

These are easy cookies for kids to help with. Let them each create their own herd of reindeer.

You can use small candies instead of chocolate chips to decorate the cookies. Do a test bake to see if they hold up to baking temperature. If not, just attach them to the baked cookies with a little melted chocolate.

Cookies as Gifts

The one gift that will never be returned or re-gifted! Homemade cookies are the perfect choice for a thank-you or hostess gift or as a present for a college student. No matter what the occasion, cookies are sure to be a tasty hit.

Message Platter: Look for inexpensive platters at the dollar store or dollar section of your discount store. Write a simple message, such as "Thanks" or "Happy Anniversary," in melted chocolate or with packaged cookie icing near the edge of the plate. Let harden before arranging cookies on platter (lined with a paper doily), leaving room for the words to show. Wrap with plastic wrap or see-through colored plastic gift wrap secured with ribbon.

Unusual Containers: To make giving cookies even more fun, put them in unusual containers. Flower pots, clear big vases or colorful new sand buckets make great choices. Line with plastic wrap, waxed paper or tissue paper. Provide a cushion at the bottom—so the cookies won't break—with a layer of shredded paper for gift baskets or crumpled tissue paper or cloth napkin.

← Decorate for the Occasion: Craft stores are a mecca for great containers for cookies. Consider decorative tins, Chinese take-out containers, wooden or paper boxes or decorative bags. Decorate plain containers to suit the giving theme. For a birthday or anniversary, scan and glue photos of the person(s) on the container. Use clip art, ribbons, buttons, etc., for embellishment.

Large Cookie in Envelope: Place one large cookie on a square of waxed paper, the size of the cookie. Place the waxed paper on a larger decorative sheet of heavy-weight paper (measure the diameter of the cookie and use a square of paper that's double the diameter.) Fold the corners of paper to the middle of the cookie (overlapping edges slightly); secure with a self-sticking seal. Or use CD envelopes to hold individual cookies.

Re-Use/Recycle Containers: Re-use take-out restaurant containers. Many restaurants use sturdy plastic containers with clear lids for your take-out order. Hand-wash, dry and keep on hand for easy cookie gift-giving.

→ Pretty Glass or Cup: Use a martini glass, tea cup, coffee mug, etc., picked up at garage sales for dramatic presentations. Wrap in colored plastic gift wrap or tulle fabric with a ribbon. The container continues to be a gift long after the cookies are eaten!

Separate for Interest: Add interest and keep cookies from breaking by tightly lining up several cookies next to each other in paper baking cups and arranging several of these filled cups in a baking pan or drawer organizer or on a platter.

Color in the Empty Spaces: Fill spaces between cookies given in flat containers with small, colorful candies to add interest and to help keep cookies from moving and breaking.

Raspberry Poinsettia Blossoms (page 142)

Gingersnap Sandwich Cookies
with Lemon Buttercream Frosting

PREP TIME: 1 hour 10 minutes **START TO FINISH:** 3 hours 40 minutes **34 sandwich cookies**

COOKIES

½	**cup butter or margarine, softened**
¼	**cup granulated sugar**
¼	**cup packed brown sugar**
½	**cup molasses**
¼	**cup cold water**
2½	**cups all-purpose flour**
2	**teaspoons ground ginger**
2	**teaspoons ground cinnamon**
1	**teaspoon baking soda**
½	**teaspoon ground cloves**
¼	**teaspoon salt**

FROSTING

3	**cups powdered sugar**
½	**cup butter, softened**
2	**teaspoons grated lemon peel**
3	**to 4 teaspoons lemon juice**
3	**to 4 teaspoons milk**

1 In large bowl, beat ½ cup butter and the sugars with electric mixer on medium speed until light and fluffy. Beat in molasses and water until blended (mixture may look curdled). On low speed, beat in flour, ginger, cinnamon, baking soda, cloves and salt. Divide dough in half; wrap each half in plastic wrap. Refrigerate about 2 hours or until chilled.

2 Heat oven to 350°F. Line cookie sheets with cooking parchment paper. On well-floured surface, roll half of dough at a time to ⅛-inch thickness (keep remaining dough refrigerated). Cut with 2-inch round cookie cutter. Using large end of a piping tip or ½-inch round canapé cutter, cut a hole in center of half of the cutouts. Carefully transfer to cookie sheets, placing ½ inch apart. Reroll scraps.

3 Bake 9 to 12 minutes or until set in center. Cool 2 minutes; remove from cookie sheets to cooling racks. Cool completely, about 30 minutes.

4 In large bowl, beat frosting ingredients on medium speed until light and fluffy. Spread about 1 heaping teaspoon frosting on each whole cookie; top with cutout cookie. If desired, sprinkle additional grated lemon peel on frosting in center.

1 Sandwich Cookie: Calories 150; Total Fat 6g (Saturated Fat 3.5g; Trans Fat 0g); Cholesterol 15mg; Sodium 95mg; Total Carbohydrate 25g (Dietary Fiber 0g); Protein 1g **Exchanges:** ½ Starch, 1 Other Carbohydrate, 1 Fat **Carbohydrate Choices:** 1½

Sweet Success Tips

For faster chilling time, roll half of the dough at a time between two sheets of parchment paper. Refrigerate about 15 minutes.

For the best flavor, be sure to use spices that are no older than 6 months.

Here's My Heart Gingerbread Pals

PREP TIME: 1 hour 25 minutes START TO FINISH: 2 hours 25 minutes 2½ dozen cookies

¼ cup light molasses
2 tablespoons water
⅔ cup butter or margarine
½ cup packed brown sugar
1 egg
2¼ cups all-purpose flour
1 teaspoon ground ginger
1 teaspoon ground cinnamon
½ teaspoon baking soda
½ teaspoon salt
¼ teaspoon ground cloves
4 oz vanilla-flavored candy coating (almond bark)
4 teaspoons red decorating sugar

1 In 3-quart saucepan, cook and stir molasses and water over medium heat until hot; remove from heat. Stir in butter and brown sugar until smooth. Stir in remaining ingredients except candy coating and decorating sugar. Divide dough in half; shape into 2 rounds. Wrap each in plastic wrap; refrigerate 1 hour.

2 Heat oven to 350°F. On floured surface, roll 1 round of dough ⅛ inch thick. Cut with floured 3- to 3½-inch gingerbread boy and girl cookie cutters. With 1-inch heart-shaped cutter, cut out small heart in center of each cookie. On one ungreased cookie sheet, place gingerbread cutouts. On second ungreased cookie sheet, place hearts. Repeat with second round.

3 Bake hearts 5 to 7 minutes, gingerbread cookies 7 to 9 minutes, or until set. Remove from cookie sheets to cooling racks.

4 In small microwavable bowl, microwave candy coating on High 1 minute; stir until smooth. Frost each heart with coating; immediately sprinkle with red sugar. Place dot of melted coating on back of heart; place on hand of each gingerbread cookie or near cutout heart on body of cookie. Decorate as desired.

1 Cookie: Calories 110; Total Fat 5g (Saturated Fat 3g; Trans Fat 0g); Cholesterol 20mg; Sodium 95mg; Total Carbohydrate 15g (Dietary Fiber 0g); Protein 1g **Exchanges:** ½ Starch, ½ Other Carbohydrate, 1 Fat **Carbohydrate Choices:** 1

Sweet Success Tip

These saucepan cookies are easy to stir up—you don't need a mixer.

Cherry Tea Cakes

PREP TIME: 1 hour 10 minutes **START TO FINISH:** 1 hour 40 minutes   **5 dozen cookies**

1 cup powdered sugar

1 cup butter or margarine, softened

2 teaspoons maraschino cherry liquid

½ teaspoon almond extract

3 or 4 drops red food color

2¼ cups all-purpose flour

½ teaspoon salt

½ cup drained maraschino cherries, chopped

½ cup white vanilla baking chips

1 Heat oven to 350°F. In large bowl, beat powdered sugar, butter, cherry liquid, almond extract and food color with electric mixer on medium speed until blended. On low speed, beat in flour and salt. Stir in cherries.

2 Shape dough into 1-inch balls. On ungreased cookie sheets, place balls 2 inches apart.

3 Bake 8 to 10 minutes or until edges are light golden brown. Remove from cookie sheets to cooling racks. Cool 20 to 30 minutes.

4 In 1-quart resealable freezer plastic bag, place baking chips; seal bag. Microwave on High 35 to 50 seconds, squeezing chips in bag every 15 seconds, until chips are melted and smooth. Cut small tip from bottom corner of bag; drizzle melted chips over cookies.

1 Cookie: Calories 60; Total Fat 3.5g (Saturated Fat 2.5g; Trans Fat 0g); Cholesterol 10mg; Sodium 45mg; Total Carbohydrate 7g (Dietary Fiber 0g); Protein 0g **Exchanges:** ½ Other Carbohydrate, ½ Fat **Carbohydrate Choices:** ½

Chocolate-Drizzled Cherry Bars

PREP TIME: 20 minutes START TO FINISH: 1 hour 55 minutes   64 bars

¾ **cup butter or margarine, softened**

¾ **cup sugar**

1 **egg**

2¼ **cups all-purpose flour**

¼ **teaspoon salt**

¼ **cup cherry-flavored gelatin (from 4-serving-size box)**

¾ **cup semisweet chocolate chips**

¾ **teaspoon vegetable oil**

1 Heat oven to 350°F. In large bowl, beat butter and sugar with electric mixer on medium speed until creamy. Beat in egg until well blended. On low speed, beat in flour, salt and dry gelatin until soft dough forms. Press dough in bottom of ungreased 13×9-inch pan.

2 Bake 11 to 14 minutes or until center is set. Cool in pan completely, about 30 minutes.

3 In resealable freezer plastic bag, mix chocolate chips and oil; seal bag. Microwave on High 30 to 45 seconds, squeezing chocolate in bag every 15 seconds, until smooth. Cut ¼-inch tip from corner of bag; drizzle chocolate over bars. Let stand about 1 hour or until chocolate is set. Cut into 8 by 4 rows; cut each bar in half diagonally to make triangles.

1 Bar: Calories 50; Total Fat 3g (Saturated Fat 2g; Trans Fat 0g); Cholesterol 10mg; Sodium 30mg; Total Carbohydrate 5g (Dietary Fiber 0g); Protein 0g **Exchanges:** ½ Other Carbohydrate, ½ Fat **Carbohydrate Choices:** ½

Sweet Success Tip

Try with strawberry gelatin— except use the entire 4-serving-size box.

Chocolate-Cherry Pinwheels

PREP TIME: 1 hour 15 minutes START TO FINISH: 4 hours 30 minutes   **4½ dozen cookies**

¾ **cup butter or margarine, softened**

1 **cup sugar**

2 **eggs**

3 **cups all-purpose or unbleached flour**

1 **teaspoon baking powder**

½ **teaspoon salt**

1½ **teaspoons almond extract**

¼ **cup maraschino cherries, finely chopped, drained on paper towels**

3 **drops red food color**

1 **teaspoon vanilla**

1 **tablespoon milk**

¼ **cup unsweetened baking cocoa**

1 In large bowl, beat butter, sugar and eggs with electric mixer on medium speed until smooth. Beat in flour, baking powder and salt until well blended. Place half of dough in medium bowl.

2 Beat almond extract, cherries and food color into half of dough. Divide cherry dough in half. Wrap each half of cherry dough in plastic wrap; refrigerate about 45 minutes or until firm.

3 Meanwhile, beat vanilla, milk and cocoa into remaining plain dough. Divide chocolate dough in half. Wrap each half of chocolate dough in plastic wrap; refrigerate about 45 minutes or until firm.

4 Place one part of chocolate dough between 2 sheets of waxed paper; roll into 10×7-inch rectangle. Repeat with one part of cherry dough. Refrigerate both about 30 minutes or until firm. Peel top sheets of waxed paper from both doughs. Turn cherry dough upside down onto chocolate dough; roll up doughs together, starting at long side, into a log. Wrap in plastic wrap; refrigerate 2 hours. Repeat with remaining parts of dough.

5 Heat oven to 350°F. Cut rolls of dough into ¼-inch slices with sharp knife. On ungreased cookie sheets, place slices 1 inch apart.

6 Bake 8 to 11 minutes or until surface appears dull. Remove from cookie sheets to cooling racks.

1 Cookie: Calories 70; Total Fat 3g (Saturated Fat 1.5g; Trans Fat 0g); Cholesterol 15mg; Sodium 55mg; Total Carbohydrate 10g (Dietary Fiber 0g); Protein 1g **Exchanges:** ½ Starch, ½ Fat **Carbohydrate Choices:** ½

Sweet Success Tip

Cookie dough rolls can be wrapped and refrigerated for up to 24 hours before baking. To freeze cookie dough rolls, wrap in foil or freezer-proof wrap. To thaw, let dough stand 15 to 30 minutes until easy to cut into slices.

Orange-Pecan-Ginger Cookies

PREP TIME: 1 hour 15 minutes **START TO FINISH:** 4 hours 30 minutes   **6 dozen cookies**

¾ cup butter or margarine, softened

½ cup granulated sugar

½ cup packed brown sugar

1 tablespoon grated orange peel

1 tablespoon orange juice

1 egg

2½ cups all-purpose flour

1 teaspoon baking powder

½ teaspoon salt

½ cup chopped pecans

¼ cup chopped crystallized ginger

¼ cup decorator sugar crystals

1 In large bowl, beat butter, granulated sugar and brown sugar with electric mixer on medium speed until light and fluffy. Beat in orange peel, orange juice and egg until blended. On low speed, beat in flour, baking powder and salt. Stir in pecans and ginger.

2 Divide dough in half. Shape each half into 10-inch log. Sprinkle 2 tablespoons of the sugar crystals on sheet of plastic wrap; roll 1 log in sugar to coat. Wrap log in plastic wrap. Repeat with remaining log and sugar crystals. Refrigerate about 3 hours or until very firm.

3 Heat oven to 375°F. Cut logs into ¼-inch slices. On ungreased cookie sheets, place slices 2 inches apart.

4 Bake 8 to 10 minutes or until edges start to brown and tops are light golden brown. Immediately remove from cookie sheets to cooling racks. Cool completely, about 15 minutes.

1 Cookie: Calories 60; Total Fat 2.5g (Saturated Fat 1.5g; Trans Fat 0g); Cholesterol 10mg; Sodium 40mg; Total Carbohydrate 8g (Dietary Fiber 0g); Protein 0g **Exchanges:** ½ Other Carbohydrate, ½ Fat **Carbohydrate Choices:** ½

Sweet Success Tips

These crisp, delicious cookies would be a welcome holiday treat. Stack 6 or 8 cookies, and tie with a pretty ribbon to present as a small gift.

For a special presentation, melt about ⅔ cup semisweet or milk chocolate chips in a long, narrow microwavable dish, such as a butter dish. Dip about ¼ inch of one edge of each cookie into chocolate; place on waxed paper and let stand about 40 minutes or until chocolate is set.

Caramel Cashew Thumbprints

PREP TIME: 45 minutes **START TO FINISH:** 1 hour **5 dozen cookies**

¾ cup butter, softened
¾ cup powdered sugar
1 teaspoon vanilla
1 egg
2 cups all-purpose flour
¼ teaspoon baking powder
¼ teaspoon salt
⅓ cup finely chopped cashews
15 milk chocolate squares with caramel filling (from 9.5-oz bag), unwrapped, cut into quarters
Additional chopped cashews, if desired

1 Heat oven to 375°F. In large bowl, beat butter and powdered sugar with electric mixer on low speed until mixed; beat on medium speed until creamy. Add vanilla and egg; beat until mixed, scraping bowl if necessary. On low speed, beat in flour, baking powder and salt until dough forms. Stir in cashews.

2 Shape dough into 1-inch balls. On ungreased cookie sheets, place balls 2 inches apart. Press thumb into center of each cookie to make indentation, but do not press all the way to cookie sheet.

3 Bake 7 to 9 minutes or until edges start to brown. Quickly remake indentation with end of wooden spoon handle if necessary. Remove from cookie sheets to cooling racks.

4 Place 1 chocolate candy quarter in thumbprint of each warm cookie. Let stand 3 minutes to melt; with tip of small knife, swirl slightly to fill thumbprint. Sprinkle with additional chopped cashews. Cool completely.

1 Cookie: Calories 50; Total Fat 3g (Saturated Fat 2g; Trans Fat 0g); Cholesterol 10mg; Sodium 30mg; Total Carbohydrate 6g (Dietary Fiber 0g); Protein 0g **Exchanges:** ½ Other Carbohydrate, ½ Fat **Carbohydrate Choices:** ½

Espresso Thumbprint Cookies

PREP TIME: 1 hour START TO FINISH: 1 hour 15 minutes **3½ dozen cookies**

COOKIES

- ¾ **cup sugar**
- ¾ **cup butter or margarine, softened**
- ½ **teaspoon vanilla**
- 1 **egg**
- 1¾ **cups all-purpose flour**
- 3 **tablespoons unsweetened baking cocoa**
- ¼ **teaspoon salt**
  Crushed hard peppermint candies, if desired

ESPRESSO FILLING

- ¼ **cup whipping cream**
- 2 **teaspoons instant espresso coffee granules**
- 1 **cup milk chocolate chips**
- 1 **tablespoon coffee-flavored liqueur, if desired**

1 Heat oven to 350°F. In large bowl, beat sugar, butter, vanilla and egg with electric mixer on medium speed, or mix with spoon, until well blended. Stir in flour, cocoa and salt until dough forms.

2 Shape dough by rounded teaspoonfuls into 1-inch balls. On ungreased cookie sheets, place balls about 2 inches apart. Press thumb or end of wooden spoon into center of each cookie, but do not press all the way to cookie sheet.

3 Bake 7 to 11 minutes or until edges are firm. If necessary, quickly remake indentations with end of wooden spoon. Immediately remove from cookie sheets to cooling racks. Cool completely, about 30 minutes.

4 Meanwhile, in 1-quart saucepan, mix whipping cream and instant coffee. Heat over medium heat, stirring occasionally, until steaming and coffee is dissolved. Remove from heat; stir in chocolate chips until melted. Stir in liqueur. Cool about 10 minutes or until thickened.

5 Spoon rounded ½ teaspoon espresso filling into indentation in each cookie. Top with crushed candies.

1 Cookie: Calories 90; Total Fat 5g (Saturated Fat 3.5g; Trans Fat 0g); Cholesterol 15mg; Sodium 45mg; Total Carbohydrate 10g (Dietary Fiber 0g); Protein 1g **Exchanges:** ½ Starch, 1 Fat **Carbohydrate Choices:** ½

Chocolate-Mint Thumbprints

PREP TIME: 1 hour START TO FINISH: 2 hours 15 minutes   3 dozen cookies

1 cup butter, softened

1 cup powdered sugar

1½ teaspoons peppermint extract

2 egg yolks

16 drops green food color

2¼ cups all-purpose flour

½ teaspoon baking powder

¼ teaspoon salt

¾ cup dark chocolate chips

3 tablespoons whipping cream

3 tablespoons butter

18 thin rectangular crème de menthe chocolate candies, unwrapped, cut in half diagonally

1 Heat oven to 350°F. Line cookie sheets with cooking parchment paper.

2 In large bowl, beat 1 cup butter and the powdered sugar with electric mixer on medium speed until light and fluffy. Beat in peppermint extract, egg yolks and food color until blended. On low speed, beat in flour, baking powder and salt.

3 Shape dough into 1-inch balls; place 2 inches apart on cookie sheets. Using end of handle of wooden spoon, press a deep well into center of each cookie, but do not press all the way to cookie sheet.

4 Bake 10 to 12 minutes or until set. Reshape wells with end of handle of wooden spoon if necessary. Cool 2 minutes; remove from cookie sheets to cooling racks. Cool completely, about 15 minutes.

5 In medium microwavable bowl, microwave chocolate chips, cream and 3 tablespoons butter uncovered on High 1 minute, stirring frequently, until chocolate is melted and mixture is smooth. Fill each well with about 1 teaspoon chocolate mixture; garnish with candy piece. Let stand about 1 hour or until chocolate is set.

1 Cookie: Calories 130; Total Fat 8g (Saturated Fat 5g; Trans Fat 0g); Cholesterol 30mg; Sodium 70mg; Total Carbohydrate 12g (Dietary Fiber 0g); Protein 1g **Exchanges:** 1 Other Carbohydrate, 1½ Fat **Carbohydrate Choices:** 1

Maple-Nut Biscotti

PREP TIME: 2 hours START TO FINISH: 3 hours 30 minutes   30 cookies

½   cup packed brown sugar

¼   cup granulated sugar

½   cup butter or margarine, softened

1   teaspoon maple flavor

3   eggs

3   cups all-purpose flour

2   teaspoons baking powder

¾   cup chopped walnuts

1   teaspoon vegetable oil

4   oz vanilla-flavored candy coating (almond bark), melted

1 Heat oven to 350°F. Lightly grease cookie sheets with shortening or cooking spray. In large bowl, beat sugars and butter with electric mixer on medium speed about 3 minutes or until creamy. Beat in maple flavor and eggs. Stir in flour and baking powder. Stir in walnuts. Divide dough in half. Shape each half into 10-inch log. Place logs 5 inches apart on cookie sheet; flatten to 3-inch width.

2 Bake 20 to 30 minutes or until set and edges begin to brown. Remove from cookie sheet to cooling rack. Cool 10 minutes. With serrated knife, cut rolls diagonally into ½-inch slices. Place slices, cut side down, on ungreased cookie sheets. Bake 5 to 10 minutes or until lightly browned and dry. Turn cookies over; bake 5 to 8 minutes longer or until lightly browned and dry. Remove from cookie sheets to cooling rack. Cool completely, about 15 minutes.

3 Stir oil into melted candy coating; drizzle over biscotti. Let stand until coating is dry. Store tightly covered.

1 Cookie: Calories 141; Total Fat 7g (Saturated Fat 3g); Sodium 57mg; Total Carbohydrate 18g (Dietary Fiber 1g); Protein 3g **Exchanges:** ½ Starch, ½ Other Carbohydrate **Carbohydrate Choices:** 1

Gluten-Free Fudge Crinkles

PREP TIME: 45 minutes **START TO FINISH:** 1 hour 5 minutes **3 dozen cookies**

1 box (15 oz) Betty Crocker Gluten Free devil's food cake mix

1 box (4-serving size) gluten-free chocolate instant pudding and pie filling mix

½ cup butter, melted

1 egg

¼ cup water

1 teaspoon gluten-free vanilla

Sugar

1 Heat oven to 350°F. In large bowl, mix dry cake mix and dry pudding mix. Add melted butter, egg, water and vanilla; stir until soft dough forms.

2 In small bowl, place sugar. Shape dough into 1¼-inch balls; roll in sugar. On ungreased cookie sheets, place balls about 2 inches apart; flatten slightly.

3 Bake 8 to 10 minutes or until set. Cool 2 minutes; remove from cookie sheets to cooling racks. Cool completely, about 20 minutes. Store tightly covered.

✱ *Cooking Gluten Free? Always read labels to make sure each recipe ingredient is gluten free. Products and ingredients sources can change.*

1 Cookie: Calories 80; Total Fat 3g (Saturated Fat 2g; Trans Fat 0g); Cholesterol 15mg; Sodium 100mg; Total Carbohydrate 13g (Dietary Fiber 0g); Protein 0g **Exchanges:** 1 Other Carbohydrate, ½ Fat **Carbohydrate Choices:** 1

Sweet Success Tip

Make everyone feel welcome by baking traditional holiday cookies customized for alternative diets. These fudgy gluten-free chocolate crinkles are easy to make since they start with a mix.

Glazed Toffee Bonbons

PREP TIME: 1 hour 10 minutes START TO FINISH: 1 hour 30 minutes **4 dozen cookies**

COOKIES

- ½ **cup butter or margarine, softened**
- ½ **cup packed brown sugar**
- ½ **teaspoon vanilla**
- 1 **egg**
- 1¾ **cups all-purpose flour**
- ¼ **teaspoon baking soda**
- ¼ **teaspoon salt**
- 3 **bars (1.4 oz each) chocolate-covered English toffee candy, finely chopped**

GLAZE

- ¼ **cup butter or margarine**
- ½ **cup packed brown sugar**
- 2 **tablespoons milk**
- 1⅓ **cups powdered sugar**
- ⅓ **cup semisweet chocolate chips**
- ⅓ **cup white vanilla baking chips**

1 Heat oven to 325°F. In large bowl, beat ½ cup butter, ½ cup brown sugar, the vanilla and egg with electric mixer on medium speed until light and fluffy. On low speed, beat in flour, baking soda and salt. Reserve one-third of the chopped candy for garnish. Stir remaining chopped candy into dough. Shape dough into 1-inch balls. On ungreased cookie sheets, place balls 1 inch apart.

2 Bake 11 to 14 minutes or until edges start to brown and tops of cookies feel set when tapped. Place cooling racks on waxed paper. Immediately remove cookies from cookie sheets to cooling racks.

3 Meanwhile, in 1-quart saucepan, heat ¼ cup butter, ½ cup brown sugar and milk over medium-low heat, stirring frequently, until mixture just comes to a boil and sugar is dissolved. Stir in powdered sugar; beat with whisk if necessary to remove lumps. Immediately dip tops of cookies into glaze, or spread glaze on tops of cookies. (Cookies don't need to be completely cooled, just firm and set.) Place on rack; let stand about 10 minutes or until glaze is set. If glaze starts to set in saucepan, reheat over medium-low heat and beat with whisk until softened.

4 Place chocolate chips and vanilla chips in separate small microwavable bowls. Microwave each on High 1½ to 2 minutes, stirring every 30 seconds, until melted and smooth. Using tip of spoon, drizzle each flavor generously over cookies. Sprinkle with remaining candy. Refrigerate 20 minutes to set quickly.

1 Cookie: Calories 100; Total Fat 4.5g (Saturated Fat 3g; Trans Fat 0g); Cholesterol 15mg; Sodium 55mg; Total Carbohydrate 15g (Dietary Fiber 0g); Protein 1g **Exchanges:** 1 Other Carbohydrate, 1 Fat **Carbohydrate Choices:** 1

Sweet Success Tip

You don't need to wait to drizzle the second melted chip mixture over the first melted chip mixture—just be sure not to touch the soft melted chocolate.

White Chocolate Chunk–Macadamia Cookies

PREP TIME: 35 minutes START TO FINISH: 35 minutes   2½ dozen cookies

1 cup packed brown sugar
½ cup granulated sugar
½ cup butter, softened
½ cup shortening
1 teaspoon vanilla
1 egg
2¼ cups all-purpose flour
1 teaspoon baking soda
¼ teaspoon salt
6 oz white chocolate baking bar, cut into ¼- to ½-inch chunks
1 jar (3.25 oz) macadamia nuts, coarsely chopped

1 Heat oven to 350°F. In large bowl, beat sugars, butter, shortening, vanilla and egg with electric mixer on medium speed, or mix with spoon, until light and fluffy. Stir in flour, baking soda and salt (dough will be stiff). Stir in white chocolate chunks and nuts.

2 Onto ungreased cookie sheet, drop dough by rounded tablespoonfuls about 2 inches apart.

3 Bake 10 to 12 minutes or until light brown. Cool 1 to 2 minutes; remove from cookie sheets to cooling racks.

1 Cookie: Calories 190; Total Fat 11g (Saturated Fat 4g; Trans Fat 1g); Cholesterol 15mg; Sodium 100mg; Total Carbohydrate 21g (Dietary Fiber 0g); Protein 2g **Exchanges:** 1 Starch, ½ Other Carbohydrate, 2 Fat **Carbohydrate Choices:** 1½

Chocolate-Filled Orange-Rosemary Butter Balls

PREP TIME: 1 hour START TO FINISH: 1 hour 30 minutes **2½ dozen sandwich cookies**

COOKIES

- **1 cup butter, softened**
- **½ cup powdered sugar**
- **1 tablespoon grated orange peel**
- **1 tablespoon finely chopped fresh rosemary leaves**
- **¼ teaspoon salt**
- **1 teaspoon vanilla**
- **2 cups all-purpose flour**
- **½ teaspoon baking powder**
- **¼ cup coarse white decorator sugar crystals, if desired**

FILLING

- **½ cup dark chocolate chips**
- **2 tablespoons whipping cream**

1 Heat oven to 400°F. In large bowl, beat butter, powdered sugar, orange peel, rosemary, salt and vanilla with electric mixer on low speed until mixed; beat on medium speed until creamy. On low speed, beat in flour and baking powder until dough forms.

2 In small bowl, place decorator sugar. Shape dough into 60 (1-inch) balls. Roll in sugar. On ungreased cookie sheets, place balls 2 inches apart. Press lightly with tines of fork to flatten slightly.

3 Bake 6 to 8 minutes or just until edges start to brown. Remove from cookie sheets to cooling racks; cool completely.

4 Meanwhile, in small microwavable bowl, microwave chocolate chips and whipping cream uncovered on High in 15-second intervals until chips can be stirred smooth. Refrigerate until cooled and mixture starts to set, about 10 minutes.

5 For each sandwich cookie, spread about ½ teaspoon filling on bottom of 1 cookie. Press bottom of second cookie over filling. Let stand until set.

1 Sandwich Cookie: Calories 110; Total Fat 7g (Saturated Fat 4.5g; Trans Fat 0g); Cholesterol 20mg; Sodium 75mg; Total Carbohydrate 10g (Dietary Fiber 0g); Protein 1g **Exchanges:** ½ Other Carbohydrate, 1½ Fat **Carbohydrate Choices:** ½

Sweet Success Tips

Place filled cookies sideways in individual petit four paper cups or mini paper baking cups.

If you bake 2 cookie sheets at a time, switch their positions in the oven halfway through baking.

Pistachio-Cranberry Biscotti

PREP TIME: 25 minutes START TO FINISH: 2 hours 10 minutes   **4 dozen cookies**

½ **cup butter or margarine, softened**

1 **cup sugar**

1 **teaspoon grated orange peel**

3 **eggs**

2½ **cups all-purpose flour**

1 **cup pistachio nuts, finely ground (1 cup)**

3 **teaspoons baking powder**

¼ **teaspoon salt**

¾ **cup sweetened dried cranberries**

½ **cup pistachio nuts**

⅔ **cup white vanilla baking chips, melted**

1 Heat oven to 325°F. Line cookie sheet with cooking parchment paper.

2 In large bowl, beat butter and sugar with electric mixer on medium-high speed until light and fluffy. Add orange peel and eggs, one at a time, beating thoroughly after each addition. On low speed, beat in flour, 1 cup ground nuts, baking powder and salt. Stir in cranberries and ½ cup nuts.

3 Divide dough in half. On one side of cookie sheet, shape half of dough into 10-inch log. Repeat with remaining dough on same cookie sheet.

4 Bake 30 to 35 minutes or until toothpick inserted in center comes out clean. Cool 25 minutes; remove from cookie sheet to cutting board. Cut logs crosswise into ½-inch slices; discard ends. Place slices, cut side down, on cookie sheets.

5 Bake about 18 minutes longer, turning once, until biscotti are crisp and light brown. Immediately remove from cookie sheets to cooling racks. Cool completely, about 30 minutes. Drizzle one side with melted baking chips; let stand until set before storing in tightly covered container.

1 Cookie: Calories 110; Total Fat 5g (Saturated Fat 2.5g; Trans Fat 0g); Cholesterol 20mg; Sodium 70mg; Total Carbohydrate 14g (Dietary Fiber 0g); Protein 2g **Exchanges:** ½ Starch, ½ Other Carbohydrate, 1 Fat **Carbohydrate Choices:** 1

Sweet Success Tip

Try dried cherries instead of cranberries.

Toffee-Pecan Bars (page 200)

chapter four

brownies
and bars

Apricot-Macadamia Caramel Bars

PREP TIME: 30 minutes **START TO FINISH:** 1 hour 30 minutes **25 bars**

SHORTBREAD COOKIE CRUST

- ¾ **cup butter or margarine, softened**
- ¼ **cup packed brown sugar**
- 1½ **cups all-purpose flour**
- ½ **teaspoon salt**

TOPPING

- 24 **vanilla caramels, unwrapped**
- ¼ **cup whipping cream**
- 1 **package (7 oz) dried apricots, chopped (about 1⅓ cups)**
- 1 **jar (6 oz) macadamia nuts, coarsely chopped (about 1⅓ cups)**

DRIZZLE

- ¼ **cup semisweet chocolate chips**
- 1 **teaspoon vegetable oil**

1 Heat oven to 350°F. In medium bowl, beat butter and brown sugar until creamy. Add flour and salt; mix until soft dough forms. With floured hands, press dough in bottom of ungreased 9-inch square pan. Bake 25 to 30 minutes or until center is set.

2 Meanwhile, in 1-quart saucepan, heat caramels and whipping cream over medium-low heat, stirring constantly, until caramels are melted and mixture is smooth. Remove from heat; stir in apricots and macadamia nuts. Spoon mixture evenly over crust; spread carefully.

3 In small microwavable bowl, microwave chocolate chips and oil uncovered on High 30 to 45 seconds, stirring every 15 seconds, until melted and smooth. Drizzle over bars.

4 Refrigerate 1 hour or until set. Cut into 5 rows by 5 rows.

1 Bar: Calories 210; Total Fat 13g (Saturated Fat 5g; Trans Fat 0g); Cholesterol 15mg; Sodium 105mg; Total Carbohydrate 20g (Dietary Fiber 1g); Protein 2g **Exchanges:** ½ Starch, 1 Other Carbohydrate, 2½ Fat **Carbohydrate Choices:** 1

Sweet Success Tips

To keep apricots from sticking to knife during chopping, dip blade in hot water.

Cashews or pecans can be substituted for the macadamia nuts.

Pecan-Praline Bacon Bars

PREP TIME: 30 minutes START TO FINISH: 2 hours 10 minutes   32 bars

CRUST

1½ cups all-purpose flour

½ cup packed dark brown sugar

1 cup butter or margarine, softened

1 package (2.1 oz) precooked bacon, cut into ¼-inch slices

PRALINE FROSTING

½ cup whipping cream

⅓ cup butter or margarine

1½ cups packed dark brown sugar

1½ cups powdered sugar

1 teaspoon vanilla

1½ cups pecan halves

1 Heat oven to 325°F. In medium bowl, stir together flour and ½ cup brown sugar. Beat in 1 cup butter with electric mixer on medium speed until blended; stir in bacon. Press in bottom of ungreased 13×9-inch pan. Bake 20 to 25 minutes or until center is set. Cool completely, about 30 minutes.

2 In 1-quart saucepan, heat whipping cream, ⅓ cup butter and 1½ cups brown sugar to boiling over medium heat, stirring frequently. Boil and stir 1 minute; remove from heat. Using whisk, stir in powdered sugar and the vanilla until smooth.

3 Spread praline frosting over cooled crust; sprinkle with pecans. Let stand 30 to 45 minutes until frosting is set but not firm. Cut into 8 rows by 4 rows. Store covered in refrigerator.

1 Bar: Calories 220; Total Fat 13g (Saturated Fat 6g; Trans Fat 0g); Cholesterol 25mg; Sodium 105mg; Total Carbohydrate 24g (Dietary Fiber 0g); Protein 2g **Exchanges:** ½ Starch, 1 Other Carbohydrate, 2½ Fat **Carbohydrate Choices:** 1½

Sweet Success Tip

To prevent frosting from cracking, be sure to cut bars 30 to 45 minutes after frosting. Frosting will be slightly warm but set.

Banana-Cashew Bars
with Browned Butter Frosting

PREP TIME: 35 minutes **START TO FINISH:** 1 hour 40 minutes   **24 bars**

BARS

1	cup granulated sugar
1	cup mashed very ripe bananas (2 medium)
⅓	cup butter or margarine, softened
2	eggs
1	cup all-purpose flour
1	teaspoon baking powder
½	teaspoon baking soda
¼	teaspoon salt
½	cup chopped cashews

FROSTING

½	cup butter (do not use margarine)
3¼	cups powdered sugar
1	teaspoon vanilla
1	to 3 tablespoons milk

GARNISH

24	cashew halves, if desired

1 Heat oven to 350°F. Grease 13×9-inch pan with shortening or cooking spray. In large bowl, mix granulated sugar, bananas, ⅓ cup butter and the eggs until blended. Stir in flour, baking powder, baking soda and salt until combined. Stir in cashews; spread batter in pan. Bake 22 to 26 minutes or until toothpick inserted in center comes out clean. Cool completely, about 40 minutes.

2 In 2-quart saucepan, heat ½ cup butter over medium heat, stirring constantly, until golden brown; remove from heat. Using spoon, gradually beat in powdered sugar. Stir in vanilla and the milk, 1 tablespoon at a time, until frosting is smooth and desired spreading consistency. Immediately spread over cooled bars. Score into 6 rows by 4 rows, making shallow cuts in frosting. Top center of each bar with cashew half, pressing in lightly. Cut bars on scored lines.

1 Bar: Calories 210; Total Fat 8g (Saturated Fat 4.5g; Trans Fat 0g); Cholesterol 35mg; Sodium 125mg; Total Carbohydrate 32g (Dietary Fiber 0g); Protein 1g **Exchanges:** ½ Starch, 1½ Other Carbohydrate, 1½ Fat **Carbohydrate Choices:** 2

Sweet Success Tips

When making frosting, watch butter carefully to make sure it doesn't burn.

Since browned butter frosting sets up quickly, do not make it until the bars have cooled.

Cinnamon-Fig Bars
with Orange Buttercream Frosting

PREP TIME: 30 minutes **START TO FINISH:** 2 hours 15 minutes   **16 bars**

FILLING

- ¼ **cup granulated sugar**
- 1¼ **cups water**
- 1 **bag (7 oz) dried Mission figs, stems removed, chopped (about 1⅓ cups)**

CRUST

- ¾ **cup all-purpose flour**
- ¼ **cup quick-cooking oats**
- ¼ **cup packed brown sugar**
- 1 **teaspoon ground cinnamon**
- ½ **cup butter or margarine, softened**

FROSTING

- 3 **tablespoons butter or margarine, softened**
- 1½ **cups powdered sugar**
- 3 **to 4 teaspoons milk**
- 1 **teaspoon grated orange peel**

1 In 1-quart saucepan, boil filling ingredients over medium-high heat, stirring frequently, until figs are tender and most of liquid is absorbed. Remove from heat; cool 5 to 10 minutes. Pour fig mixture into food processor. Cover; process, using quick on-and-off motions, until figs are pureed; set aside.

2 Heat oven to 350°F. Grease 8-inch square pan with shortening or cooking spray. In large bowl, combine crust ingredients with electric mixer on low speed until crumbly. Press in bottom of pan. Bake 25 to 30 minutes or until center is set. Spread filling over crust. Bake 6 to 10 minutes longer or just until filling sets. Cool completely, about 1 hour 15 minutes.

3 In medium bowl, beat 3 tablespoons butter with electric mixer on medium speed until blended. Add powdered sugar. Beat on low speed, adding milk, 1 teaspoon at a time, until mixture is smooth and desired spreading consistency. Stir in orange peel. Carefully spread over cooled bars. Cut into 4 rows by 4 rows.

1 Bar: Calories 200; Total Fat 8g (Saturated Fat 5g; Trans Fat 0g); Cholesterol 20mg; Sodium 60mg; Total Carbohydrate 31g (Dietary Fiber 1g); Protein 1g **Exchanges:** ½ Starch, 1½ Other Carbohydrate, 1½ Fat **Carbohydrate Choices:** 2

Sweet Success Tips

Shop for figs in the dried fruit section at the supermarket.

Baking these bars for a special occasion? To cut bars neatly, line pan with foil, extending foil several inches over shorter ends of pan. Spray foil; press crust in pan. When you are ready to cut bars, use the extra foil at ends to lift bars from pan. Peel back foil to easily cut perfect bars.

Lemon Bars

PREP TIME: 10 minutes START TO FINISH: 2 hours   25 bars

1 cup all-purpose flour
½ cup butter, softened
¼ cup powdered sugar
2 eggs
1 cup granulated sugar
2 teaspoons grated lemon peel
2 tablespoons lemon juice
½ teaspoon baking powder
¼ teaspoon salt
Additional powdered sugar

1 Heat oven to 350°F. In medium bowl, mix flour, butter and ¼ cup powdered sugar with spoon, until well mixed. Press in ungreased 8- or 9-inch square pan, building up ½-inch edges.

2 Bake crust 20 minutes; remove from oven. In medium bowl, beat all remaining ingredients except additional powdered sugar with electric mixer on high speed about 3 minutes or until light and fluffy. Pour over hot crust.

3 Bake 25 to 30 minutes longer or until no indentation remains when touched lightly in center. Cool completely in pan on cooling rack, about 1 hour. Dust with powdered sugar. Cut into 5 rows by 5 rows.

1 Bar: Calories 100; Total Fat 4g (Saturated Fat 2g; Trans Fat 0g); Cholesterol 25mg; Sodium 65mg; Total Carbohydrate 14g (Dietary Fiber 0g); Protein 1g **Exchanges:** 1 Other Carbohydrate, 1 Fat **Carbohydrate Choices:** 1

Lemon-Coconut Bars: Stir ½ cup flaked coconut into egg mixture in step 2.

Mojito Bars

PREP TIME: 15 minutes **START TO FINISH:** 2 hours 50 minutes **24 bars**

3 tablespoons light rum or 1½ teaspoons rum extract plus 3 tablespoons water

16 fresh mint leaves, chopped

¾ cup butter or margarine, softened

½ cup powdered sugar

2 cups all-purpose flour

4 eggs

1½ cups granulated sugar

¼ teaspoon salt

2 teaspoons grated lime peel

⅔ cup fresh lime juice (from 6 limes)

2 to 3 drops green food color, if desired

2 tablespoons milk

1 tablespoon powdered sugar

1 In small bowl, mix rum and chopped mint. Set aside.

2 Heat oven to 350°F. Lightly spray 13×9-inch pan with cooking spray. In large bowl, beat butter and ½ cup powdered sugar with electric mixer on medium speed. Beat in 1¾ cups of the flour on low speed just until well combined. Press in pan. Bake 22 to 25 minutes or until set and lightly browned.

3 Meanwhile, in large bowl, beat eggs and granulated sugar with whisk. Add remaining ¼ cup flour and the salt; beat with whisk until blended. Mix in lime peel, lime juice, food color and milk.

4 Place strainer over medium bowl; pour rum mixture into strainer. Press mixture with back of spoon through strainer to drain liquid from leaves; discard leaves. Mix strained liquid into egg mixture with whisk until well combined. Pour over partially baked crust. Bake 25 to 27 minutes longer or until center is set.

5 Cool completely, about 1 hour. Sprinkle with powdered sugar. Cut into 6 rows by 4 rows. Store bars tightly covered in refrigerator.

1 Bars: Calories 170; Total Fat 7g (Saturated Fat 4g; Trans Fat 0g); Cholesterol 50mg; Sodium 75mg; Total Carbohydrate 24g (Dietary Fiber 0g); Protein 2g **Exchanges:** ½ Starch, 1 Other Carbohydrate, 1½ Fat **Carbohydrate Choices:** 1½

Sweet Success Tip

If desired, omit mint leaves and substitute ½ teaspoon mint extract. Add extract with the rum as directed.

Toffee Bars

PREP TIME: 20 minutes **START TO FINISH:** 1 hour 25 minutes   **32 bars**

1 cup butter, softened
1 cup packed brown sugar
1 teaspoon vanilla
1 egg yolk
2 cups all-purpose flour
¼ teaspoon salt
⅔ cup milk chocolate chips
   or 3 bars (1.55 oz each)
   milk chocolate, chopped
½ cup chopped nuts

1 Heat oven to 350°F. In large bowl, stir butter, brown sugar, vanilla and egg yolk until well mixed. Stir in flour and salt (dough will be stiff). Press dough in ungreased 13×9-inch pan.

2 Bake 25 to 30 minutes or until very light brown (crust will be soft, do not overbake). Immediately sprinkle chocolate chips over hot crust. Let stand about 5 minutes or until chips are soft; spread evenly. Sprinkle with nuts. Cool 30 minutes in pan on cooling rack. For easiest cutting, cut into 8 rows by 4 rows while warm.

1 Bar: Calories 140; Total Fat 8g (Saturated Fat 3.5g; Trans Fat 0g); Cholesterol 25mg; Sodium 65mg; Total Carbohydrate 15g (Dietary Fiber 0g); Protein 1g **Exchanges:** 1 Other Carbohydrate, 1½ Fat **Carbohydrate Choices:** 1

Double-Toffee Bars: Stir in ½ cup toffee bits with the flour and salt.

Toffee-Pecan Bars

PREP TIME: 30 minutes **START TO FINISH:** 2 hours **48 bars**

CRUST

- ¾ **cup butter or margarine, softened**
- ⅓ **cup packed brown sugar**
- 1 **egg**
- 2 **cups all-purpose flour**

FILLING

- 1 **cup butter or margarine**
- ¾ **cup packed brown sugar**
- ¼ **cup light corn syrup**
- 2 **cups coarsely chopped pecans**
- 1 **cup swirled milk chocolate and caramel chips (from 10-oz bag)**

1 Heat oven to 375°F. Grease bottom and sides of 15×10×1-inch pan with shortening or cooking spray (do not use dark pan).

2 In large bowl, beat ¾ cup butter and ⅓ cup brown sugar with electric mixer on medium speed until light and fluffy. Add egg; beat until well blended. On low speed, beat in flour until dough begins to form. Press dough in pan.

3 Bake 12 to 17 minutes or until edges are light golden brown. Meanwhile, in 2-quart saucepan, heat 1 cup butter, ¾ cup brown sugar and the corn syrup to boiling over medium heat, stirring frequently. Boil 2 minutes without stirring.

4 Quickly stir pecans into corn syrup mixture; spread over partially baked crust. Bake 20 to 23 minutes longer or until filling is golden brown and bubbly.

5 Immediately sprinkle chocolate chips evenly over hot bars. Let stand 5 minutes to soften. With rubber spatula, gently swirl melted chips over bars. Cool completely, about 1 hour. Cut into 6 rows by 4 rows to make 24 squares, then cut each square in half to make triangles. Store covered in refrigerator.

1 Bar: Calories 160; Total Fat 11g (Saturated Fat 5g; Trans Fat 0g); Cholesterol 20mg; Sodium 50mg; Total Carbohydrate 14g (Dietary Fiber 0g); Protein 1g **Exchanges:** ½ Starch, ½ Other Carbohydrate, 2 Fat **Carbohydrate Choices:** 1

Sweet Success Tips

Try using raspberry-flavored chocolate chips instead of the swirled chips.

Coarsely chopped walnuts can be used instead of the pecans.

Brownie and Bar Success Secrets

For brownies and bars to turn out perfectly every time, it's all about the pan you use and tricks for cutting them.

Choosing the Right Pan

Use the exact size of pan called for in the recipe when baking bars or brownies. If made in too big of a pan, bars will be hard and overbaked. Bars made in pans that are too small can be doughy in the center and have hard edges.

Shiny metal pans are recommended for baking bars. They reflect heat and prevent the bottom from getting too brown and hard. Check at minimum bake time; bake longer if needed.

Follow the manufacturer's directions when using dark, nonstick or glass baking pans; they may recommend reducing the oven temperature by 25°F. Check for doneness 3 to 5 minutes before the minimum bake time given in the recipe.

Cutting Bars Perfectly

Line the Pan: Lining the pan with foil before baking makes it easy to cut bars—and is great for quick cleanup! Turn the pan upside-down. Tear off a piece of foil longer than the pan. Smooth the foil around the pan bottom and sides and then remove. Flip the pan over, and gently fit the shaped foil into the pan.

When the bars or brownies are cool, lift them out of the pan, using the edges of foil as handles. Peel back the foil and cut the bars as directed.

Use a Plastic Knife: Our food stylists have found that plastic knives work best for cutting brownies and soft, sticky bars such as Lemon Bars (page 194). They also prevent your pans from getting scratched, as they could if using a metal knife.

Peanut Butter Crunch Bars (page 216)

Snickerdoodle Bars

PREP TIME: 20 minutes **START TO FINISH:** 1 hour 45 minutes   **24 bars**

BARS

2⅓	cups all-purpose flour
1¼	teaspoons baking powder
½	teaspoon salt
¾	cup butter or margarine, softened
1¼	cups granulated sugar
½	cup packed brown sugar
3	eggs
1	teaspoon vanilla

CINNAMON FILLING

1	tablespoon granulated sugar
1	tablespoon ground cinnamon

GLAZE

1	cup powdered sugar
1	to 2 tablespoons milk
¼	teaspoon vanilla

1 Heat oven to 350°F. Spray or grease bottom only of 13×9-inch pan with cooking spray. In small bowl, mix flour, baking powder and salt; set aside.

2 In large bowl, beat butter with electric mixer on high speed until creamy. Beat in sugars. Gradually beat in eggs and vanilla until well mixed. On low speed, beat in flour mixture until well mixed.

3 Spoon half the batter into pan; spread evenly. In small bowl, mix cinnamon filling ingredients; sprinkle evenly over batter.

4 Drop teaspoon-size amounts of remaining batter evenly over cinnamon filling mixture.

5 Bake 20 to 25 minutes or until golden brown and toothpick inserted in center comes out clean. Cool completely, about 1 hour.

6 In small bowl, stir glaze ingredients until smooth and thin enough to drizzle. Drizzle over bars. Cut into 6 rows by 4 rows.

1 Bar: Calories 190; Total Fat 7g (Saturated Fat 4g; Trans Fat 0g); Cholesterol 40mg; Sodium 125mg; Total Carbohydrate 30g (Dietary Fiber 0g); Protein 2g **Exchanges:** ½ Starch, 1½ Other Carbohydrate, 1½ Fat **Carbohydrate Choices:** 2

Sweet Success Tips

These bars are especially suitable for picnics and packing for traveling. Bars with soft frostings should be avoided because the frosting may melt. Cut into bars, and pack between sheets of waxed paper in sealed plastic food containers. For optimum packing, wrap each individual brownie or bar cookie in plastic wrap.

If desired, sprinkle ⅓ cup cinnamon chips or chopped toasted pecans over cinnamon-sugar filling in center of bars.

Apple Crumble Bars

PREP TIME: 15 minutes **START TO FINISH:** 3 hours 40 minutes   **24 bars**

CRUST

2½	cups all-purpose flour
1	cup butter or margarine, softened
¾	cup granulated sugar
½	teaspoon salt

FILLING

3½	cups apple pie filling (from two 21-oz cans)

CRUMBLE

1	cup all-purpose flour
1	cup quick-cooking oats
¾	cup packed brown sugar
1	teaspoon ground cinnamon
¼	teaspoon ground nutmeg
10	tablespoons butter, cut into small pieces

1 Heat oven to 375°F. Grease 13×9-inch pan with shortening or cooking spray. In large bowl, beat crust ingredients with electric mixer on low speed until mixture looks like coarse crumbs. Press in pan.

2 Bake 15 minutes or until golden brown. Cool about 30 minutes. Reduce oven temperature to 350°F.

3 Spoon pie filling evenly over crust. In medium bowl, mix 1 cup flour, the oats, brown sugar, cinnamon and nutmeg. Add 10 tablespoons butter; mix with fork or fingers until crumbly. Sprinkle mixture over filling; press lightly.

4 Bake 40 minutes or until light brown. Cool completely, about 2 hours. Cut into 6 rows by 4 rows.

1 bar: Calories 283; Total Fat 13g (Saturated Fat 8g); Sodium 75mg; Total Carbohydrate 41g (Dietary Fiber 1g); Protein 3g **Exchanges:** 1 Starch, 1½ Other Carbohydrate, 2½ Fat **Carbohydrate Choices:** 2½

Caramel Apple-Nut Bars

PREP TIME: 15 minutes **START TO FINISH:** 2 hours 20 minutes   **36 bars**

- 2 cups all-purpose flour
- 2 cups quick-cooking oats
- 1½ cups packed brown sugar
- 1 teaspoon baking soda
- ½ teaspoon salt
- 1¼ cups butter or margarine, softened
- ½ cup caramel topping
- 3 tablespoons all-purpose flour
- 1 medium apple, peeled, chopped (1 cup)
- ½ cup coarsely chopped pecans

1 Heat oven to 350°F. Grease bottom and sides of 13×9-inch pan with shortening or cooking spray. In large bowl, beat 2 cups flour, the oats, brown sugar, baking soda, salt and butter with electric mixer on low speed until crumbly, or mix with spoon. Press about 3 cups of mixture in pan. Bake 10 minutes.

2 Meanwhile, in small bowl, mix caramel topping and 3 tablespoons flour. Sprinkle apple and pecans over partially baked crust. Drizzle with caramel mixture. Sprinkle with remaining crust mixture.

3 Bake 20 to 25 minutes longer or until golden brown. Cool completely, about 1 hour 30 minutes. Cut into 6 rows by 6 rows.

1 Bar: Calories 160; Total Fat 8g (Saturated Fat 4g; Trans Fat 0g); Cholesterol 15mg; Sodium 150mg; Total Carbohydrate 22g (Dietary Fiber 1g); Protein 1g **Exchanges:** ½ Starch, 1 Other Carbohydrate, 1½ Fat **Carbohydrate Choices:** 1½

Pumpkin-Spice Bars
with Cream Cheese Frosting

PREP TIME: 20 minutes **START TO FINISH:** 2 hours 50 minutes   **49 bars**

BARS

- **4 eggs**
- **2 cups granulated sugar**
- **1 cup vegetable oil**
- **1 can (15 oz) pumpkin (not pumpkin pie mix)**
- **2 cups all-purpose flour**
- **2 teaspoons baking powder**
- **1 teaspoon baking soda**
- **½ teaspoon salt**
- **2 teaspoons ground cinnamon**
- **½ teaspoon ground ginger**
- **¼ teaspoon ground cloves**
- **1 cup raisins, if desired**

CREAM CHEESE FROSTING

- **1 package (8 oz) cream cheese, softened**
- **¼ cup butter or margarine, softened**
- **2 to 3 teaspoons milk**
- **1 teaspoon vanilla**
- **4 cups powdered sugar**
- **½ cup chopped walnuts, if desired**

1 Heat oven to 350°F. Spray 15×10×1-inch pan with cooking spray.

2 In large bowl, beat eggs, granulated sugar, oil and pumpkin with whisk until smooth. Stir in flour, baking powder, baking soda, salt, cinnamon, ginger and cloves. Stir in raisins. Spread in pan.

3 Bake 25 to 30 minutes or until toothpick inserted in center comes out clean and bars spring back when touched lightly in center. Cool completely, about 2 hours.

4 In medium bowl, beat cream cheese, butter, milk and vanilla with electric mixer on low speed until smooth. Gradually beat in powdered sugar, 1 cup at a time, on low speed until smooth and spreadable. Spreading frosting over bars. Sprinkle with walnuts. Cut into 7 rows by 7 rows. Store covered in refrigerator.

1 Bar: Calories 170; Total Fat 7g (Saturated Fat 2.5g; Trans Fat 0g); Cholesterol 25mg; Sodium 95mg; Total Carbohydrate 23g (Dietary Fiber 0g); Protein 1g **Exchanges:** ½ Starch, 1 Other Carbohydrate, 1½ Fat **Carbohydrate Choices:** 1½

Sweet Success Tips

In a pinch, use 2½ teaspoons pumpkin pie spice instead of the cinnamon, ginger and cloves.

Plain canned pumpkin is not sweetened and doesn't have flavoring added; pumpkin pie mix contains sugar and spices.

Pumpkin Cheesecake Squares

PREP TIME: 20 minutes START TO FINISH: 3 hours 5 minutes   **16 bars**

BASE

- **1 cup all-purpose flour**
- **¾ cup packed brown sugar**
- **½ cup butter or margarine**
- **1 cup quick-cooking oats**
- **½ cup finely chopped walnuts**

FILLING

- **1 package (8 oz) cream cheese, softened**
- **¾ cup sugar**
- **1 can (15 oz) pumpkin (not pumpkin pie mix)**
- **1½ teaspoons ground cinnamon**
- **1 teaspoon ground ginger**
- **3 eggs**

TOPPING

- **2 cups sour cream**
- **⅓ cup sugar**
- **½ teaspoon vanilla**
- **Additional finely chopped walnuts, if desired**

1 Heat oven to 350°F. Spray 13×9-inch pan with cooking spray. In medium bowl, mix flour and brown sugar. Using pastry blender, cut in butter until mixture looks like coarse crumbs. Stir in oats and ½ cup walnuts. Press in bottom of pan; bake 15 minutes.

2 In large bowl, beat filling ingredients with electric mixer on medium speed until well blended. Pour over hot base. Bake 20 to 25 minutes longer or until set and dry in center.

3 Meanwhile, in small bowl, mix topping ingredients. Drop mixture by spoonfuls over pumpkin layer; spread evenly over hot filling. Bake about 5 minutes or until topping is set. Cool completely, about 2 hours. Sprinkle with additional chopped walnuts. Cut into 4 rows by 4 rows. Store covered in refrigerator.

1 Bar: Calories 340; Total Fat 19g (Saturated Fat 11g; Trans Fat 0.5g); Cholesterol 50mg; Sodium 110mg; Total Carbohydrate 37g (Dietary Fiber 2g); Protein 4g **Exchanges:** 1 Starch, 1½ Other Carbohydrate, 3½ Fat **Carbohydrate Choices:** 2½

Sweet Success Tip

Don't want to make a pie? Try these bars instead. They can be made up to a day ahead of time.

Frosted Cinnamon-Ginger Bars

PREP TIME: 15 minutes **START TO FINISH:** 1 hour 35 minutes **24 bars**

BARS

- ¾ cup butter or margarine, softened
- ½ cup packed brown sugar
- 1 egg
- ⅓ cup molasses
- 2½ cups all-purpose flour
- 2 teaspoons baking soda
- ½ teaspoon ground cinnamon
- ½ teaspoon ground ginger
- ½ teaspoon ground cloves
- ¼ teaspoon salt

TOPPING

- ½ teaspoon granulated sugar
- ¼ teaspoon ground cinnamon
- 1 cup Betty Crocker Whipped vanilla frosting

1 Heat oven to 350°F. In large bowl, beat butter and brown sugar with electric mixer on medium speed until well blended. Beat in egg until well blended. Beat in molasses until creamy. On low speed, beat in remaining bar ingredients until soft dough forms. Press dough in bottom of ungreased 13×9-inch pan.

2 Bake 15 to 18 minutes or until edges look dry and center springs back when touched gently with finger. Cool completely, about 1 hour.

3 In small bowl, mix granulated sugar and ¼ teaspoon cinnamon. Spread frosting over bars; sprinkle with cinnamon-sugar mixture. Cut into 6 rows by 4 rows.

1 Bar: Calories 170; Total Fat 8g (Saturated Fat 4g; Trans Fat 0.5g); Cholesterol 25mg; Sodium 180mg; Total Carbohydrate 23g (Dietary Fiber 0g); Protein 1g **Exchanges:** ½ Starch, 1 Other Carbohydrate, 1½ Fat **Carbohydrate Choices:** 1½

Sweet Success Tip

Add a little crunch to these bars by mixing 1½ cups chopped walnuts into the batter.

Chewy Raspberry Almond Bars

PREP TIME: 20 minutes **START TO FINISH:** 2 hours **16 bars**

1½ cups quick-cooking oats

1½ cups all-purpose flour

¾ cup packed light brown sugar

½ teaspoon salt

¾ cup cold butter or margarine

1 egg, beaten

¾ cup seedless red raspberry jam

1 cup fresh raspberries (6 oz)

½ cup sliced almonds

1 Heat oven to 375°F. Spray 9-inch square pan with baking spray with flour.

2 In large bowl, mix oats, flour, brown sugar and salt. Cut in butter, using pastry blender or fork, until mixture looks like coarse crumbs. Reserve 1 cup mixture for topping. To remaining mixture, stir in egg until just moistened.

3 Press dough firmly and evenly into bottom of pan, using fingers or bottom of measuring cup. Spread with jam. Arrange raspberries over jam. Stir almonds into reserved crumb mixture; sprinkle evenly over raspberries.

4 Bake 30 to 35 minutes or until top is golden. Cool 1 hour in pan on cooling rack. Cut into 4 rows by 4 rows.

1 Bar: Calories 260; Total Fat 11g (Saturated Fat 6g; Trans Fat 0g); Cholesterol 35mg; Sodium 150mg; Total Carbohydrate 36g (Dietary Fiber 2g); Protein 3g **Exchanges:** 2 Starch, ½ Other Carbohydrate, 1½ Fat **Carbohydrate Choices:** 2½

Chewy Blueberry Almond Bars: Substitute fresh blueberries for the raspberries and blueberry preserves for the raspberry jam.

Sweet Success Tip

If you don't have baking spray with flour, grease the pan with cooking spray and sprinkle lightly with flour.

Date Bars

PREP TIME: 30 minutes **START TO FINISH:** 1 hour 5 minutes   **36 bars**

DATE FILLING

- 3 cups chopped pitted dates (1 lb)
- 1½ cups water
- ¼ cup granulated sugar

BARS

- 1 cup packed brown sugar
- 1 cup butter, softened
- 1¾ cups all-purpose or whole wheat flour
- 1½ cups quick-cooking oats
- ½ teaspoon baking soda
- ½ teaspoon salt

1 In 2-quart saucepan, cook filling ingredients over low heat about 10 minutes, stirring constantly, until thickened. Cool 5 minutes.

2 Heat oven to 400°F. Grease bottom and sides of 13×9-inch pan with shortening.

3 In large bowl, stir brown sugar and butter until well mixed. Stir in flour, oats, baking soda and salt until crumbly. Press half of the crumb mixture evenly in bottom of pan. Spread with filling. Top with remaining crumb mixture; press lightly.

4 Bake 25 to 30 minutes or until light brown. Cool 5 minutes in pan on cooling rack. Cut into 6 rows by 6 rows while warm.

1 Bar: Calories 150; Total Fat 5g (Saturated Fat .5g; Trans Fat 0g); Cholesterol 15mg; Sodium 85mg; Total Carbohydrate 253g (Dietary Fiber 2g); Protein 2g **Exchanges:** 1Starch, ½ Other Carbohydrate, 1 Fat **Carbohydrate Choices:** 1½

Fig Bars: Substitute 3 cups chopped dried figs for the dates.

Peanut Butter Crunch Bars

PREP TIME: 15 minutes **START TO FINISH:** 2 hours 45 minutes **36 bars**

1 cup sugar

½ cup butter or margarine, softened

½ cup peanut butter

2 tablespoons milk

1 teaspoon vanilla

1 egg

1½ cups whole wheat flour

½ teaspoon baking soda

½ teaspoon salt

1 cup semisweet chocolate chips (6 oz)

½ cup chopped honey-roasted peanuts

1 Heat oven to 350°F. Spray 13×9-inch pan with cooking spray. In large bowl, beat sugar, butter and peanut butter with electric mixer until light and fluffy. Add milk, vanilla and egg; beat until well blended. Add flour, baking soda and salt; mix well. Spread in pan.

2 Bake 19 to 24 minutes or until edges are golden brown. Immediately sprinkle with chocolate chips; let stand 5 minutes.

3 Using metal spatula, spread softened chips to frost bars. Sprinkle with peanuts. Cool completely in pan on cooling rack, about 2 hours. Cut into 6 rows by 6 rows.

1 Bar: Calories 130; Total Fat 7g (Saturated Fat 3g; Trans Fat 0g); Cholesterol 15mg; Sodium 95mg; Total Carbohydrate 13g (Dietary Fiber 1g); Protein 2g **Exchanges:** ½ Starch, ½ Other Carbohydrate, 1½ Fat **Carbohydrate Choices:** 1

Sweet Success Tip

Try using your other favorite chips, such as dark or milk chocolate.

Triple-Nut Bars

PREP TIME: 35 minutes **START TO FINISH:** 1 hour 50 minutes   **36 bars**

CRUST

- ¾ **cup butter or margarine, softened**
- ½ **cup packed brown sugar**
- ½ **teaspoon almond extract**
- 1½ **cups all-purpose flour**

TOPPING

- 1 **cup butter or margarine**
- 1½ **cups packed brown sugar**
- ¼ **cup honey**
- ¼ **cup light corn syrup**
- ½ **teaspoon vanilla**
- 1 **cup walnut pieces**
- 1 **cup unblanched or blanched whole almonds**
- 1 **cup pecan halves**

1 Heat oven to 350°F. In medium bowl, beat ¾ cup butter, ½ cup brown sugar and the almond extract with electric mixer on medium-low speed until blended. On low speed, beat in flour until soft dough forms. Press dough in bottom of ungreased 13×9-inch pan. Bake 17 to 20 minutes or until golden brown.

2 Meanwhile, in 2-quart saucepan, cook 1 cup butter, 1½ cups brown sugar, the honey, corn syrup and vanilla over medium-high heat 12 to 15 minutes, stirring frequently, until mixture comes to a full rolling boil. Boil 1 to 2 minutes, stirring frequently. Remove from heat.

3 Sprinkle walnuts, almonds and pecans over crust. Pour brown sugar mixture over nuts. Bake 13 to 15 minutes longer or until top of mixture is bubbly. Cool completely, about 1 hour. Cut into 6 rows by 6 rows.

1 Bar: Calories 230; Total Fat 15g (Saturated Fat 6g; Trans Fat 0g); Cholesterol 25mg; Sodium 70mg; Total Carbohydrate 21g (Dietary Fiber 1g); Protein 2g **Exchanges:** 1½ Other Carbohydrate, 3 Fat **Carbohydrate Choices:** 1½

Fully Loaded Bars

PREP TIME: 20 minutes **START TO FINISH:** 1 hour 50 minutes   **36 bars**

¾ cup packed brown sugar

¾ cup butter or margarine, softened

1 egg

1½ cups all-purpose flour

1 cup old-fashioned or quick-cooking oats

1 bag (14 oz) caramels, unwrapped

⅓ cup half-and-half

1 cup semisweet chocolate chunks

1 cup coarsely chopped mixed nuts

¼ cup broken pretzel twists

1 Heat oven to 350°F. Grease 13×9-inch pan with shortening or cooking spray. In large bowl, beat brown sugar, butter and egg with electric mixer on medium speed, or mix with spoon. Stir in flour and oats. Spread in pan.

2 Bake 15 to 20 minutes or until light golden brown. Meanwhile, in 1-quart saucepan, heat caramels and half-and-half over low heat, stirring occasionally, until caramels are melted.

3 Pour caramel mixture over crust. Sprinkle with chocolate chunks, nuts and pretzels.

4 Bake 5 to 8 minutes longer or until chocolate is softened. Cool about 1 hour or until chocolate is set. Cut into 6 rows by 6 rows.

1 Bar: Calories 180; Total Fat 9g (Saturated Fat 4g; Trans Fat 0g); Cholesterol 20mg; Sodium 80mg; Total Carbohydrate 23g (Dietary Fiber 1g); Protein 2g **Exchanges:** 1½ Other Carbohydrate, 2 Fat **Carbohydrate Choices:** 1½

Sweet Success Tip

Pop these crunchy-chewy bars into the refrigerator to quickly cool them.

No-Bake Chocolate–Peanut Butter Candy Bars

PREP TIME: 15 minutes START TO FINISH: 45 minutes   **32 bars**

24	creme-filled chocolate sandwich cookies
4	cups miniature marshmallows
¼	cup butter or margarine
1	cup semisweet chocolate chips (6 oz)
1	can (14 oz) sweetened condensed milk
1	bag (10 oz) peanut butter chips (1⅔ cups)
¼	cup creamy peanut butter
1	cup coarsely chopped honey-roasted peanuts
4	Nature Valley® peanut butter crunchy granola bars (2 pouches from 8.9-oz box), crushed
1	teaspoon vegetable oil

1 Line bottom and sides of 13×9-inch (3-quart) glass baking dish with foil, leaving foil hanging over 2 opposite sides of pan. In food processor bowl with metal blade, process cookies until finely chopped.

2 In 2-quart saucepan, cook marshmallows and butter over low heat, stirring constantly, until melted. Stir in chopped cookies and ¾ cup of the chocolate chips until well mixed. Press in bottom of baking dish.

3 In microwavable bowl, microwave condensed milk and peanut butter chips uncovered on High 60 seconds, stirring once until smooth. Stir in peanut butter. Stir in peanuts and granola bars. Spread over chocolate layer.

4 In small microwavable bowl, microwave remaining ¼ cup chocolate chips and the oil uncovered on High 30 seconds or until chips can be stirred smooth. Drizzle chocolate diagonally over peanut butter layer. Refrigerate until set. Remove bars from pan, using foil to lift. Cut into 8 rows by 4 rows.

1 Bar: Calories 240; Total Fat 12g (Saturated Fat 4g; Trans Fat 0g); Cholesterol 10mg; Sodium 130mg; Total Carbohydrate 29g (Dietary Fiber 1g); Protein 5g **Exchanges:** 2 Starch, 2 Fat **Carbohydrate Choices:** 2

Sweet Success Tip

To easily crush granola bars, leave them in their pouches. Gently pound with meat mallet or rolling pin to break them up. Or, crumble them into a large resealable plastic bag and roll with a rolling pin.

Eggnog Cheesecake Bars

PREP TIME: 20 minutes START TO FINISH: 2 hours 25 minutes   24 bars

CRUST

- **2 cups graham cracker crumbs (32 squares)**
- **¾ cup butter or margarine, melted**
- **½ cup blanched whole almonds, finely chopped**
- **¼ cup packed brown sugar**
- **1 tablespoon ground cinnamon**

FILLING

- **2 packages (8 oz each) cream cheese, softened**
- **¼ cup granulated sugar**
- **¼ cup packed brown sugar**
- **2 teaspoons ground nutmeg**
- **½ cup whipping cream**
- **1 teaspoon vanilla**
- **2 eggs**

TOPPING

- **½ cup blanched whole almonds, finely chopped, toasted★**

1 Heat oven to 350°F. In large bowl, stir crust ingredients until well blended. Press mixture in bottom of ungreased 13×9-inch pan. Bake 8 minutes.

2 In clean large bowl, beat cream cheese with electric mixer on medium speed until softened. Gradually beat in granulated sugar, ¼ cup brown sugar, the nutmeg, cream and vanilla. Beat in eggs, one at a time, until creamy. Pour mixture over crust.

3 Bake 30 to 35 minutes longer or until center is set. Sprinkle with ½ cup toasted almonds; press in slightly. Cool 1 hour 30 minutes. Cut into 6 rows by 4 rows, using thin knife and wiping blade occasionally. Store covered in refrigerator.

★To toast almonds, bake in shallow pan at 350°F 3 to 5 minutes, stirring occasionally, until golden brown.

1 Bar: Calories 460; Total Fat 36g (Saturated Fat 19g; Trans Fat 1g); Cholesterol 110mg; Sodium 300mg; Total Carbohydrate 28g (Dietary Fiber 2g); Protein 7g **Exchanges:** 2 Other Carbohydrate, 1 High-Fat Meat, 5½ Fat **Carbohydrate Choices:** 2

Sweet Success Tip

Try crushed vanilla wafer cookies instead of the graham cracker crumbs.

Crunchy Peanut Butter Blast Brownies

PREP TIME: 20 minutes **START TO FINISH:** 1 hour 50 minutes **24 brownies**

BROWNIES

- 1 **box (1 lb 2.3 oz) Betty Crocker fudge brownie mix**
- ¼ **cup water**
- ⅔ **cup vegetable oil**
- 2 **eggs**
- 1 **cup semisweet chocolate chips (6 oz)**
- 15 **peanut-shaped peanut butter-filled sandwich cookies, chopped**

TOPPING

- 1 **bag (10 oz) peanut butter chips**
- ¼ **cup creamy peanut butter**
- ½ **cup chopped salted cocktail peanuts**

1 Heat oven to 350°F. Grease bottom only of 13×9-inch pan with shortening or cooking spray.

2 In medium bowl, stir brownie mix, water, oil and eggs until well blended. Stir in chocolate chips and cookies; spread in pan. Bake 24 to 26 minutes or until toothpick inserted 2 inches from side of pan comes out clean or almost clean. Cool 30 minutes.

3 In small microwavable bowl, microwave peanut butter chips and peanut butter uncovered on High 45 to 60 seconds, stirring every 15 seconds, until melted and smooth. Spread over cooled brownies; sprinkle with peanuts. Cover and refrigerate 40 minutes or until topping is set. Cut into 6 rows by 4 rows.

1 Brownie: Calories 320; Total Fat 17g (Saturated Fat 4g; Trans Fat 0g); Cholesterol 20mg; Sodium 180mg; Total Carbohydrate 37g (Dietary Fiber 1g); Protein 4g **Exchanges:** 1 Starch, 1½ Other Carbohydrate, 3½ Fat **Carbohydrate Choices:** 2½

Sweet Success Tip

For added texture, substitute crunchy peanut butter for creamy.

Hazelnut-Mocha Brownies

PREP TIME: 20 minutes START TO FINISH: 1 hour 35 minutes   24 brownies

BROWNIES

- 1 box (1 lb 2.3 oz) Betty Crocker fudge brownie mix
- ¼ cup water
- ⅔ cup vegetable oil
- 2½ teaspoons instant espresso coffee powder or granules
- 2 eggs
- 1 cup chopped hazelnuts (filberts)

FROSTING

- 1 cup powdered sugar
- ½ cup hazelnut spread with cocoa
- 2 tablespoons butter or margarine, softened
- 2 to 3 tablespoons milk

1 Heat oven to 350°F. Grease bottom only of 13×9-inch pan with shortening or cooking spray. In medium bowl, stir brownie mix, water, oil, espresso powder and eggs until well blended. Stir in hazelnuts; spread in pan. Bake 24 to 26 minutes or until toothpick inserted 2 inches from side of pan comes out clean or almost clean. Cool completely, about 40 minutes.

2 In medium bowl, beat powdered sugar, hazelnut spread, butter and 1 tablespoon milk with electric mixer on low speed until blended. Beat in additional milk, 1 tablespoon at a time, until desired spreading consistency. Frost cooled brownies. Let stand about 15 minutes or until frosting sets. Cut into 6 rows by 4 rows.

1 Brownie: Calories 240; Total Fat 13g (Saturated Fat 2g; Trans Fat 0g); Cholesterol 20mg; Sodium 90mg; Total Carbohydrate 29g (Dietary Fiber 0g); Protein 1g **Exchanges:** ½ Starch, 1½ Other Carbohydrate, 2½ Fat **Carbohydrate Choices:** 2

Sweet Success Tips

Hazelnut spread with cocoa can be found near the peanut butter at the supermarket.

Don't enjoy mocha flavor? Just leave out the espresso coffee powder.

Pretzel Brownie Bars

PREP TIME: 25 minutes **START TO FINISH:** 1 hour 55 minutes   **32 bars**

CRUST

1½	cups crushed pretzels
¼	cup granulated sugar
½	cup butter or margarine, melted

BROWNIES

1	box (1 lb 2.3 oz) Betty Crocker fudge brownie mix
¼	cup water
⅔	cup vegetable oil
2	eggs

FROSTING

1	cup powdered sugar
2	tablespoons butter or margarine, softened
2	squares (1 oz each) unsweetened chocolate, melted
1	teaspoon vanilla
2	to 3 tablespoons milk
½	cup crushed pretzels

1 Heat oven to 350°F. In medium bowl, mix crust ingredients. Press in ungreased 13×9-inch pan. Bake 8 minutes; cool 10 minutes.

2 In medium bowl, stir brownie ingredients until blended. Carefully spread batter over cooled crust. Bake 24 to 26 minutes or until toothpick inserted 2 inches from side of pan comes out clean or almost clean. Cool completely in pan on cooling rack, about 1 hour.

3 In medium bowl, beat powdered sugar, 2 tablespoons butter, melted chocolate and the vanilla with electric mixer on low speed until combined. Beat in 1 tablespoon milk until blended. Beat in additional milk, 1 tablespoon at a time, until frosting is desired spreading consistency. Frost cooled brownies; sprinkle with crushed pretzels. Cut into 8 rows by 4 rows.

1 Bar: Calories 190; Total Fat 10g (Saturated Fat 3.5g; Trans Fat 0g); Cholesterol 25mg; Sodium 135mg; Total Carbohydrate 23g (Dietary Fiber 0g); Protein 1g **Exchanges:** ½ Starch, 1 Other Carbohydrate, 2 Fat **Carbohydrate Choices:** 1½

Sweet Success Tip

Use a food processor to easily crush pretzels.

Chocolate Brownies

PREP TIME: 25 minutes START TO FINISH: 3 hours 10 minutes   16 brownies

⅔   cup butter

5   oz unsweetened baking chocolate, chopped

1¾ cups sugar

2   teaspoons vanilla

3   eggs

1   cup all-purpose flour

½   cup chopped walnuts, toasted if desired*

Chocolate or mocha frosting, if desired

1 Heat oven to 350°F. Grease bottom and sides of 9-inch square pan with shortening.

2 In 1-quart saucepan, melt butter and chocolate over low heat, stirring constantly. Cool 5 minutes.

3 In medium bowl, beat sugar, vanilla and eggs with electric mixer on high speed 5 minutes. Beat in chocolate mixture on low speed, scraping bowl occasionally. Beat in flour just until blended, scraping bowl occasionally. Stir in walnuts. Spread in pan.

4 Bake 40 to 45 minutes or just until brownies begin to pull away from sides of pan. Cool completely in pan on cooling rack, about 2 hours. Frost with frosting. Cut into 4 rows by 4 rows.

*To toast walnuts, heat oven to 350°F. Spread walnuts in ungreased shallow pan. Bake uncovered 6 to 10 minutes, stirring occasionally, until light brown.

1 Brownie: Calories 310; Total Fat 18g (Saturated Fat 8g; Trans Fat 0g); Cholesterol 60mg; Sodium 65mg; Total Carbohydrate 31g (Dietary Fiber 2g); Protein 4g **Exchanges:** 1 Starch, 1 Other Carbohydrate, 3½ Fat **Carbohydrate Choices:** 2

Chocolate-Peanut Butter Brownies: Substitute ⅓ cup crunchy peanut butter for ⅓ cup of the butter. Omit walnuts. Before baking, arrange 16 miniature chocolate-covered peanut butter cup candies, unwrapped, over top. Press into batter so tops of cups are even with top of batter.

Double Chocolate Brownies: Stir in ½ cup semisweet or dark chocolate chips after adding the flour in step 3.

Ultimate Fudge Mocha Brownies

PREP TIME: 20 minutes **START TO FINISH:** 2 hours 25 minutes **32 brownies**

BROWNIES

- ½ **cup semisweet chocolate chips**
- ½ **cup butter or margarine**
- 1 **cup packed dark brown sugar**
- 2 **eggs**
- 2 **tablespoons coffee-flavored liqueur**
- 1 **teaspoon vanilla**
- ¾ **cup all-purpose flour**
- 2 **tablespoons unsweetened baking cocoa**
- ½ **teaspoon salt**

FROSTING

- ⅓ **cup butter or margarine, softened**
- 2 **cups powdered sugar**
- 2 **tablespoons coffee-flavored liqueur**

GLAZE

- ½ **cup whipping cream**
- 1 **tablespoon light corn syrup**
- 1 **cup semisweet chocolate chips (6 oz)**

1 Heat oven to 350°F. Line 8-inch square pan with foil; spray foil with cooking spray.

2 In 3-quart saucepan, melt ½ cup chocolate chips and ½ cup butter over low heat, stirring constantly; remove from heat. Cool completely. Stir in brown sugar, eggs, 2 tablespoons liqueur and the vanilla with whisk. Stir in flour, cocoa and salt. Spread evenly in pan. Bake 20 minutes or until center is set. Cool completely.

3 In medium bowl, beat frosting ingredients with electric mixer on medium speed until smooth and spreadable. Frost brownies. Refrigerate at least 15 minutes. In small microwavable bowl, microwave glaze ingredients on High 1 minute; stir. Microwave 15 seconds longer; stir until melted and smooth. Pour glaze over frosting; spread to cover. Refrigerate until set. With wet knife, cut into 8 rows by 4 rows. Store covered in refrigerator.

1 Brownie: Calories 173; Total Fat 9g (Saturated Fat 5g); Sodium 87g; Total Carbohydrate 23g (Dietary Fiber 1g); Protein 1g **Exchanges:** 1½ Other Carbohydrate, 1½ Fat **Carbohydrate Choices:** 1½

Chocolate-Cashew Brownies

PREP TIME: 45 minutes **START TO FINISH:** 2 hours 40 minutes **24 brownies**

BROWNIES

- **1 cup butter or margarine, softened**
- **¾ cup granulated sugar**
- **½ cup packed brown sugar**
- **1 teaspoon vanilla**
- **2 eggs**
- **1¾ cups all-purpose flour**
- **¾ cup unsweetened baking cocoa**
- **1 teaspoon salt**
- **½ teaspoon baking soda**
- **1 cup semisweet chocolate chips (6 oz)**
- **¾ cup miniature marshmallows**
- **½ cup chopped cashews**

FROSTING

- **3 cups powdered sugar**
- **¼ cup butter or margarine, softened**
- **½ teaspoon vanilla**
- **3 to 4 tablespoons half-and-half or milk**
- **¼ teaspoon unsweetened baking cocoa**
- **Additional cashews, if desired**

1 Heat oven to 350°F. Spray 13×9-inch pan with cooking spray.

2 In large bowl, beat 1 cup butter with electric mixer on medium speed until smooth and creamy. Beat in sugars, 1 teaspoon vanilla and the eggs until smooth. On low speed, beat in flour, ¾ cup cocoa, the salt and baking soda until soft dough forms. Stir in chocolate chips, marshmallows and cashews. Spread mixture in pan.

3 Bake 15 to 20 minutes or until set. Cool completely, about 1 hour.

4 In small bowl, mix all frosting ingredients except cocoa and cashews, adding enough of the half-and-half until frosting is smooth and spreadable. Frost brownies. Sprinkle with ¼ teaspoon cocoa and additional cashews. Let stand about 30 minutes or until frosting is set. Cut into 6 rows by 4 rows.

1 Brownie: Calories 300; Total Fat 14g (Saturated Fat 8g; Trans Fat 0g); Cholesterol 40mg; Sodium 150mg; Total Carbohydrate 41g (Dietary Fiber 1g); Protein 3g **Exchanges:** 1 Starch, 1½ Other Carbohydrate, 2½ Fat **Carbohydrate Choices:** 3

Outrageous Caramel-Fudge Brownies

PREP TIME: 30 minutes START TO FINISH: 3 hours   **24 brownies**

- 1 **bag (14 oz) caramels, unwrapped**
- ½ **cup evaporated milk (from 12-oz can)**
- 1 **cup butter or margarine**
- 2 **cups sugar**
- 2 **teaspoons vanilla**
- 4 **eggs, slightly beaten**
- 1¼ **cups all-purpose flour**
- ¾ **cup unsweetened baking cocoa**
- ¼ **teaspoon salt**
- 1 **bag (11.5 or 12 oz) semisweet chocolate chunks (2 cups)**
- 1½ **cups chopped pecans**
- 1 **teaspoon vegetable oil**

1 Heat oven to 350°F. Grease bottom and sides of 13×9-inch pan with shortening or cooking spray. In 3-quart saucepan, heat caramels and milk over low heat, stirring frequently, until caramels are melted and smooth.

2 In 2-quart saucepan, melt butter over low heat; remove from heat. Stir in sugar, vanilla and eggs until well blended. Stir in flour, cocoa and salt. Stir in 1½ cups of the chocolate chunks and 1 cup of the pecans. Spread evenly in pan.

3 Gently and evenly drizzle melted caramel over batter, preventing large pockets of caramel and preventing caramel from reaching bottom of brownies. (Caramel can cover entire surface of batter.) Bake 35 to 40 minutes or until set.

4 In 1-quart saucepan, heat remaining ½ cup chocolate chunks and the oil over low heat, stirring frequently, until smooth. Drizzle over warm brownies. Sprinkle with remaining ½ cup pecans; press in lightly. Cool 20 minutes. Refrigerate about 1 hour 30 minutes or until chocolate is set. Cut into 6 rows by 4 rows. If refrigerated longer, let stand at room temperature 20 minutes before serving.

1 Brownie: Calories 380; Total Fat 20g (Saturated Fat 9g; Trans Fat 0g); Cholesterol 60mg; Sodium 140mg; Total Carbohydrate 46g (Dietary Fiber 2g); Protein 4g **Exchanges:** 1 Starch, 2 Other Carbohydrate, 4 Fat **Carbohydrate Choices:** 3

Sweet Success Tip

Instead of using all semisweet chocolate chunks, you could substitute white vanilla baking chips for part or all of the semisweet chunks.

Dulce-Frosted Chipotle Brownies

PREP TIME: 20 minutes START TO FINISH: 2 hours 5 minutes   **16 brownies**

1   **box Betty Crocker Premium Brownies Chocolate Chunk**

   Water, vegetable oil and eggs called for on brownie mix box

1   **teaspoon ground cinnamon**

½   **to ¾ teaspoon chipotle chile powder**

2   **cups powdered sugar**

¼   **cup dulce de leche (caramelized sweetened condensed milk) (from 13.4-oz can)**

2   **tablespoons butter or margarine, softened**

2   **tablespoons milk**

1   **teaspoon vanilla**

1 Heat oven to 350°F. Grease or spray bottom of 8-inch pan.

2 Make brownie batter as directed on box, adding cinnamon and chipotle powder until well blended. Spread in pan. Bake 39 to 42 minutes or until toothpick inserted 2 inches from edge comes out almost clean. Cool 1 hour 5 minutes.

3 In medium bowl, beat powdered sugar, dulce de leche, butter, milk and vanilla with electric mixer on low speed until smooth and creamy. Spread onto cooled brownies. Cut into 4 rows by 4 rows.

1 Brownie: Calories 270; Total Fat 9g (Saturated Fat 3g; Trans Fat 0g); Cholesterol 20mg; Sodium 120mg; Total Carbohydrate 45g (Dietary Fiber 1g); Protein 1g **Exchanges:** ½ Starch, 2½ Other Carbohydrate, 2 Fat **Carbohydrate Choices:** 3

Sweet Success Tips

Look for cans of dulce de leche next to sweetened condensed milk in your grocery store. Dulce de leche is similar to sweetened condensed milk, but it has been caramelized and is much thicker.

Dulce [DOOL-say] is Spanish for "sweet," and generally refers to an intensely sweet confection made with sugar and cream. Leche [LAY-chay] is the Spanish word for "milk."

Pumpkin Swirl Brownies

PREP TIME: 15 minutes **START TO FINISH:** 2 hours 30 minutes   **16 brownies**

FILLING

- **1 package (3 oz) cream cheese, softened**
- **½ cup canned pumpkin (not pumpkin pie mix)**
- **1 egg**
- **3 tablespoons sugar**
- **1 teaspoon ground cinnamon**
- **¼ teaspoon ground nutmeg**

BROWNIES

- **1 box Betty Crocker Premium Brownies Ultimate Fudge**
- **¼ cup vegetable oil**
- **2 tablespoons water**
- **1 egg**

1 Heat oven to 350°F. Grease bottom only of 9-inch square pan with shortening or cooking spray. In small bowl, beat filling ingredients with electric mixer on low speed until smooth. Set aside.

2 Make brownie batter as directed on box, using ¼ cup oil, 2 tablespoons water and the egg. Spread three-fourths of the batter in pan. Spoon filling by tablespoonfuls evenly over batter. Spoon remaining brownie batter over filling. Cut through batter several times with knife for marbled design.

3 Bake 40 to 45 minutes or until toothpick inserted 1 inch from side of pan comes out almost clean. Cool 1 hour 30 minutes. Cut into 4 rows by 4 rows. Store covered in refrigerator.

1 Brownie: Calories 210; Total Fat 8g (Saturated Fat 3g; Trans Fat 0g); Cholesterol 30mg; Sodium 140mg; Total Carbohydrate 33g (Dietary Fiber 1g); Protein 2g **Exchanges:** ½ Starch, 1½ Other Carbohydrate, 1½ Fat **Carbohydrate Choices:** 2

Chocolate Chip Blonde Brownies

PREP TIME: 15 minutes **START TO FINISH:** 3 hours 45 minutes **24 brownies**

⅔ **cup butter or margarine, softened**

2 **cups packed brown sugar**

2 **teaspoons vanilla**

2 **eggs**

2 **cups all-purpose flour**

2 **teaspoons baking powder**

1 **teaspoon salt**

1 **bag (12 oz) semisweet chocolate chips (2 cups)**

1 Heat oven to 350°F. Spray bottom only of 13×9-inch pan with cooking spray, or grease with butter.

2 In large bowl, beat butter, brown sugar, vanilla and eggs with electric mixer on medium-high speed until blended. On low speed, beat in flour, baking powder and salt until soft dough forms. Spread in pan. Sprinkle chocolate chips evenly over top.

3 Bake 25 to 30 minutes or until edges are golden brown. Cool completely, about 3 hours. Cut into 6 rows by 4 rows.

1 Brownie: Calories 240; Total Fat 10g (Saturated Fat 6g; Trans Fat 0g); Cholesterol 30mg; Sodium 190mg; Total Carbohydrate 35g (Dietary Fiber 1g); Protein 2g **Exchanges:** 1 Starch, 1½ Other Carbohydrate, 2 Fat **Carbohydrate Choices:** 2

Gluten-Free Peanut Butter Cookie Candy Bars

PREP TIME: 30 minutes START TO FINISH: 2 hours 35 minutes   36 bars

COOKIE BASE

- 1 box Betty Crocker Gluten Free chocolate chip cookie mix

  Butter, gluten-free vanilla and egg called for on cookie mix box

FILLING

- ⅓ cup light corn syrup
- 3 tablespoons butter, softened
- 3 tablespoons peanut butter
- 1 tablespoon plus 1½ teaspoons water
- 1¼ teaspoons gluten-free vanilla

  Dash salt
- 3½ cups gluten-free powdered sugar

CARAMEL LAYER

- 1 bag (14 oz) gluten-free caramels, unwrapped
- 2 tablespoons water
- 1½ cups dry-roasted peanuts

TOPPING

- 1 bag (11.5 oz) milk chocolate chips (2 cups)

1 Heat oven to 350°F. Make cookie dough as directed on box using butter, vanilla and egg. In ungreased 13×9-inch pan, press dough evenly. Bake 18 to 20 minutes or until light golden brown. Cool about 30 minutes.

2 In large bowl, beat all filling ingredients except powdered sugar with electric mixer on medium speed until creamy and smooth. Gradually beat in powdered sugar until well blended (filling will be thick). Press filling over cookie base.

3 In medium microwavable bowl, microwave caramels and 2 tablespoons water uncovered on High 2 to 4 minutes, stirring twice, until caramels are melted. Stir in peanuts. Spread evenly over filling. Refrigerate about 15 minutes or until caramel layer is firm.

4 In small microwavable bowl, microwave chocolate chips uncovered on High 1 to 2 minutes, stirring once, until melted. Spread evenly over caramel layer. Refrigerate about 1 hour or until chocolate is set. Cut into 6 rows by 6 rows. Store covered at room temperature.

★ *Cooking Gluten Free? Always read labels to make sure each recipe ingredient is gluten free. Products and ingredients sources can change.*

1 Bar: Calories 290; Total Fat 12g (Saturated Fat 5g; Trans Fat 0g); Cholesterol 20mg; Sodium 140mg; Total Carbohydrate 42g (Dietary Fiber 1g); Protein 3g **Exchanges:** ½ Starch, 2½ Other Carbohydrate, 2½ Fat **Carbohydrate Choices:** 3

Sweet Success Tip

Powdered sugar is usually gluten free since it's blended with cornstarch to keep it fluffy. However, some manufacturers use wheat products instead of cornstarch, so always check the label when purchasing.

Peanut Butter Rocky Road Brownies

PREP TIME: 20 minutes START TO FINISH: 2 hours 30 minutes   24 brownies

1   box (1 lb, 2.3 oz) Betty Crocker fudge brownie mix

Water, vegetable oil and eggs called for on brownie mix box

1   jar (7 oz) marshmallow creme

½   cup creamy peanut butter

1   tablespoon milk

30   miniature chocolate-covered peanut butter cup candies, unwrapped, chopped

½   cup chopped salted peanuts

¼   cup semisweet chocolate chips

¼   teaspoon vegetable oil

1 Heat oven to 350°F. Grease bottom only of 13×9-inch pan with shortening or cooking spray.

2 Make and bake brownie mix as directed on box. Cool completely.

3 In medium bowl, beat marshmallow creme, peanut butter and milk with electric mixer on medium speed until smooth and creamy. Spread over cooled brownies. Sprinkle with chopped peanut butter candies and peanuts.

4 In small microwavable bowl, microwave chocolate chips and ¼ teaspoon oil uncovered on High 30 to 60 seconds, stirring once, until melted. Drizzle over brownies. Let stand about 30 minutes or until chocolate is set. Cut into 6 rows by 4 rows.

1 Brownie: Calories 280; Total Fat 14g (Saturated Fat 3.5g; Trans Fat 0g); Cholesterol 20mg; Sodium 160mg; Total Carbohydrate 34g (Dietary Fiber 2g); Protein 4g **Exchanges:** 1 Starch, 1½ Other Carbohydrate, 2½ Fat **Carbohydrate Choices:** 2

Sweet Success Tip

Cut these rich brownies into bite-size squares and serve in decorative papers.

Gluten-Free Strawberry Truffle Brownies

PREP TIME: 30 minutes START TO FINISH: 2 hours 30 minutes   20 brownies

BROWNIES

- 1 **box Betty Crocker Gluten Free brownie mix**
- **Melted butter and eggs called for on brownie mix box**

STRAWBERRY TRUFFLE TOPPING

- 1 **cup white vanilla baking chips (6 oz)**
- ¼ **cup butter, cut into pieces**
- ½ **cup gluten-free powdered sugar**
- ½ **cup strawberry jam**
- 3 **to 4 drops gluten-free red food color, if desired**

CHOCOLATE GLAZE

- ½ **cup semisweet chocolate chips**
- 2 **tablespoons butter**
- 2 **tablespoons light corn syrup**
- **Additional gluten-free powdered sugar, if desired**

1 Heat oven to 350°F. Spray bottom only of 9-inch square pan with cooking spray. Make brownie batter as directed on box. Spread batter in pan. Bake 26 to 30 minutes or until toothpick inserted comes out almost clean. Cool in pan on cooling rack 30 minutes.

2 In microwavable bowl, microwave white chips and ¼ cup butter on Medium-High (70%) 1 to 2 minutes, stirring once, until butter is melted. Stir until smooth. Add ½ cup powdered sugar and jam; stir until smooth. Stir in food color. Spread over brownies. Chill 30 minutes.

3 Melt chocolate chips and 2 tablespoons butter. Stir in corn syrup. Drizzle over topping; spread gently to cover. Chill until set, about 30 minutes. Sprinkle with powdered sugar. Cut into 5 rows by 4 rows. Store tightly covered in refrigerator.

★ *Cooking Gluten Free? Always read labels to make sure each recipe ingredient is gluten free. Products and ingredients sources can change.*

1 Brownie: Calories 260; Total Fat 12g (Saturated Fat 7g; Trans Fat 0g); Cholesterol 35mg; Sodium 115mg; Total Carbohydrate 37g (Dietary Fiber 1g); Protein 2g **Exchanges:** ½ Starch, 2 Other Carbohydrate, 2 Fat **Carbohydrate Choices:** 2½

Raspberry Truffle Brownies: Use seedless raspberry preserves for the strawberry jam.

Sweet Success Tip

If your jar of strawberry preserves is in the refrigerator, measure out what you need and allow it to come to room temperature so it will blend into the white chocolate mixture more easily.

Oatmeal Brownies

PREP TIME: 25 minutes **START TO FINISH:** 3 hours 10 minutes **48 brownies**

CRUST AND TOPPING

2½	cups quick-cooking or old-fashioned oats
¾	cup all-purpose flour
¾	cup packed brown sugar
½	teaspoon baking soda
¾	cup butter or margarine, melted

FILLING

4	oz unsweetened baking chocolate
⅔	cup butter or margarine
2	cups granulated sugar
1	teaspoon vanilla
4	eggs
1¼	cups all-purpose flour
1	teaspoon baking powder
1	teaspoon salt

1 Heat oven to 350°F. Spray 13×9-inch pan with cooking spray.

2 In large bowl, mix oats, ¾ cup flour, the brown sugar and baking soda. Stir in melted butter. Reserve ¾ cup oat mixture for topping. Press remaining oat mixture in pan. Bake 10 minutes. Cool 5 minutes.

3 Meanwhile, in 3-quart saucepan, heat chocolate and ⅔ cup butter over low heat, stirring occasionally, until melted; remove from heat. Stir in granulated sugar, vanilla and eggs. Stir in 1¼ cups flour, the baking powder and salt.

4 Spread filling over crust. Sprinkle with reserved oat mixture. Bake about 30 minutes longer or until center is set and oat mixture turns golden brown (do not overbake). Cool completely, about 2 hours. Cut into 8 rows by 6 rows.

1 Brownie: Calories 150; Total Fat 7g (Saturated Fat 4.5g; Trans Fat 0g); Cholesterol 30mg; Sodium 120mg; Total Carbohydrate 20g (Dietary Fiber 1g); Protein 2g **Exchanges:** 1½ Other Carbohydrate, 1½ Fat **Carbohydrate Choices:** 1

Sweet Success Tips

Unsweetened baking chocolate is bitter in flavor and used primarily in baking.

To keep brownies longer, wrap tightly, label and freeze up to 6 months.

Black Forest Dream Bars (page 309)

contest-winning cookies and bars

Joyful Almond Cookies

{ **Cookie Contest Winner** Whitney Gilbert }

PREP TIME: 50 minutes START TO FINISH: 50 minutes   **3 dozen cookies**

1 **pouch Betty Crocker chocolate chip cookie mix**

½ **cup butter or margarine, softened**

½ **teaspoon almond extract**

1 **egg**

2 **cups flaked coconut**

⅔ **cup chopped toasted almonds★**

1 Heat oven to 375°F. In large bowl, stir cookie mix, butter, almond extract and egg until soft dough forms. Stir in ½ cup of the coconut and the almonds; mix well.

2 Roll dough into 36 (1-inch) balls. Dough will be sticky. Roll balls in remaining coconut until well coated. Place 2 inches apart on ungreased cookie sheets.

3 Bake 9 to 11 minutes or until light golden brown. Cool 2 minutes; remove from cookie sheets to cooling racks. Cool completely. Store covered at room temperature.

★*To toast almonds, heat oven to 350°F. Spread almonds in ungreased shallow pan. Bake 6 to 10 minutes, stirring occasionally, until light brown*

1 Cookie: Calories 120; Total Fat 7g (Saturated Fat 4g; Trans Fat 0g); Cholesterol 15mg; Sodium 85mg; Total Carbohydrate 13g (Dietary Fiber 0g); Protein 1g **Exchanges:** 1 Other Carbohydrate, 1½ Fat **Carbohydrate Choices:** 1

Maple Walnut White Chocolate Chip Cookies

{ **Cookie Contest Winner** Molly Deere }

PREP TIME: 45 minutes **START TO FINISH:** 45 minutes   **2 dozen cookies**

1 pouch Betty Crocker sugar cookie mix
½ cup butter or margarine, softened
1 tablespoon maple flavor
1 egg
1½ cups white vanilla baking chips
1 cup chopped walnuts

1 Heat oven to 350°F. In large bowl, stir cookie mix, butter, maple flavor and egg until soft dough forms. Stir in baking chips and walnuts.

2 Using small cookie scoop or tablespoon, drop dough 2 inches apart on ungreased cookie sheets.

3 Bake 13 to 14 minutes or until edges are golden brown. Cool 2 minutes; remove from cookie sheets to cooling racks. Cool completely. Store covered at room temperature.

1 Cookie: Calories 230; Total Fat 13g (Saturated Fat 7g; Trans Fat 1g); Cholesterol 20mg; Sodium 120mg; Total Carbohydrate 26g (Dietary Fiber 0g); Protein 2g **Exchanges:** 1 Starch, ½ Other Carbohydrate, 2½ Fat **Carbohydrate Choices:** 2

Sweet Success Tip

Semisweet, dark or milk chocolate chips can be used for the white vanilla chips.

Almond Poppy Tea Cookies

{ **Cookie Contest Winner** Joan Cossette }

PREP TIME: 1 hour START TO FINISH: 1 hour   **3 dozen cookies**

1   **pouch Betty Crocker sugar cookie mix**

⅓   **cup all-purpose flour**

1   **tablespoon poppy seed**

½   **cup butter or margarine, softened**

1   **package (3 oz) cream cheese, softened**

2   **teaspoons almond extract**

1   **egg**

¼   **cup sliced almonds, if desired**

1   **cup powdered sugar**

3   **to 4 teaspoons water**

1 Heat oven to 350°F. In large bowl, stir cookie mix, flour, poppy seed, butter, cream cheese, 1 teaspoon of the almond extract and the egg until soft dough forms.

2 Roll dough into 1¼-inch balls. On ungreased cookie sheets, place balls 2 inches apart. Press with fingers to slightly flatten. Top each with 5 sliced almonds arranged to form a star.

3 Bake 9 to 11 minutes or until edges are light golden brown. Cool 3 minutes; remove from cookie sheets to cooling racks.

4 In small bowl, mix powdered sugar, remaining 1 teaspoon almond extract and enough water to give glaze spreading consistency. Spread glaze over warm cookies. Store cooled cookies tightly covered in single layer at room temperature.

1 Cookie: Calories 110; Total Fat 5g (Saturated Fat 2.5g; Trans Fat 0.5g); Cholesterol 15mg; Sodium 70mg; Total Carbohydrate 15g (Dietary Fiber 0g); Protein 1g **Exchanges:** ½ Starch, ½ Other Carbohydrate, 1 Fat **Carbohydrate Choices:** 1

Choco-Cherry Double Delights

{ **Cookie Contest Winner** Diana Neves }

PREP TIME: 45 minutes **START TO FINISH:** 1 hour   **2½ dozen cookies**

1⅓ cups whole maraschino cherries, well drained

1 pouch Betty Crocker double chocolate chunk cookie mix

2 tablespoons vegetable oil

1 tablespoon water

1 egg, beaten

½ cup chopped macadamia nuts

1 teaspoon powdered sugar

1 Heat oven to 375°F. Cut 15 of the maraschino cherries in half; set aside for topping cookies. Chop remaining cherries.

2 In large bowl, stir cookie mix, oil, water and egg until soft dough forms. Stir in chopped cherries and nuts.

3 Onto ungreased cookie sheets, drop dough by rounded teaspoonfuls 2 inches apart. Press 1 cherry half lightly into center of each cookie.

4 Bake 7 to 9 minutes or until set. Cool 2 minutes; remove from cookie sheets to cooling racks. Cool completely, about 15 minutes. Before serving, sprinkle with powdered sugar. Store loosely covered at room temperature.

1 Cookie: Calories 110; Total Fat 4g (Saturated Fat 1.5g; Trans Fat 0g); Cholesterol 5mg; Sodium 75mg; Total Carbohydrate 17g (Dietary Fiber 0g); Protein 1g **Exchanges:** ½ Starch, ½ Other Carbohydrate, 1 Fat **Carbohydrate Choices:** 1

Sweet Success Tips

Because of their high fat content, macadamia nuts should be stored in the refrigerator or freezer. All types of nuts keep well in the freezer, so you can always be prepared when the cookie-baking bug strikes!

Have almonds, walnuts or pecans on hand, but no macadamia nuts? Feel free to substitute in this recipe.

Citrus-Kissed Fig Thumbprints

{ **Cookie Contest Winner** Edwina Gadsby }

PREP TIME: 55 minutes **START TO FINISH:** 55 minutes **4 dozen cookies**

- 1 **pouch Betty Crocker sugar cookie mix**
- 3 **tablespoons all-purpose flour**
- ½ **cup butter or margarine, melted**
- 1 **teaspoon grated lemon peel**
- 1 **teaspoon grated orange peel**
- ½ **teaspoon vanilla**
- 1 **egg**
- ⅓ **cup fig preserves**
- 1 **teaspoon coarse sugar, if desired**

1 Heat oven to 375°F. In large bowl, stir cookie mix, flour, butter, lemon peel, orange peel, vanilla and egg until soft dough forms.

2 Roll dough into 1-inch balls. On ungreased cookie sheets, place balls 2 inches apart. Press thumb into center of each cookie to make indentation, but do not press all the way to cookie sheet. Spoon about ¼ teaspoon preserves into each indentation.

3 Bake 7 to 9 minutes or until edges are light golden brown. Cool 2 minutes; remove from cookie sheets to cooling racks. Sprinkle with coarse sugar. Store cooled cookies tightly covered at room temperature.

1 Cookie: Calories 70; Total Fat 3g (Saturated Fat 1.5g; Trans Fat 0g); Cholesterol 10mg; Sodium 45mg; Total Carbohydrate 10g (Dietary Fiber 0g); Protein 0g **Exchanges:** ½ Other Carbohydrate, ½ Fat **Carbohydrate Choices:** ½

Sweet Success Tip

Grating lemon and orange peel is a breeze when you use a handheld fine grater. Look for them where kitchen supplies are sold.

Cranberry Pistachio Cookies

{ Cookie Contest Winner Virginia Kocen **}**

PREP TIME: 1 hour START TO FINISH: 1 hour   **4 dozen cookies**

1 pouch Betty Crocker sugar cookie mix

1 box (4-serving size) pistachio instant pudding and pie filling mix

¼ cup all-purpose flour

½ cup butter or margarine, melted

2 eggs

1 cup dry-roasted salted pistachio nuts, chopped

½ cup dried cranberries, chopped

1 Heat oven to 350°F. In large bowl, stir cookie mix, pudding mix and flour. Stir in butter and eggs until soft dough forms. Add nuts and cranberries; mix well.

2 Using small cookie scoop or teaspoon, drop dough 2 inches apart onto ungreased cookie sheets. Press with fingers to slightly flatten.

3 Bake 9 to 11 minutes or until edges are light golden brown. Cool 2 minutes; remove from cookie sheets to cooling racks. Store cooled cookies tightly covered at room temperature.

1 Cookie: Calories 90; Total Fat 4.5g (Saturated Fat 1.5g; Trans Fat 0g); Cholesterol 15mg; Sodium 85mg; Total Carbohydrate 12g (Dietary Fiber 0g); Protein 1g **Exchanges:** 1 Other Carbohydrate, 1 Fat **Carbohydrate Choices:** 1

Sweet Success Tip

Use a food processor to quickly chop the nuts and cranberries.

Iced Cinnamon-Pecan Biscotti

{ **Gold Medal Flour Scratch Bakers' Club Baking Contest Winner** Christine Yang }

PREP TIME: 40 minutes **START TO FINISH:** 2 hours 25 minutes **16 cookies**

COOKIES

- **2** cups all-purpose flour
- **1½** teaspoons baking powder
- **1** teaspoon ground cinnamon
- **½** cup granulated sugar
- **¼** teaspoon salt
- **½** cup unsalted butter or regular butter, softened
- **1** teaspoon vanilla
- **2** eggs

FILLING

- **½** cup packed brown sugar
- **¼** cup unsalted butter or regular butter, softened
- **1** teaspoon ground cinnamon
- **1** cup chopped toasted pecans*

ICING

- **½** cup powdered sugar
- **2** teaspoons milk
- **1** teaspoon light corn syrup
- **¼** teaspoon vanilla

1 Heat oven to 350°F. Line cookie sheet with cooking parchment paper. In medium bowl, mix flour, baking powder and 1 teaspoon cinnamon.

2 In large bowl, beat granulated sugar, salt and ½ cup butter with electric mixer on medium speed until light and fluffy. Add 1 teaspoon vanilla. Beat in eggs, one at a time, until well blended. Gradually add flour mixture, beating until well blended.

3 Place dough on cookie sheet. With floured fingers, press dough into rectangle, 14×10 inches. In small bowl, mix together brown sugar, ¼ cup softened butter, 1 teaspoon cinnamon and ¾ cup of the pecans. Spread brown sugar mixture evenly over dough to within ½ inch of edges of dough. Using parchment paper to lift dough, fold long sides of dough over center ⅓ of dough, overlapping one side over the other. Shape dough into log, 12×3 inches. Press remaining ¼ cup pecans on top.

4 Bake 28 to 30 minutes or until light golden brown. Cool on cookie sheet 15 minutes. Leaving baked cookie on parchment paper, carefully remove from cookie sheet to cutting board. Using serrated knife, cut crosswise into ¾-inch slices. Carefully place slices cut side down on cookie sheet. Bake 15 to 18 minutes or until light golden brown. Cool completely on cookie sheet, about 30 minutes.

5 In small bowl, stir together powdered sugar and milk. Add corn syrup and ¼ teaspoon vanilla; blend until smooth. Drizzle over cooled biscotti.

*To toast pecans, heat oven to 350°F. Spread pecans in ungreased shallow pan. Bake uncovered 6 to 10 minutes, stirring occasionally, until light brown.

1 Cookie: Calories 270; Total Fat 15g (Saturated Fat 6g; Trans Fat 0g); Cholesterol 50mg; Sodium 120mg; Total Carbohydrate 30g (Dietary Fiber 1g); Protein 3g **Exchanges:** 1 Starch, 1 Other Carbohydrate, 3 Fat **Carbohydrate Choices:** 2

Red Velvet Rich and Creamy Cookies

{ **Cookie Contest Winner** Joanne Opdahl }

PREP TIME: 1 hour START TO FINISH: 1 hour 15 minutes   **3 dozen cookies**

1   **pouch Betty Crocker sugar cookie mix**

⅓   **cup unsweetened baking cocoa**

¼   **cup butter or margarine, softened**

¼   **cup sour cream**

1   **tablespoon red food color**

1   **egg**

¾   **to 1 cup Betty Crocker Rich & Creamy cream cheese frosting**

¼   **cup chopped nuts**

1 Heat oven to 375°F. In large bowl, stir cookie mix, cocoa, butter, sour cream, food color and egg until soft dough forms.

2 Shape dough into 1-inch balls. Onto ungreased cookie sheets, place balls 2 inches apart.

3 Bake 8 to 9 minutes or until set. Cool 2 minutes; remove from cookie sheets to cooling racks. Cool completely, about 15 minutes.

4 Frost cooled cookies with frosting. Sprinkle with nuts. Store tightly covered at room temperature.

1 Cookie: Calories 110; Total Fat 4.5g (Saturated Fat 1.5g; Trans Fat 1g); Cholesterol 10mg; Sodium 70mg; Total Carbohydrate 16g (Dietary Fiber 0g); Protein 1g **Exchanges:** ½ Starch, ½ Other Carbohydrate, 1 Fat **Carbohydrate Choices:** 1

Sweet Success Tips

Chopped walnuts are delicious sprinkled on these frosted cookies, or try chopped pecans. Lightly toast them first, if you like, to bring out the flavor.

Store the leftover cream cheese frosting in its container in the refrigerator, and use it to frost some cupcakes. It would be great on carrot cake cupcakes!

Butter Pecan Thumbprints

{ **Celebrate the Season—Fall Baking Contest Winner** Mary Shivers }

PREP TIME: 1 hour 10 minutes **START TO FINISH:** 1 hour 40 minutes   **3 dozen cookies**

COOKIES

- **1 cup packed light brown sugar**
- **½ cup unsalted butter, softened**
- **1 egg, beaten**
- **2 teaspoons vanilla**
- **1½ cups all-purpose flour**
- **¼ teaspoon baking soda**
- **⅛ teaspoon kosher (coarse) salt**
- **1½ cups finely chopped pecans**

FILLING

- **⅓ cup packed light brown sugar**
- **2 tablespoons all-purpose flour**
- **1 cup finely chopped pecans**
- **2 tablespoons unsalted butter, softened**

1 Heat oven to 325°F. Grease cookie sheets with shortening or cooking spray, or line with cooking parchment paper or silicone baking mat.

2 In large bowl, beat 1 cup brown sugar, ½ cup butter, the egg and vanilla with electric mixer on low speed. Stir in 1½ cups flour, the baking soda and salt. Stir in 1½ cups pecans.

3 In small bowl, mix ⅓ cup brown sugar, 2 tablespoons flour and 1 cup pecans. Stir in 2 tablespoons butter with fork until mixture is crumbly.

4 Shape dough into 1½-inch balls. Place balls 2 inches apart on cookie sheets. Press thumb into center of each cookie to make indentation, but do not press all the way to cookie sheet. Fill each indentation with about 1 teaspoon of filling.

5 Bake 10 to 15 minutes or until edges are golden brown. Cool 5 minutes; remove from cookie sheets to cooling racks.

1 Cookie: Calories 150; Total Fat 9g (Saturated Fat 2.5g; Trans Fat 0g); Cholesterol 15mg; Sodium 20mg; Total Carbohydrate 16g (Dietary Fiber 1g); Protein 1g **Exchanges:** 1 Other Carbohydrate, 2 Fat **Carbohydrate Choices:** 1

Sweet Success Tip

Use a thimble or the end of a wooden spoon to make uniform indentations in cookie dough.

Raspberry Pistachio Thumbprints

{ **Celebrate the Season—Holiday Cookie Contest Winner** Laura Murphy }

PREP TIME: 1 hour 20 minutes **START TO FINISH:** 1 hour 50 minutes   **3½ dozen cookies**

1   cup butter or margarine, softened

½   cup powdered sugar

2   cups all-purpose flour

¼   teaspoon salt

1   teaspoon vanilla

1   cup finely chopped roasted pistachio nuts

1   jar (12 oz) red raspberry jam

2   tablespoons powdered sugar

1 Heat oven to 325°F. In large bowl, beat butter and ½ cup powdered sugar with electric mixer on medium speed until creamy. Stir in flour, salt, vanilla and nuts.

2 Shape dough into 1¼-inch balls. On ungreased cookie sheets, place balls about 1 inch apart. Press thumb into center of each cookie to make indentation, but do not press all the way to cookie sheet.

3 Bake 15 to 17 minutes or until set but not browned. Quickly remake indentation with end of wooden spoon handle if necessary. Remove from cookie sheets to cooling racks; cool completely, about 30 minutes.

4 Fill each thumbprint with 1 rounded teaspoonful of jam. Sprinkle 2 tablespoons powdered sugar over jam-filled centers.

1 Cookie: Calories 110; Total Fat 6g (Saturated Fat 3g; Trans Fat 0g); Cholesterol 10mg; Sodium 60mg; Total Carbohydrate 13g (Dietary Fiber 0g); Protein 1g **Exchanges:** ½ Starch, ½ Other Carbohydrate, 1 Fat **Carbohydrate Choices:** 1

Sweet Success Tips

A food processor works great for finely chopping the pistachio nuts.

You can substitute strawberry jam or your favorite flavor for the raspberry.

Chocolate-Marshmallow Pillows

{ **Cookie Contest Winner** *Kristina Vanni* }

PREP TIME: 45 minutes **START TO FINISH:** 1 hour 5 minutes   **2 dozen cookies**

COOKIES

- 1 **pouch Betty Crocker double chocolate chunk cookie mix**
- ¼ **cup vegetable oil**
- 2 **tablespoons water**
- 1 **egg**
- ⅔ **cup chopped pecans**
- 12 **large marshmallows, cut in half**

FROSTING

- 1 **cup semisweet chocolate chips (6 oz)**
- ⅓ **cup whipping cream**
- 1 **teaspoon butter or margarine**
- 1 **teaspoon vanilla**
- ½ **cup powdered sugar**

1 Heat oven to 350°F. In large bowl, stir cookie mix, oil, water, egg and pecans until soft dough forms.

2 Onto ungreased cookie sheets, drop dough by rounded tablespoonfuls 2 inches apart.

3 Bake 7 minutes. Remove from oven; immediately press marshmallow half lightly, cut side down, on top of cookie. Bake 1 to 2 minutes longer or just until marshmallows begin to soften. Cool 2 minutes; remove from cookie sheets to cooling racks. Cool completely, about 15 minutes.

4 Meanwhile, in 1-quart nonstick saucepan, melt chocolate chips over low heat, stirring until smooth. Remove from heat. Add whipping cream, butter and vanilla; blend well. Stir in powdered sugar until smooth.

5 Spread frosting over each cooled cookie, covering marshmallow. Let stand until frosting is set.

1 Cookie: Calories 200; Total Fat 10g (Saturated Fat 3.5g; Trans Fat 0g); Cholesterol 15mg; Sodium 100mg; Total Carbohydrate 27g (Dietary Fiber 0g); Protein 1g **Exchanges:** 2 Other Carbohydrate, 2 Fat **Carbohydrate Choices:** 2

Sweet Success Tip

Lightly spray kitchen scissors with cooking spray to make cutting marshmallows easy.

Dark Chocolate–Glazed Orange Macaroons

{ **Celebrate the Season—Holiday Cookie Contest Winner** Holly Bauer }

PREP TIME: 1 hour START TO FINISH: 2 hours 15 minutes   2½ dozen cookies

2⅔ cups firmly packed flaked coconut

⅔ cup sugar

¼ cup all-purpose flour

4 egg whites

½ cup finely chopped pecans

1 tablespoon grated orange peel

2 teaspoons vanilla

½ teaspoon almond extract

3 oz dark baking chocolate, chopped

1 Heat oven to 325°F. Line cookie sheets with cooking parchment paper or silicone baking mat.

2 In large bowl, mix coconut, sugar and flour. Stir in egg whites, pecans, orange peel, vanilla and almond extract. Onto cookie sheet, drop dough by tablespoonfuls 2 inches apart.

3 Bake 18 to 22 minutes or until golden. Remove from cookie sheets to cooling racks; cool completely.

4 In small resealable freezer plastic bag, place chocolate; seal bag. Microwave on High about 1 minute or until softened. Gently squeeze bag until chocolate is smooth; cut off tiny corner of bag. Squeeze bag to drizzle chocolate over cookies. Let stand until set.

1 Cookie: Calories 100; Total Fat 5g (Saturated Fat 3.5g; Trans Fat 0g); Cholesterol 0mg; Sodium 30mg; Total Carbohydrate 10g (Dietary Fiber 1g); Protein 1g **Exchanges:** ½ Starch, 1 Fat **Carbohydrate Choices:** ½

Sweet Success Tip

When you need to separate an egg, take them right out of the fridge before separating, as chilled eggs separate easier.

Chocolate–Peanut Butter Cookie Treats

{ **Cookie Contest Winner** Jamie Emerson }

PREP TIME: 1 hour **START TO FINISH:** 1 hour 15 minutes   **3 dozen cookies**

COOKIES

- **1** pouch Betty Crocker peanut butter cookie mix
- **3** tablespoons vegetable oil
- **1** tablespoon water
- **1** egg

COATING

- **1** cup semisweet chocolate chips (6 oz)
- **¼** cup butter or margarine
- **¼** cup peanut butter
- **1** teaspoon vanilla
- **1½** to 2 cups powdered sugar

1 Heat oven to 375°F. In large bowl, stir cookie mix, oil, water and egg until soft dough forms.

2 Shape dough into 1-inch balls. On ungreased cookie sheets, place balls 2 inches apart.

3 Bake 8 to 9 minutes or until edges are light golden brown. Cool 2 minutes; remove from cookie sheets to cooling racks. Cool completely, about 15 minutes.

4 In small microwavable bowl, microwave chocolate chips, butter and peanut butter uncovered on High 1 minute to 1 minute 30 seconds; stir until smooth. Stir in vanilla.

5 Place 1½ cups powdered sugar in 1-gallon resealable food-storage plastic bag; set aside. Place 12 cooled cookies in large bowl. Pour one-third of chocolate mixture over cookies in bowl. Using rubber spatula, toss cookies gently to coat. Place cookies in bag with powdered sugar; seal bag. Gently turn bag to coat cookies. Remove cookies from bag to cooling rack to set. Repeat with 12 more cookies and half of remaining chocolate mixture; repeat again until all cookies are coated, adding additional powdered sugar to bag as needed.

1 Cookie: Calories 140; Total Fat 7g (Saturated Fat 2.5g; Trans Fat 0g); Cholesterol 10mg; Sodium 90mg; Total Carbohydrate 18g (Dietary Fiber 0g); Protein 2g **Exchanges:** ½ Starch, ½ Other Carbohydrate, 1½ Fat **Carbohydrate Choices:** 1

Ginger-Lemon Delights

{ **Cookie Contest Winner** Donna Deteau }

PREP TIME: 50 minutes **START TO FINISH:** 1 hour 10 minutes   **3 dozen cookies**

COOKIES

- **1 pouch Betty Crocker sugar cookie mix**
- **½ cup shortening**
- **¼ cup mild-flavor (light) molasses**
- **1 tablespoon ground ginger**
- **1¼ teaspoons ground cinnamon**
- **1 teaspoon ground cloves**
- **1 egg**

GLAZE AND TOPPING

- **1 cup powdered sugar**
- **1 teaspoon grated lemon peel**
- **4 teaspoons lemon juice**
- **¼ cup finely chopped crystallized ginger**

1 Heat oven to 375°F. In large bowl, stir cookie ingredients until very soft dough forms (dough will be sticky).

2 Onto ungreased cookie sheets, drop dough with 1 tablespoon–size cookie scoop or by tablespoonfuls about 2 inches apart.

3 Bake 8 to 10 minutes or until edges are light golden brown. Cool 2 minutes; remove from cookie sheets to cooling racks. Cool completely, about 30 minutes.

4 In small bowl, stir powdered sugar, lemon peel and lemon juice until smooth. Spread glaze on cookies. Sprinkle with crystallized ginger.

1 Cookie: Calories 110; Total Fat 4.5g (Saturated Fat 1g; Trans Fat 1g); Cholesterol 5mg; Sodium 45mg; Total Carbohydrate 18g (Dietary Fiber 0g); Protein 0g **Exchanges:** 1 Other Carbohydrate, 1 Fat **Carbohydrate Choices:** 1

Sweet Success Tip

Crystallized ginger is fresh gingerroot cooked in a candy syrup and coated with coarse sugar. Look for it next to the fresh herbs in your supermarket.

Best-Ever Chewy Gingerbread Cookies

{ **Celebrate the Season—Holiday Cookie Contest Winner** Shannon Bills }

PREP TIME: 1 hour 30 minutes START TO FINISH: 3 hours 30 minutes   7½ dozen cookies

1   cup plus 2 tablespoons
     unsalted butter, softened

1   cup packed brown sugar

1   egg

¼   cup plus 2 tablespoons
     molasses

2½ cups all-purpose flour

2¼ teaspoons baking soda

½   teaspoon kosher (coarse)
     salt

1   tablespoon ground ginger

1   tablespoon ground
     cinnamon

2   teaspoons ground cloves

1½ teaspoons ground nutmeg

½   teaspoon ground allspice

⅔   cup granulated or coarse
     sugar

1 In large bowl, beat butter and brown sugar with electric mixer on medium speed until light and fluffy, about 5 minutes. Beat in egg and molasses. Stir in remaining ingredients except granulated sugar. Cover; refrigerate at least 2 hours.

2 Heat oven to 350°F. Line cookie sheets with cooking parchment paper or silicone baking mat. In small bowl, place granulated sugar. Shape dough into 1-inch balls; roll in sugar. On cookie sheets, place balls 2 inches apart.

3 Bake 8 to 10 minutes or just until set and soft in center. Cool 2 minutes; remove from cookie sheets to cooling racks. Store tightly covered up to 1 week.

1 Cookie: Calories 50; Total Fat 2.5g (Saturated Fat 1.5g; Trans Fat 0g); Cholesterol 10mg; Sodium 45mg; Total Carbohydrate 8g (Dietary Fiber 0g); Protein 0g **Exchanges:** ½ Other Carbohydrate, ½ Fat **Carbohydrate Choices:** ½

Sweet Success Tips

Look for cooking parchment paper with the waxed paper, foil and plastic wrap at the grocery store. Silicone baking mats are becoming widely available and are now sold in a variety of stores.

You can use light or dark molasses in this recipe.

Pumpkin-Pecan Spice Cookies

{ **Celebrate the Season—Fall Baking Contest Winner** Debra Keil }

PREP TIME: 1 hour 5 minutes **START TO FINISH:** 1 hour 35 minutes   **3½ dozen cookies**

1½ **cups packed light brown sugar**

½ **cup butter or margarine, softened**

2 **eggs**

½ **cup canned pumpkin (not pumpkin pie mix)**

3 **teaspoons vanilla**

2¾ **cups all-purpose flour**

2 **teaspoons baking powder**

1 **teaspoon ground cinnamon**

½ **teaspoon salt**

½ **teaspoon ground ginger**

¼ **teaspoon ground nutmeg**

⅛ **teaspoon ground allspice**

⅛ **teaspoon ground cloves**

Pinch ground cardamom

1⅓ **cups finely chopped pecans**

½ **cup white vanilla baking chips**

4 **oz vanilla-flavored candy coating (almond bark), chopped**

1 Heat oven to 350°F. Grease cookie sheets with shortening or cooking spray, or line with cooking parchment paper or silicone baking mat.

2 In large bowl, beat brown sugar, butter, eggs, pumpkin and vanilla with electric mixer on medium speed. Stir in flour, baking powder and spices. Stir in pecans and baking chips. Drop dough by tablespoonfuls onto cookie sheet.

3 Bake 10 to 14 minutes or until edges are lightly browned. Remove from cookie sheets to cooling racks. Cool completely, about 30 minutes.

4 Place candy coating in small resealable freezer plastic bag; seal bag. Microwave on High about 1 minute or until softened. Gently squeeze bag until coating is smooth; cut off tiny corner of bag. Squeeze bag to drizzle coating over cookies. Let stand until set.

1 Cookie: Calories 140; Total Fat 7g (Saturated Fat 3g; Trans Fat 0g); Cholesterol 15mg; Sodium 80mg; Total Carbohydrate 18g (Dietary Fiber 0g); Protein 2g **Exchanges:** 1 Other Carbohydrate, 1½ Fat **Carbohydrate Choices:** 1

Sweet Success Tips

When buying canned pumpkin, check the label to be sure it's not pumpkin pie mix, which contains sugar and spices.

Try cooked winter squash in place of the pumpkin.

Glazed Bohemian Anise Cookies

{ **Celebrate the Season—Holiday Cookie Contest Winner** David Dahlman }

PREP TIME: 1 hour 5 minutes **START TO FINISH:** 1 hour 50 minutes   **2½ dozen cookies**

COOKIES

- ¾ **cup butter, softened**
- ½ **cup sugar**
- 1 **egg**
- 1 **teaspoon grated lemon peel**
- 1¾ **cups all-purpose flour**
- 1 **teaspoon ground cinnamon**
- ¼ **teaspoon ground cloves**
- ¼ **teaspoon ground nutmeg**
- ¼ **teaspoon pepper**
- 1 **teaspoon anise seed**
- 2 **tablespoons all-purpose flour**

GLAZE AND TOPPING

- ¾ **cup white vanilla baking chips**
- 1 **teaspoon oil**
- ¼ **teaspoon anise extract**
- ¼ **cup chopped almonds, toasted***

1 Heat oven to 350°F. In large bowl, beat butter and sugar with electric mixer on medium speed until smooth. Beat in egg and lemon peel. Stir in 1¾ cups flour, the cinnamon, cloves, nutmeg, pepper and anise seed.

2 Shape dough into 1¼-inch balls. On ungreased cookie sheets, place balls about 1 inch apart. Dip bottom of drinking glass into 2 tablespoons flour; press each ball until about ¼ inch thick.

3 Bake 11 to 14 minutes or until edges are light golden brown. Remove from cookie sheets to cooling racks. Cool 15 minutes.

4 In a small microwavable bowl, microwave baking chips and oil on High 10 seconds; stir. Microwave in additional 10-second intervals until mixture can be stirred smooth. Stir in anise extract. Spoon into small resealable food-storage plastic bag; cut off tiny corner of bag. Squeeze bag to drizzle glaze over cookies. Immediately sprinkle with almonds. Let stand until set, about 30 minutes.

**To toast almonds, heat oven to 350°F. Spread almonds in ungreased shallow pan. Bake uncovered 6 to 10 minutes, stirring occasionally, until light brown.*

1 Cookie: Calories 130; Total Fat 8g (Saturated Fat 4.5g; Trans Fat 0g); Cholesterol 20mg; Sodium 40mg; Total Carbohydrate 14g (Dietary Fiber 0g); Protein 1g **Exchanges:** 1 Other Carbohydrate, 1½ Fat **Carbohydrate Choices:** 1

Frosted Tropical Coconut Bursts

{ **Cookie Contest Winner** Pat Muzzy }

PREP TIME: 1 hour 10 minutes **START TO FINISH:** 1 hour 10 minutes   **3 dozen cookies**

COOKIES

- **1 pouch Betty Crocker sugar cookie mix**
- **½ cup butter or margarine, softened**
- **1 egg**
- **1 cup dried tropical three-fruit mix**
- **½ cup coconut**

GLAZE

- **1 cup powdered sugar**
- **½ teaspoon coconut extract**
- **1 to 2 tablespoons milk**

1 Heat oven to 375°F. In large bowl, stir cookie mix, butter and egg until soft dough forms. Stir in fruit mix and coconut until well mixed.

2 Onto ungreased cookie sheets, drop dough by rounded tablespoonfuls 2 inches apart.

3 Bake 8 to 9 minutes or until golden brown around edges. Cool 2 minutes; remove from cookie sheets to cooling racks. Cool completely, about 15 minutes.

4 In small bowl, stir powdered sugar, coconut extract and enough milk until glaze is spreadable. Spread glaze over tops of cooled cookies.

1 Cookie: Calories 120; Total Fat 4.5g (Saturated Fat 2.5g; Trans Fat 0.5g); Cholesterol 15mg; Sodium 65mg; Total Carbohydrate 17g (Dietary Fiber 0g); Protein 0g **Exchanges:** 1 Other Carbohydrate, 1 Fat **Carbohydrate Choices:** 1

White Chocolate–Cranberry Cookies

{ **Celebrate the Season—Holiday Cookie Contest Winner** Laura Abeloe }

PREP TIME: 55 minutes START TO FINISH: 1 hour 25 minutes   3 dozen cookies

¾ **cup butter or margarine, softened**

¾ **cup packed light brown sugar**

½ **cup granulated sugar**

2 **teaspoons vanilla**

1 **teaspoon almond extract, if desired**

1 **egg**

1¾ **cups all-purpose flour**

½ **teaspoon baking soda**

¼ **teaspoon salt**

1 **cup white vanilla baking chips (6 oz)**

1 **cup sweetened dried cranberries**

1 Heat oven to 350°F. In large bowl, beat butter, brown sugar, granulated sugar, vanilla, almond extract and egg with electric mixer on medium speed until well mixed. Stir in flour, baking soda and salt. Stir in baking chips and cranberries.

2 Onto ungreased cookie sheets, drop dough by rounded tablespoonfuls about 2 inches apart.

3 Bake 12 to 15 minutes or until light brown. Cool 2 to 3 minutes; remove from cookie sheets to cooling racks.

1 Cookie: Calories 130; Total Fat 6g (Saturated Fat 3.5g; Trans Fat 0g); Cholesterol 15mg; Sodium 70mg; Total Carbohydrate 18g (Dietary Fiber 0g); Protein 1g **Exchanges:** ½ Starch, ½ Other Carbohydrate, 1 Fat **Carbohydrate Choices:** 1

Sweet Success Tip

When using brown sugar in baking, it's important to firmly pack the brown sugar into the measuring cup for best results.

Cran-Orange 'n Date-Nut Cookies

{ **Cookie Contest Winner** Barbara Estabrook }

PREP TIME: 55 minutes **START TO FINISH:** 1 hour   **3½ dozen cookies**

⅓ cup dried cranberries

¼ cup chopped orange slice candies

¼ cup coarsely chopped dates

2 tablespoons fresh orange juice

1 pouch Betty Crocker sugar cookie mix

2 tablespoons all-purpose flour

½ teaspoon ground cinnamon

¼ teaspoon ground ginger

⅓ cup butter or margarine, melted

1 teaspoon grated orange peel

1 egg

1 cup chopped pistachio nuts

½ cup flaked coconut

1 Heat oven to 375°F. In small bowl, mix cranberries, candies, dates and orange juice; set aside. In large bowl, stir cookie mix, flour, cinnamon and ginger until blended. Stir in butter, orange peel and egg until soft dough forms. Stir in cranberry mixture, nuts and coconut.

2 Onto ungreased cookie sheets, drop dough by teaspoonfuls 2 inches apart.

3 Bake 10 to 12 minutes or until edges are light golden brown. Cool 5 minutes; remove from cookie sheets to cooling racks. Store cooled cookies tightly covered.

1 Cookie: Calories 100; Total Fat 4.5g (Saturated Fat 1.5g; Trans Fat 0g); Cholesterol 10mg; Sodium 50mg; Total Carbohydrate 13g (Dietary Fiber 0g); Protein 1g **Exchanges:** ½ Starch, ½ Other Carbohydrate, 1 Fat **Carbohydrate Choices:** 1

Buckeye Delights

{ **Cookie Contest Winner** Pam Correll }

PREP TIME: 1 hour 5 minutes **START TO FINISH:** 2 hours 5 minutes   **3 dozen cookie cups**

COOKIE BASE

- **1 pouch Betty Crocker sugar cookie mix**
- **⅓ cup unsweetened baking cocoa**
- **½ cup butter or margarine, softened**
- **1 egg**

FILLING

- **½ cup powdered sugar**
- **½ cup peanut butter**
- **2 tablespoons butter or margarine, softened**
- **1 teaspoon vanilla**
- **¼ teaspoon salt**

TOPPING

- **½ cup whipping cream**
- **1 cup plus 2 tablespoons semisweet chocolate chips**
- **1 tablespoon peanut butter**

1 Heat oven to 350°F. Place mini foil candy cups (about 1¼ inch) in each of 36 mini muffin cups. In large bowl, stir cookie base ingredients until soft dough forms. Press about 1 tablespoon dough into each foil cup. Bake 8 to 10 minutes or until puffy and set. Cool completely, about 30 minutes. Remove from pan.

2 In small bowl, mix filling ingredients until well blended. Press about 1 teaspoon mixture on top of each cooled cookie.

3 In 1-quart saucepan, heat whipping cream just to boiling over low heat, stirring occasionally; remove from heat. Stir in 1 cup of the chocolate chips. Refrigerate about 30 minutes or until cooled. Spread about 2 teaspoons chocolate mixture over each cookie cup.

4 Place remaining 2 tablespoons chocolate chips and 1 tablespoon peanut butter in resealable food-storage plastic bag; partially seal bag. Microwave uncovered on High 30 to 60 seconds or until softened; knead to mix. Cut off small tip from one corner of bag. Squeeze bag to drizzle chocolate mixture over each cookie cup. Refrigerate about 30 minutes or until set. Store covered in refrigerator.

1 Cookie Cup: Calories 160; Total Fat 9g (Saturated Fat 4.5g; Trans Fat 0.5g); Cholesterol 20mg; Sodium 100mg; Total Carbohydrate 17g (Dietary Fiber 0g); Protein 2g **Exchanges:** 1 Starch, 1½ Fat **Carbohydrate Choices:** 1

Sweet Success Tip

Buckeye candies are peanut butter balls dipped in chocolate. The name comes from their resemblance to the nut of the buckeye tree.

Gluten-Free Peanut Butter Cookie Cups

{ **Celebrate the Season—Holiday Cookie Contest Winner** Michelle Bowman }

PREP TIME: 55 minutes **START TO FINISH:** 1 hour 30 minutes   **5 dozen cookies**

1   box Betty Crocker Gluten Free chocolate chip cookie mix

1   egg

½   cup butter, softened

1   teaspoon gluten-free vanilla

½   cup creamy peanut butter

60   miniature chocolate-covered peanut butter cup candies, unwrapped

1 Heat oven to 375°F. Place mini paper baking cup in each of 24 mini muffin cups.

2 In large bowl, mix cookie mix, egg, butter and vanilla with spoon. Stir in peanut butter. Shape dough into 1-inch balls. Place balls in muffin cups.

3 Bake 9 to 11 minutes or until just lightly browned. Immediately press peanut butter cup candy into center of each cookie. Cool 5 minutes before removing from pans to cooling rack; cool completely. Repeat with remaining dough.

✱ *Cooking Gluten Free? Always read labels to make sure each recipe ingredient is gluten free. Products and ingredients sources can change.*

1 Cookie: Calories 100; Total Fat 5g (Saturated Fat 2g; Trans Fat 0g); Cholesterol 10mg; Sodium 80mg; Total Carbohydrate 11g (Dietary Fiber 0g); Protein 1g **Exchanges:** ½ Starch, ½ Other Carbohydrate, 1 Fat **Carbohydrate Choices:** 1

Dark Chocolate–Apricot Cookies

{ **Cookie Contest Winner** Pat Muzzy }

PREP TIME: 1 hour **START TO FINISH:** 3 hours   **3 dozen cookies**

1   **pouch Betty Crocker sugar cookie mix**

½   **cup butter or margarine, softened**

¼   **teaspoon orange extract**

1   **egg**

1   **cup chopped dried apricots**

1   **package (12 oz) dark chocolate chips**

1 Heat oven to 375°F. In large bowl, stir cookie mix, butter, orange extract and egg until soft dough forms. Stir in apricots until blended.

2 Onto ungreased cookie sheets, drop dough by rounded teaspoonfuls 2 inches apart.

3 Bake 8 to 10 minutes or until edges are light golden brown. Cool 3 minutes; remove from cookie sheets to cooling racks. Cool completely, about 15 minutes.

4 In small microwavable bowl, microwave chocolate chips uncovered on High 1 to 2 minutes, stirring every 30 seconds, until chips are melted. Dip each cookie halfway into melted chocolate, letting excess drip off. Place on waxed paper; let stand until chocolate is set, at least 2 hours. To quickly set chocolate, refrigerate cookies 15 minutes. Store between sheets of waxed paper in tightly covered container at room temperature.

1 Cookie: Calories 140; Total Fat 7g (Saturated Fat 3.5g; Trans Fat 0.5g); Cholesterol 15mg; Sodium 60mg; Total Carbohydrate 19g (Dietary Fiber 1g); Protein 1g **Exchanges:** ½ Starch, 1 Other Carbohydrate, 1 Fat **Carbohydrate Choices:** 1

Sweet Success Tip

Dried fruit can be sticky to chop. Try dipping kitchen scissors in water to cut the dried apricots into small pieces.

Chocolate Chip–Oatmeal Shortbread Cookies

{ **Celebrate the Season—Holiday Cookie Contest Winner** Laurie De Hamer }

PREP TIME: 1 hour 5 minutes **START TO FINISH:** 1 hour 20 minutes   **4½ dozen cookies**

- 1   cup butter, softened
- 1   cup powdered sugar
- 1½   cups all-purpose flour
- ½   teaspoon baking soda
- 2   teaspoons vanilla
- 1   cup quick-cooking oats
- 1   bag (12 oz) miniature semisweet chocolate chips

1 Heat oven to 325°F. In large bowl, beat butter and powdered sugar with electric mixer on medium speed until light and fluffy. Stir in flour, baking soda, vanilla and oats. Stir in chocolate chips.

2 Onto ungreased cookie sheets, drop dough by teaspoonfuls 2 inches apart.

3 Bake 11 to 13 minutes or until lightly browned. Cool 1 minute; remove from cookie sheets to cooling racks.

1 Cookie: Calories 90; Total Fat 5g (Saturated Fat 3.5g; Trans Fat 0g); Cholesterol 10mg; Sodium 35mg; Total Carbohydrate 10g (Dietary Fiber 0g); Protein 1g **Exchanges:** ½ Other Carbohydrate, 1 Fat **Carbohydrate Choices:** ½

Mint Chocolate Chip Cookies

{ **Cookie Contest Winner** Patti Bullock }

PREP TIME: 25 minutes **START TO FINISH:** 40 minutes   **3 dozen cookies**

1 **pouch Betty Crocker sugar cookie mix**

½ **cup butter or margarine, softened**

¼ **to ½ teaspoon mint extract**

6 **to 8 drops green food color**

1 **egg**

1 **cup crème de menthe baking chips**

1 **cup semisweet chocolate chunks**

1 Heat oven to 350°F. In large bowl, stir cookie mix, butter, mint extract, food color and egg until soft dough forms. Stir in baking chips and chocolate chunks.

2 Using small cookie scoop or teaspoon, drop dough 2 inches apart onto ungreased cookie sheets.

3 Bake 8 to 10 minutes or until set. Cool 3 minutes; remove from cookie sheets to cooling racks. Store cooled cookies tightly covered at room temperature.

1 Cookie: Calories 130; Total Fat 7g (Saturated Fat 3.5g; Trans Fat 0.5g); Cholesterol 15mg; Sodium 60mg; Total Carbohydrate 16g (Dietary Fiber 0g); Protein 1g **Exchanges:** 1 Other Carbohydrate, 1½ Fat **Carbohydrate Choices:** 1

Spicy Ginger Shortbreads

{ **Celebrate the Season—Fall Baking Contest Winner** Nadine Mesch }

PREP TIME: 1 hour **START TO FINISH:** 3 hours   **3 dozen cookies**

¾ **cup butter, softened**

¼ **cup granulated sugar**

1 **teaspoon grated lemon peel**

1 **egg yolk**

1¼ **cups all-purpose flour**

1 **teaspoon five-spice powder**

¼ **cup finely chopped crystallized ginger**

¼ **cup finely chopped pecans**

1 **tablespoon all-purpose flour**

GLAZE

¼ **cup white vanilla baking chips**

½ **cup powdered sugar**

1 **tablespoon water**

1 In large bowl, beat butter, granulated sugar, lemon peel and egg yolk with electric mixer on medium speed until light and fluffy. Stir in 1¼ cups flour and the five-spice powder until dough holds together. Stir in ginger and pecans.

2 Place dough on smooth surface sprinkled with 1 tablespoon flour. Divide dough in half. Shape each half into 6-inch log. Wrap in plastic wrap; refrigerate 1 hour.

3 Heat oven to 350°F. Grease cookie sheets with shortening or cooking spray, or line with cooking parchment paper or silicone baking mat. Cut dough into ¼-inch slices. Place 1 inch apart on cookie sheets.

4 Bake 8 to 10 minutes or until light golden brown. Remove from cookie sheets to cooling racks. Cool completely, about 30 minutes.

5 In small microwavable bowl, microwave baking chips uncovered on High 30 to 60 seconds, stirring once, until softened and chips can be stirred smooth. Stir in powdered sugar and water. Add additional water, if needed, to achieve glaze consistency. Drizzle glaze over cookies. Let stand until set.

1 Cookie: Calories 80; Total Fat 5g (Saturated Fat 3g; Trans Fat 0g); Cholesterol 15mg; Sodium 30mg; Total Carbohydrate 8g (Dietary Fiber 0g); Protein 0g **Exchanges:** ½ Other Carbohydrate, 1 Fat **Carbohydrate Choices:** ½

Sweet Success Tip

Five-spice powder typically consists of equal parts cinnamon, cloves, fennel seed, star anise and Szechuan peppercorns. Look for it with other spices at the grocery store.

Mega-Bucks Shortbread

{ **Gold Medal Flour Scratch Bakers' Club Baking Contest Winner** Lori Falce }

PREP TIME: 20 minutes **START TO FINISH:** 2 hours 20 minutes   **36 bars**

¾ cup butter, softened

¼ cup packed brown sugar

1½ cups all-purpose flour

½ teaspoon salt

½ cup chopped dry-roasted macadamia nuts

1 can (14 oz) sweetened condensed milk (not evaporated)

1 bag (12 oz) white vanilla baking chips (2 cups)

4 oz dried pineapple, finely chopped (¾ cup)

1 bag (12 oz) semisweet chocolate chips (2 cups)

1 tablespoon butter

¼ cup whipping cream

1 Heat oven to 350°F. In medium bowl, beat ¾ cup softened butter and the brown sugar until creamy. Add flour and salt; mix until soft dough forms. Stir in nuts. Press in ungreased 9-inch square pan. Bake 25 to 30 minutes or until light golden brown. Cool 10 minutes.

2 In medium microwavable bowl, microwave sweetened condensed milk and vanilla baking chips uncovered on High 1 to 2 minutes, stirring every 30 seconds, until chips are completely melted and mixture is smooth. Stir in dried pineapple. Pour over shortbread in pan. Refrigerate about 1 hour 30 minutes or until set.

3 In small microwavable bowl, microwave chocolate chips, 1 tablespoon butter and the whipping cream uncovered on High 1 to 2 minutes, stirring every 30 seconds, until chips are completely melted. Spread over pineapple layer. Refrigerate about 1 hour or until set. For 36 bars, cut into 6 rows by 6 rows. Store covered in refrigerator.

1 Bar: Calories 220; Total Fat 12g (Saturated Fat 8g; Trans Fat 0g); Cholesterol 15mg; Sodium 100mg; Total Carbohydrate 26g (Dietary Fiber 1g); Protein 2g **Exchanges:** ½ Starch, 1 Other Carbohydrate, 2½ Fat **Carbohydrate Choices:** 2

Chocolate and Orange Pecan Shortbread

{ **Celebrate the Season—Holiday Cookie Contest Winner** Amy Tong }

PREP TIME: 1 hour 30 minutes **START TO FINISH:** 2 hours 15 minutes   **2 dozen cookies**

1½ **cups unsalted butter, softened**
 1 **cup sugar**
 2 **tablespoons grated orange peel**
 1 **teaspoon vanilla**
 1 **teaspoon orange extract**
3½ **cups all-purpose flour**
 ¼ **teaspoon salt**
1½ **cups finely chopped pecans**
 1 **cup miniature semisweet chocolate chips**

1 Heat oven to 350°F. In large bowl, beat butter and sugar with electric mixer on medium speed until combined. Beat in orange peel, vanilla and orange extract. On low speed, beat in flour and salt. Stir in pecans and chocolate chips.

2 Divide dough in half; shape into 2 flat rounds. Wrap 1 round in plastic wrap.

3 On floured surface, roll unwrapped dough about ½ inch thick. Cut into 2½-inch circles with plain or fluted cookie cutter (or cut into desired shapes). On ungreased cookie sheets, place cookies about 1 inch apart. Repeat with second round.

4 Bake 15 to 19 minutes or until edges begin to brown. Remove from cookie sheets to cooling racks.

1 Cookie: Calories 290; Total Fat 19g (Saturated Fat 9g; Trans Fat 0g); Cholesterol 30mg; Sodium 25mg; Total Carbohydrate 28g (Dietary Fiber 1g); Protein 3g **Exchanges:** 1 Starch, 1 Other Carbohydrate, 3½ Fat **Carbohydrate Choices:** 2

Sweet Success Tip

Don't use too much flour on your work surface when rolling the dough, as it could affect the texture of the baked cookies.

Chewy Cranberry-Oatmeal Cookies
with Orange Icing

{ **Celebrate the Season—Holiday Cookie Contest Winner** Ungala Gillespie }

PREP TIME: 45 minutes **START TO FINISH:** 1 hour   **2 dozen cookies**

COOKIES

- ¾ **cup butter or margarine, softened**
- 1 **cup packed light brown sugar**
- 2 **eggs**
- 2 **teaspoons vanilla**
- 2 **teaspoons grated orange peel**
- 2 **cups quick-cooking oats**
- 1 **cup all-purpose flour**
- ⅔ **teaspoon baking soda**
- 1 **teaspoon ground cinnamon**
- 1 **cup sweetened dried cranberries**

ICING

- 1 **cup powdered sugar**
- ¼ **teaspoon vanilla**
- 3 **to 4 teaspoons orange juice**

1 Heat oven to 350°F. In large bowl, beat butter, brown sugar, eggs, vanilla and orange peel with electric mixer on medium speed until light and fluffy, or mix with spoon. Stir in remaining cookie ingredients.

2 Onto ungreased cookie sheets, drop dough by tablespoonfuls 2 inches apart.

3 Bake 11 to 14 minutes or until golden brown. Remove from cookie sheets to cooling racks; cool completely, about 15 minutes.

4 In small bowl, stir powdered sugar, vanilla and enough orange juice until thin enough to drizzle. Spoon into small resealable food-storage plastic bag; cut off tiny corner of bag. Squeeze bag to drizzle icing over cookies.

1 Cookie: Calories 180; Total Fat 7g (Saturated Fat 4g; Trans Fat 0g); Cholesterol 35mg; Sodium 85mg; Total Carbohydrate 27g (Dietary Fiber 1g); Protein 2g **Exchanges:** ½ Starch, 1½ Other Carbohydrate, 1½ Fat **Carbohydrate Choices:** 2

Sweet Success Tip

You'll need 1 medium orange for the grated peel in the cookie dough and the juice in the icing.

Memory Lane Oatmeal Peanut Butter Creme Sandwiches

{ **Cookie Contest Winner** Nancy Elliott }

PREP TIME: 1 hour **START TO FINISH:** 1 hour 15 minutes   **20 sandwich cookies**

COOKIES

- **1   pouch Betty Crocker oatmeal cookie mix**
- **¼   cup packed brown sugar**
- **½   cup butter or margarine, softened**
- **½   cup creamy peanut butter**
- **1   tablespoon water**
- **1   egg**

FILLING

- **1   cup creamy peanut butter**
- **½   cup Betty Crocker Rich & Creamy vanilla frosting**
- **4   teaspoons milk**

1 Heat oven to 375°F. In large bowl, stir cookie mix, brown sugar, butter, ½ cup peanut butter, the water and egg until soft dough forms.

2 Roll dough into 40 (1¼-inch) balls. On ungreased cookie sheets, place balls 2 inches apart. Press with fingers to slightly flatten.

3 Bake 9 to 10 minutes or until light golden brown. Cool 3 minutes; remove from cookie sheets to cooling racks. Cool completely, about 15 minutes.

4 In small bowl, stir filling ingredients until well blended. For each sandwich cookie, spread about 1 tablespoon filling on bottom of 1 cookie; top with another cookie, bottom side down. Press together lightly, twisting slightly. Store tightly covered at room temperature.

1 Sandwich Cookie: Calories 300; Total Fat 17g (Saturated Fat 5g; Trans Fat 0.5g); Cholesterol 25mg; Sodium 230mg; Total Carbohydrate 31g (Dietary Fiber 1g); Protein 7g **Exchanges:** 1 Starch, 1 Other Carbohydrate, ½ Medium-Fat Meat, 3 Fat **Carbohydrate Choices:** 2

Sweet Success Tip

Spray your measuring cup with cooking spray before measuring the peanut butter, and the peanut butter will slide right out!

Apricot Bars with Cardamom-Butter Glaze

{ **Cookie Contest Winner** Patrice Hurd }

PREP TIME: 1 hour 10 minutes **START TO FINISH:** 2 hours 45 minutes   **32 bars**

FILLING

- **1** large orange
- **2** cups chopped dried apricots
- **¼** cup granulated sugar
- **⅔** cup water
- **2** tablespoons butter or margarine

COOKIE BASE

- **1** pouch Betty Crocker sugar cookie mix
- **1** teaspoon ground cardamom
- **½** cup cold butter or margarine
- **¼** teaspoon almond extract
- **1** egg, slightly beaten
- **½** cup sliced almonds, coarsely chopped

GLAZE

- **½** cup powdered sugar
- **2** tablespoons butter or margarine, melted
- **¼** teaspoon ground cardamom
- **¼** teaspoon almond extract
- **1** to 2 teaspoons warm water

1 Heat oven to 350°F. Spray bottom and sides of 13×9-inch pan with cooking spray. Grate 2 teaspoons peel and squeeze juice from orange. In 2-quart saucepan, heat orange juice, orange peel, apricots, granulated sugar and ⅔ cup water to boiling over medium heat, stirring occasionally. Reduce heat to medium-low; simmer 15 minutes, stirring occasionally. Remove from heat. Add 2 tablespoons butter; stir until melted. Mash filling with fork or potato masher until fairly smooth. Set aside.

2 In large bowl, mix cookie mix and 1 teaspoon cardamom. Cut in ½ cup butter, using pastry blender or fork, until mixture looks like coarse crumbs. Add almond extract and egg; toss with fork to combine. Reserve 1 cup crumb mixture.

3 Press remaining crumb mixture in bottom of pan. Bake 15 minutes.

4 Spoon filling evenly over warm cookie base. Stir almonds into reserved crumb mixture; sprinkle over filling. Bake 25 to 30 minutes longer or until topping is light golden brown. Cool 10 minutes.

5 In small bowl, stir glaze ingredients, using enough warm water until glaze is thin enough to drizzle. Place glaze in small resealable food-storage plastic bag; seal bag. Cut off small tip from one corner of bag. Squeeze bag to drizzle glaze over warm bars. Cool completely, about 1 hour. Cut into 8 rows by 4 rows. Store covered at room temperature.

1 Bar: Calories 150; Total Fat 7g (Saturated Fat 3g; Trans Fat 0.5g); Cholesterol 20mg; Sodium 80mg; Total Carbohydrate 21g (Dietary Fiber 1g); Protein 1g **Exchanges:** 1½ Other Carbohydrate, 1½ Fat **Carbohydrate Choices:** 1½

Sweet Success Tip

No cardamom? It's a unique aromatic spice, a member of the ginger family and also a bit pricey. If you leave it out of the recipe, the flavor will be different, but you'll still get a delicious bar. Go ahead and try it.

Butter Pecan Chews

{ **Celebrate the Season—Holiday Cookie Contest Winner** Lisa Chambers }

PREP TIME: 20 minutes **START TO FINISH:** 2 hours 35 minutes   **36 bars**

1½ **cups all-purpose flour**

3 **tablespoons granulated sugar**

¾ **cup butter or margarine, softened**

3 **eggs, separated**

2½ **cups packed light brown sugar**

1 **teaspoon vanilla**

½ **teaspoon salt**

1 **cup chopped pecans**

¾ **cup flaked coconut**

2 **tablespoons powdered sugar**

1 Heat oven to 375°F. Grease 13×9-inch pan with butter.

2 In medium bowl, mix flour, granulated sugar and butter. Press mixture in bottom of pan. Bake 12 to 14 minutes or until light brown.

3 Meanwhile, in large bowl, beat egg yolks, brown sugar, vanilla and salt with electric mixer. Stir in pecans and coconut. In small bowl, beat egg whites with electric mixer until foamy. Fold into egg yolk mixture.

4 Remove partially baked crust from oven. Spread filling evenly over crust. Reduce oven temperature to 350°F.

5 Bake 25 to 30 minutes longer or until deep golden brown and center is set. Sprinkle powdered sugar over bars. Cool on cooling rack. Cut into 6 rows by 6 rows.

1 Bar: Calories 160; Total Fat 7g (Saturated Fat 3.5g; Trans Fat 0g); Cholesterol 30mg; Sodium 75mg; Total Carbohydrate 22g (Dietary Fiber 0g); Protein 1g **Exchanges:** 1½ Other Carbohydrate, 1½ Fat **Carbohydrate Choices:** 1½

Sweet Success Tip

With a flavor like pecan pie, these rich and buttery bars would be perfect for Thanksgiving or Christmas and would also be great to take to a potluck gathering or bake sale.

Snow Covered Crunch Bars

{ **Cookie Contest Winner** Laura Eckel }

PREP TIME: 20 minutes **START TO FINISH:** 1 hour 30 minutes   **36 bars**

1   **pouch Betty Crocker sugar cookie mix**
1   **cup butter or margarine, softened**
1   **egg**
1   **package (12 oz) semisweet chocolate chips (2 cups)**
2½   **cups peanut butter**
6   **cups Rice Chex® cereal**
½   **to 1 cup powdered sugar**

1 Heat oven to 375°F. Spray 13×9-inch baking pan with cooking spray. In large bowl, stir cookie mix, ½ cup of the butter and the egg until soft dough forms. Press dough in bottom of pan. Bake 10 to 12 minutes or until edges are light golden brown. Cool 15 minutes.

2 In large microwavable bowl, microwave chocolate chips and remaining ½ cup butter on High about 1½ minutes, stirring after 1 minute, until melted and smooth. Add peanut butter; mix until well blended.

3 Place cereal in 1-gallon resealable food-storage plastic bag; seal bag. Using your hands, gently break cereal into small pieces. Gently stir cereal into chocolate mixture until cereal is coated. Spread cereal mixture evenly over cookie crust; gently press. Sprinkle with powdered sugar. Refrigerate about 1 hour or until bars are set. Cut into 6 rows by 6 rows. Store covered at room temperature.

1 Bar: Calories 300; Total Fat 18g (Saturated Fat 7g; Trans Fat 0.5g); Cholesterol 20mg; Sodium 200mg; Total Carbohydrate 27g (Dietary Fiber 1g); Protein 6g **Exchanges:** 1½ Starch, ½ Other Carbohydrate, 3½ Fat **Carbohydrate Choices:** 2

Sweet Success Tip

Package up larger size bars for bake sale success.

Crème Brûlée Cheesecake Bars

{ Cookie Contest Winner Jeanne Holt **}**

PREP TIME: 15 minutes **START TO FINISH:** 4 hours 20 minutes   **36 bars**

1 pouch Betty Crocker sugar cookie mix

1 box (4-serving size) French vanilla instant pudding and pie filling mix

2 tablespoons packed brown sugar

½ cup butter or margarine, melted

2½ teaspoons vanilla

2 whole eggs

2 packages (8 oz each) cream cheese, softened

½ cup sour cream

½ cup granulated sugar

3 egg yolks

⅔ cup toffee bits, finely crushed

1 Heat oven to 350°F. Lightly spray bottom and sides of 13×9-inch pan with cooking spray.

2 In large bowl, stir cookie mix, pudding mix, brown sugar, butter, 1 teaspoon of the vanilla and 1 whole egg until soft dough forms. Press dough in bottom and ½ inch up sides of pan.

3 In small bowl, beat cream cheese, sour cream and granulated sugar with electric mixer on medium speed until smooth. Add remaining whole egg, 3 egg yolks and remaining 1½ teaspoons vanilla; beat until smooth. Spread over crust in pan.

4 Bake 30 to 35 minutes or until set in center. Immediately sprinkle top with crushed toffee bits. Cool 30 minutes. Refrigerate about 3 hours or until chilled. Cut into 9 rows by 4 rows. Store covered in refrigerator.

1 Bar: Calories 190; Total Fat 11g (Saturated Fat 6g; Trans Fat 1g); Cholesterol 55mg; Sodium 160mg; Total Carbohydrate 20g (Dietary Fiber 0g); Protein 2g **Exchanges:** ½ Starch, 1 Other Carbohydrate, 2 Fat **Carbohydrate Choices:** 1

Sweet Success Tip

To crush the toffee bits, place in a small resealable food-storage plastic bag; pound with a rolling pin or flat side of a meat mallet.

Berry Best Lemon Bars

{ **Cookie Contest Winner** Carole Holt }

PREP TIME: 30 minutes **START TO FINISH:** 3 hours 30 minutes   **20 bars**

1 pouch Betty Crocker
  oatmeal cookie mix

½ cup butter or margarine,
  softened

1 egg

2 cups fresh blueberries

½ cup blueberry jam

2 cups prepared lemon
  pie filling

2½ cups frozen (thawed)
  whipped topping

1 Heat oven to 375°F. Lightly spray bottom and sides of 13×9-inch pan with cooking spray. In large bowl, stir cookie mix, butter and egg until soft dough forms. Reserve ⅓ cup of the cookie dough. Press remaining dough in bottom of pan. Bake 15 to 18 minutes or until golden brown. Cool completely, about 30 minutes.

2 Meanwhile, shape reserved cookie dough into 5 balls. Place on ungreased cookie sheet. Bake 8 to 9 minutes or until light golden brown. Cool 2 minutes; remove from cookie sheet to cooling rack. Cool completely, about 15 minutes.

3 In small bowl, mix blueberries and jam. Spread over cookie crust. Carefully spread lemon pie filling over blueberry layer. Spread whipped topping over lemon layer. Crumble cookies; sprinkle over whipped topping. Refrigerate at least 2 hours or until chilled. To serve, cut into 5 rows by 4 rows. Store covered in refrigerator.

1 Bar: Calories 230; Total Fat 8g (Saturated Fat 4.5g; Trans Fat 0g); Cholesterol 25mg; Sodium 220mg; Total Carbohydrate 36g (Dietary Fiber 0g); Protein 3g **Exchanges:** 1 Starch, 1½ Other Carbohydrate, 1½ Fat **Carbohydrate Choices:** 2½

Sweet Success Tip

Cut bars into bite-size squares for a dessert buffet.

Mochachino Dessert Bars
with White Mocha Drizzle

{ **Cookie Contest Winner** Brett Youman }

PREP TIME: 20 minutes START TO FINISH: 1 hour 45 minutes   **20 bars**

1   **pouch Betty Crocker double chocolate chunk cookie mix**

¼   **cup vegetable oil**

3   **tablespoons strong brewed coffee (room temperature)**

1   **egg**

½   **cup coarsely chopped macadamia nuts**

½   **cup flaked coconut, toasted**

½   **cup whipping cream**

3   **oz white chocolate baking squares, coarsely chopped**

2   **tablespoons coarsely chopped macadamia nuts**

1   Heat oven to 350°F. Line 9-inch square pan with foil. Spray foil with cooking spray.

2   In large bowl, stir cookie mix, oil, 2 tablespoons of the coffee, the egg, ½ cup macadamia nuts and coconut until soft dough forms. Spread in bottom of pan.

3   Bake 20 to 25 minutes or just until set. Cool completely, about 1 hour.

4   In small microwavable bowl, microwave whipping cream, white chocolate and remaining 1 tablespoon coffee uncovered on High about 1 minute 30 seconds, stirring every 30 seconds, until chocolate is melted and mixture is smooth.

5   Use foil to lift bars from pan; remove foil. Cut into 5 rows by 4 rows. Place bars on dessert plates. Spoon warm drizzle over bars; sprinkle with 2 tablespoons macadamia nuts. Serve immediately. Store bars tightly covered at room temperature. Store leftover drizzle covered in refrigerator.

To toast coconut, heat oven to 350°F. Spread coconut in ungreased shallow pan. Bake uncovered 5 to 7 minutes, stirring occasionally, until golden brown.

1 Bar: Calories 210; Total Fat 12g (Saturated Fat 5g; Trans Fat 0g); Cholesterol 20mg; Sodium 125mg; Total Carbohydrate 24g (Dietary Fiber 0g); Protein 2g **Exchanges:** ½ Starch, 1 Other Carbohydrate, 2½ Fat **Carbohydrate Choices:** 1½

Sweet Success Tip

Wait to drizzle the bars until just before serving. So if you won't be serving all of the bars the day you make them, store the bars and drizzle separately. The bars can stay at room temperature, but the drizzle needs to be refrigerated.

Pumpkin Streusel Cheesecake Bars

{ **Cookie Contest Winner** Judy Castranova }

PREP TIME: 45 minutes **START TO FINISH:** 3 hours   **24 bars**

COOKIE CRUST

- 1 pouch Betty Crocker oatmeal cookie mix
- ½ cup crushed gingersnap cookies
- ½ cup finely chopped pecans
- ½ cup cold butter or margarine

FILLING

- 2 packages (8 oz each) cream cheese, softened
- 1 cup sugar
- 1 cup canned pumpkin (not pumpkin pie mix)
- 2 tablespoons all-purpose flour
- 1 tablespoon pumpkin pie spice
- 2 tablespoons whipping cream
- 2 eggs

TOPPINGS

- ⅓ cup chocolate topping
- ⅓ cup caramel topping

1 Heat oven to 350°F. In large bowl, stir together cookie mix, crushed cookies and pecans. Cut in butter, using pastry blender or fork, until mixture looks like coarse crumbs. Reserve 1 cup mixture. Press remaining mixture in bottom of ungreased 13×9-inch pan. Bake 10 minutes. Cool 10 minutes.

2 Meanwhile, in large bowl, beat cream cheese and sugar with electric mixer on medium speed until smooth. Add remaining filling ingredients; beat until well blended. Pour over warm cookie crust. Sprinkle with reserved cookie crust mixture.

3 Bake 35 to 40 minutes or until center is set. Cool 30 minutes. Refrigerate about 2 hours or until chilled.

4 Before serving, place each topping in a small food-storage plastic bag, snip off a small corner of each bag and squeeze to drizzle chocolate and caramel toppings over bars. Cut into 6 rows by 4 rows. Store covered in refrigerator.

1 Bar: Calories 280; Total Fat 14g (Saturated Fat 7g; Trans Fat 0g); Cholesterol 50mg; Sodium 200mg; Total Carbohydrate 35g (Dietary Fiber 1g); Protein 4g **Exchanges:** 1 Starch, 1½ Other Carbohydrate, 2½ Fat **Carbohydrate Choices:** 2

Sweet Success Tip

A food processor can be used for even easier preparation. Place cookie crust ingredients in processor bowl; pulse until mixture looks like coarse crumbs. Reserve 1 cup. Press remaining cookie crust mixture in pan. Place filling ingredients in processor bowl; pulse until well blended. Continue recipe as directed.

Cranberry Crumb Bars

{ **Celebrate the Season—Holiday Cookie Contest Winner** Katie Goodman }

PREP TIME: 20 minutes START TO FINISH: 4 hours   24 bars

CRUST AND TOPPING

2½ cups all-purpose flour

1 cup sugar

½ cup ground slivered almonds

1 teaspoon baking powder

¼ teaspoon salt

1 cup cold butter

1 egg

¼ teaspoon ground cinnamon

FILLING

4 cups fresh or frozen cranberries

1 cup sugar

Juice of ½ orange (4 teaspoons)

1 tablespoon cornstarch

1 teaspoon vanilla

1 Heat oven to 375°F. Grease 13×9-inch pan with butter or cooking spray.

2 In large bowl, mix flour, 1 cup sugar, the almonds, baking powder and salt. Cut in butter, using pastry blender (or pulling 2 table knives through ingredients in opposite directions), until mixture looks like coarse crumbs. Stir in egg. Press 2½ cups of crumb mixture in bottom of pan. Stir cinnamon into remaining crumb mixture; set aside.

3 In medium bowl, stir together all filling ingredients. Spoon evenly over crust. Spoon reserved crumb mixture evenly over filling.

4 Bake 45 to 55 minutes or until top is light golden brown. Cool completely. Refrigerate until chilled. Cut into 6 rows by 4 rows. Store tightly covered in refrigerator.

1 Bar: Calories 210; Total Fat 9g (Saturated Fat 5g; Trans Fat 0g); Cholesterol 30mg; Sodium 105mg; Total Carbohydrate 30g (Dietary Fiber 1g); Protein 2g **Exchanges:** 1 Starch, ½ Fruit, ½ Other Carbohydrate, 1½ Fat **Carbohydrate Choices:** 2

Sweet Success Tips

A food processor works great for grinding the almonds. You will need about ⅔ cup slivered almonds to measure ½ cup ground almonds.

Stock up on cranberries while they're abundant in stores. Just toss them in the freezer and use as you need them; they'll be good for about a year. If you're using frozen cranberries for this recipe, there is no need to thaw them first.

Apple Streusel Cheesecake Bars

{ **Cookie Contest Winner** Brenda Watts }

PREP TIME: 20 minutes START TO FINISH: 3 hours 40 minutes   **24 bars**

1   **pouch Betty Crocker oatmeal cookie mix**

½   **cup cold butter or margarine**

2   **packages (8 oz each) cream cheese, softened**

½   **cup sugar**

2   **tablespoons all-purpose flour**

1   **teaspoon vanilla**

1   **egg**

1   **can (21 oz) apple pie filling**

½   **teaspoon ground cinnamon**

¼   **cup chopped walnuts**

1 Heat oven to 350°F. Spray 13×9-inch pan with cooking spray. In large bowl, place cookie mix. Using pastry blender (or pulling 2 table knives through mixture in opposite directions), cut in butter until mixture looks like coarse crumbs. Reserve 1½ cups crumb mixture; press remaining crumbs in bottom of pan. Bake 10 minutes.

2 Meanwhile, in large bowl, beat cream cheese, sugar, flour, vanilla and egg with electric mixer on medium speed until smooth.

3 Spread cream cheese mixture evenly over partially baked crust. In medium bowl, mix pie filling and cinnamon. Spoon evenly over cream cheese mixture. Sprinkle reserved crumbs over top. Sprinkle with walnuts.

4 Bake 35 to 40 minutes or until light golden brown. Cool about 30 minutes. Refrigerate to chill, about 2 hours. Cut into 6 rows by 4 rows. Cover and refrigerate any remaining bars.

1 Bar: Calories 240; Total Fat 12g (Saturated Fat 7g; Trans Fat 0g); Cholesterol 40mg; Sodium 160mg; Total Carbohydrate 29g (Dietary Fiber 0g); Protein 3g **Exchanges:** 1 Starch, 1 Other Carbohydrate, 2 Fat **Carbohydrate Choices:** 2

Black Forest Dream Bars

{ **Cookie Contest Winner** Laureen Silva }

PREP TIME: 30 minutes **START TO FINISH:** 3 hours 40 minutes **20 bars**

1 **pouch Betty Crocker double chocolate chunk cookie mix**

¼ **cup vegetable oil**

1 **egg**

1 **can (21 oz) cherry pie filling**

2 **packages (8 oz each) cream cheese, softened**

½ **cup sugar**

1 **container (8 oz) frozen whipped topping, thawed**

1 Heat oven to 350°F. Lightly spray bottom and sides of 13×9-inch pan with cooking spray. In large bowl, stir cookie mix, oil and egg until soft dough forms. Onto ungreased cookie sheet, drop 3 tablespoonfuls of dough 2 inches apart to make 3 cookies. Bake 12 to 13 minutes or until set. Cool 2 minutes; remove from cookie sheet to cooling rack. Cool completely, about 15 minutes.

2 Meanwhile, press remaining cookie dough in bottom of sprayed pan. Reserve 1 cup cherry pie filling for topping; cover with plastic wrap and refrigerate. In large bowl, beat cream cheese, sugar and the remaining pie filling with electric mixer on medium speed until blended. Spread cream cheese mixture over crust in pan.

3 Bake 35 to 40 minutes or until set. Cool 30 minutes. Refrigerate about 1 hour or until chilled.

4 Spread whipped topping over cream cheese layer. Top with spoonfuls of the reserved cherry pie filling. Coarsely crumble baked cookies; sprinkle over top of bars. Refrigerate at least 1 hour for flavors to blend. To serve, cut into 5 rows by 4 rows. Store covered in refrigerator.

1 Bar: Calories 320; Total Fat 15g (Saturated Fat 8g; Trans Fat 0g); Cholesterol 35mg; Sodium 190mg; Total Carbohydrate 43g (Dietary Fiber 0g); Protein 3g **Exchanges:** ½ Starch, 2½ Other Carbohydrate, 3 Fat **Carbohydrate Choices:** 3

Sweet Success Tip

Raspberry pie filling makes a good substitution for the cherry.

Chocolate Marbled Banana Nut Bars

{ **Cookie Contest Winner** Patricia Ingalls }

PREP TIME: 20 minutes START TO FINISH: 3 hours 15 minutes   20 bars

1 pouch Betty Crocker sugar cookie mix

½ cup plus 2 tablespoons butter or margarine, softened

1 egg

¾ cup mashed very ripe banana

½ cup chopped walnuts

1¼ cups semisweet chocolate chips

1 Heat oven to 350°F. Spray bottom and sides of 9-inch square pan with cooking spray. In large bowl, stir cookie mix, ½ cup of the butter and the egg until soft dough forms. Reserve 1 cup of the dough. To the remaining dough, add mashed banana and walnuts; mix well. Spread in bottom of pan.

2 In medium microwavable bowl, microwave ¾ cup of the chocolate chips with the remaining 2 tablespoons butter on High about 1 minute, stirring after 30 seconds, until melted and smooth. Add reserved cookie dough; stir until well blended. Drop chocolate dough by spoonfuls evenly over top of banana mixture; spread gently to almost cover. Swirl chocolate mixture into banana mixture with knife for marbled design.

3 Bake 35 to 40 minutes or until toothpick inserted in center comes out clean. Cool 15 minutes.

4 In small microwavable bowl, microwave remaining ½ cup chocolate chips on High about 1 minute, stirring after 30 seconds, until melted and smooth. Put melted chocolate in small resealable food-storage plastic bag. Cut off one corner of the bag; squeeze to drizzle over bars. Cool completely, about 2 hours. Cut into 5 rows by 4 rows. Store covered at room temperature.

1 Bar: Calories 240; Total Fat 13g (Saturated Fat 6g; Trans Fat 1g); Cholesterol 25mg; Sodium 115mg; Total Carbohydrate 28g (Dietary Fiber 1g); Protein 2g **Exchanges:** 1 Starch, 1 Other Carbohydrate, 2½ Fat **Carbohydrate Choices:** 2

Sweet Success Tip

Got ripe bananas? Stir 'em up with sugar cookie mix to make yummy banana bars.

Salty Caramel Peanut Brittle Bars

{ **Cookie Contest Winner** Deborah Vanni }

PREP TIME: 15 minutes **START TO FINISH:** 2 hours 10 minutes **48 bars**

1 **pouch Betty Crocker sugar cookie mix**

¼ **cup packed brown sugar**

¾ **cup cold unsalted or salted butter, cut into pieces**

2 **cups salted cocktail peanuts**

1 **cup semisweet chocolate chips (6 oz)**

1 **jar (12.25 oz) caramel topping**

½ **teaspoon coarse sea salt**

1 Heat oven to 350°F. Spray 15×10×1-inch pan with sides with cooking spray. Reserve 3 tablespoons cookie mix.

2 Place remaining cookie mix in large bowl. Stir in brown sugar. Using pastry blender or fork, cut in butter until mixture looks like coarse crumbs. Press mixture in bottom of pan. Bake 18 minutes.

3 Immediately sprinkle cookie crust with peanuts and chocolate chips. In small microwavable bowl, microwave caramel topping on High about 30 seconds or until of drizzling consistency. Add reserved cookie mix; blend well. Drizzle evenly over peanuts and chocolate chips. Sprinkle evenly with salt.

4 Bake 12 to 14 minutes longer or until caramel is bubbly. Cool completely, about 1 hour. Refrigerate 15 minutes to set chocolate. Cut into 8 rows by 6 rows. Store covered at room temperature.

1 Bar: Calories 150; Total Fat 8g (Saturated Fat 3g; Trans Fat 0g); Cholesterol 10mg; Sodium 130mg; Total Carbohydrate 17g (Dietary Fiber 0g); Protein 2g **Exchanges:** ½ Starch, ½ Other Carbohydrate, 1½ Fat **Carbohydrate Choices:** 1

Sweet Success Tip

The secret to cutting bars easily is to line the pan with foil. Just lift out the baked bars and cut. Spray the foil for best results.

Mocha-Toffee Truffle Bars

{ **Cookie Contest Winner** Mary Shivers }

PREP TIME: 30 minutes START TO FINISH: 3 hours   **36 bars**

1 pouch Betty Crocker sugar cookie mix

½ cup butter or margarine, melted

1 egg, slightly beaten

1 can (14 oz) sweetened condensed milk (not evaporated)

1 teaspoon instant coffee granules or crystals

1 bag (11.5 oz) milk chocolate chips (2 cups)

1 bag (8 oz) toffee bits (1½ cups)

1 cup chopped pecans

1 Heat oven to 350°F. In large bowl, stir cookie mix, butter and egg until soft dough forms. Spread in bottom of ungreased 13×9-inch pan. Bake 12 to 15 minutes or until light golden brown.

2 Meanwhile, in small microwavable bowl, microwave condensed milk uncovered on High 1 minute. Stir in coffee granules until mostly dissolved; set aside.

3 Sprinkle warm crust with chocolate chips, toffee bits and pecans. Drizzle condensed milk mixture evenly over pecans.

4 Bake 23 to 27 minutes or until top is golden brown and bubbly in center. Cool completely, about 2 hours. Cut into 9 rows by 4 rows. Store covered at room temperature.

1 Bar: Calories 220; Total Fat 12g (Saturated Fat 6g; Trans Fat 0.5g); Cholesterol 20mg; Sodium 100mg; Total Carbohydrate 26g (Dietary Fiber 0g); Protein 2g **Exchanges:** ½ Starch, 1 Other Carbohydrate, 2½ Fat **Carbohydrate Choices:** 2

Peanut-Buttery Fudge Bars

{ Cookie Contest Winner Robin Wilson }

PREP TIME: 20 minutes **START TO FINISH:** 3 hours 5 minutes **24 bars**

COOKIE BASE

- **1 pouch Betty Crocker peanut butter cookie mix**
- **3 tablespoons vegetable oil**
- **1 tablespoon water**
- **1 egg**

TOPPING

- **1 cup hot fudge topping**
- **1 cup Betty Crocker Rich & Creamy cream cheese frosting**
- **¼ cup creamy peanut butter**
- **1 container (8 oz) frozen whipped topping, thawed**
- **2 bars (2.1 oz each) chocolate-covered crispy peanut-buttery candy, unwrapped, finely crushed**

1 Heat oven to 350°F. Spray bottom only of 13×9-inch pan with cooking spray.

2 In large bowl, stir cookie mix, oil, water and egg until soft dough forms. Press in bottom of pan.

3 Bake 12 to 15 minutes or until light golden brown. Cool completely, about 30 minutes.

4 Spread fudge topping over cooled cookie base. In large bowl, mix frosting and peanut butter. Gently fold in whipped topping and candy until well blended. Spoon mixture over fudge topping and carefully spread to evenly cover. Refrigerate about 2 hours or until chilled. Sprinkle with additional chocolate-covered candy, coarsely crushed, if desired. Cut into 6 rows by 4 rows. Store covered in refrigerator.

1 Bar: Calories 260; Total Fat 12g (Saturated Fat 4g; Trans Fat 0.5g); Cholesterol 10mg; Sodium 200mg; Total Carbohydrate 36g (Dietary Fiber 0g); Protein 3g **Exchanges:** 1 Starch, 1½ Other Carbohydrate, 2 Fat **Carbohydrate Choices:** 2½

Sweet Success Tip

To crush candy bars, place in small resealable food-storage plastic bag; crush with rolling pin or flat side of meat mallet.

Coconut Bonbon Bars

{ **Cookie Contest Winner** Bev Jones }

PREP TIME: 35 minutes START TO FINISH: 3 hours 55 minutes   **36 bars**

COOKIE BASE

- **1** **pouch Betty Crocker double chocolate chunk cookie mix**
- **¼** **cup vegetable oil**
- **2** **tablespoons water**
- **1** **egg**

FILLING

- **½** **cup butter, softened**
- **1** **can (14 oz) sweetened condensed milk (not evaporated)**
- **1** **teaspoon vanilla**
- **6** **cups powdered sugar**
- **1½** **cups coconut**
- **½** **cup finely chopped blanched almonds**

TOPPING

- **½** **cup whipping cream**
- **1** **bag (12 oz) semisweet chocolate chips (2 cups)**
- **½** **cup butter (do not use margarine)**

1 Heat oven to 350°F. In large bowl, stir cookie base ingredients until soft dough forms. Press in bottom of ungreased 13×9-inch pan. Bake 12 minutes. Cool completely, about 30 minutes.

2 Meanwhile, in large bowl, beat softened butter, condensed milk and vanilla with electric mixer on medium speed until smooth. Gradually beat in powdered sugar. Stir in coconut and almonds until well blended. Spread filling evenly over cooled cookie base. Cover; refrigerate about 1 hour or until filling is set.

3 Meanwhile, in 2-quart nonstick saucepan, heat topping ingredients over medium-low heat, stirring constantly, until melted and smooth. Cool about 10 minutes or until lukewarm.

4 Pour topping over filling; spread to cover filling. Refrigerate uncovered about 2 hours or until set. Before cutting into bars, let stand 10 minutes at room temperature. Cut into 9 rows by 4 rows. Store covered in refrigerator.

1 Bar: Calories 330; Total Fat 15g (Saturated Fat 8g; Trans Fat 0g); Cholesterol 25mg; Sodium 125mg; Total Carbohydrate 45g (Dietary Fiber 1g); Protein 2g **Exchanges:** ½ Starch, 2½ Other Carbohydrate, 3 Fat **Carbohydrate Choices:** 3

Sweet Success Tips

An easy variation is to leave out the almonds in the filling and then sprinkle coarsely chopped smoked almonds over the chocolate topping. It adds that salty and sweet dimension.

Cut bars into mini bite-size treats and serve in mini paper or metallic liners.

Nanaimo Cookie Bars

{ **Cookie Contest Winner** Karen Hayden }

PREP TIME: 45 minutes **START TO FINISH:** 2 hours 5 minutes   **36 bars**

COOKIE BASE

- 1 **pouch Betty Crocker double chocolate chunk cookie mix**
- 1 **cup graham cracker crumbs**
- ½ **cup chopped nut topping or chopped walnuts**
- ½ **cup flaked coconut**
- 1 **cup butter or margarine, melted**
- 1 **egg**

FILLING

- 4 **cups powdered sugar**
- 4 **tablespoons vanilla instant pudding and pie filling mix**
- ⅓ **cup butter or margarine, softened**
- ¼ **cup milk**

TOPPING

- 1 **bag (12 oz) semisweet chocolate chips (2 cups)**
- ¼ **cup butter or margarine**

1 Heat oven to 350°F. Line bottom and sides of 13×9-inch pan with foil, leaving foil overhanging at 2 opposite sides of pan.

2 In large bowl, stir cookie base ingredients until well mixed. Spread into pan; press lightly.

3 Bake 16 to 18 minutes or until set. Cool completely, about 30 minutes.

4 In another large bowl, stir together powdered sugar and dry pudding mix. Add ⅓ cup butter and the milk; beat with electric mixer on medium speed until smooth (filling will be very thick). Spoon over cookie base; press evenly to cover. Refrigerate while making topping.

5 In small microwavable bowl, microwave topping ingredients uncovered on High 1 minute to 1 minute 30 seconds, stirring every 30 seconds until melted and smooth. Spread over filling. Refrigerate uncovered until set, about 30 minutes.

6 Use foil to lift bars from pan; pull foil from sides of bars. Cut into 9 rows by 4 rows. Store covered in refrigerator.

1 Bar: Calories 270; Total Fat 14g (Saturated Fat 8g; Trans Fat 0g); Cholesterol 25mg; Sodium 150mg; Total Carbohydrate 34g (Dietary Fiber 0g); Protein 1g **Exchanges:** ½ Starch, 1½ Other Carbohydrate, 3 Fat **Carbohydrate Choices:** 2

Sweet Success Tip

Canadian legend claims that these yummy bars originated in Nanaimo, Canada, in the 1950s. Although unsubstantiated, the story is that a local housewife submitted the recipe under the name "Nanaimo Bars" for a recipe contest.

Neapolitan Cream Cheese Bars

{ Cookie Contest Winner Annie Walter **}**

PREP TIME: 20 minutes START TO FINISH: 3 hours 35 minutes   **36 bars**

1 **pouch Betty Crocker double chocolate chunk cookie mix**

½ **cup butter or margarine, melted**

3 **eggs**

2 **packages (8 oz each) cream cheese, softened**

½ **cup sugar**

1 **teaspoon vanilla**

1 **container Betty Crocker Whipped strawberry frosting**

1 Heat oven to 350°F. Spray bottom and sides of 13×9-inch pan with cooking spray. In large bowl, stir cookie mix, melted butter and 1 egg until soft dough forms. Press dough in bottom of pan. Bake 10 minutes. Cool 10 minutes.

2 Meanwhile, in large bowl, beat cream cheese, sugar, vanilla and the remaining 2 eggs with electric mixer on medium speed until smooth. Spread over cookie base.

3 Bake 30 to 35 minutes or until set. Cool 30 minutes. Spread frosting over cream cheese layer. Refrigerate about 2 hours or until chilled. Cut into 6 rows by 6 rows. Store covered in refrigerator.

1 Bar: Calories 180; Total Fat 11g (Saturated Fat 6g; Trans Fat 1g); Cholesterol 40mg; Sodium 135mg; Total Carbohydrate 20g (Dietary Fiber 0g); Protein 1g **Exchanges:** ½ Starch, 1 Other Carbohydrate, 2 Fat **Carbohydrate Choices:** 1

Sweet Success Tip

Use a wet knife for cutting cheesecake bars, wiping off crumbs after each cut.

"Lime in the Coconut" Frosted Cheesecake Bars

{ **Cookie Contest Winner** Janice Elder }

PREP TIME: 15 minutes **START TO FINISH:** 3 hours 25 minutes **24 bars**

COOKIE BASE

- 1 **pouch Betty Crocker sugar cookie mix**
- 2 **tablespoons all-purpose flour**
- ⅓ **cup butter or margarine, softened**
- 1 **egg, slightly beaten**

FILLING

- 2 **packages (8 oz each) cream cheese, softened**
- 1 **can (16 oz) cream of coconut (not coconut milk)**
- 3 **tablespoons lime juice**
- 1 **teaspoon vanilla**
- 2 **eggs**

TOPPING

- 1 **container Betty Crocker Whipped cream cheese frosting**
- 1¼ **cups coconut, toasted**＊
- 2 **teaspoons grated lime peel**

1 Heat oven to 350°F. Spray bottom and sides of 13×9-inch pan with cooking spray. In large bowl, stir cookie base ingredients until soft dough forms. Press evenly in bottom of pan. Bake 15 to 18 minutes or until golden brown. Cool 15 minutes.

2 Meanwhile, in large bowl, beat cream cheese with electric mixer on medium speed until light and fluffy. Beat in cream of coconut until well blended. Beat in lime juice, vanilla and 2 eggs until smooth. Spread over cookie base.

3 Bake 40 to 45 minutes or until set and light golden brown on edges. Cool in pan on cooling rack 30 minutes. Refrigerate 1 hour to cool completely.

4 Carefully spread frosting over filling. Sprinkle with coconut and lime peel. Cover; refrigerate 30 minutes. Cut into 6 rows by 4 rows. Store covered in refrigerator.

＊To toast coconut, spread on ungreased cookie sheet and bake at 350°F 10 to 15 minutes, stirring occasionally, until coconut is light golden brown.

1 Bar: Calories 340; Total Fat 23g (Saturated Fat 14g; Trans Fat 2g); Cholesterol 55mg; Sodium 180mg; Total Carbohydrate 29g (Dietary Fiber 0g); Protein 4g **Exchanges:** 1 Starch, 1 Other Carbohydrate, 4½ Fat **Carbohydrate Choices:** 2

Metric Conversion Guide

Volume

U.S. UNITS	CANADIAN METRIC	AUSTRALIAN METRIC
¼ teaspoon	1 mL	1 ml
½ teaspoon	2 mL	2 ml
1 teaspoon	5 mL	5 ml
1 tablespoon	15 mL	20 ml
¼ cup	50 mL	60 ml
⅓ cup	75 mL	80 ml
½ cup	125 mL	125 ml
⅔ cup	150 mL	170 ml
¾ cup	175 mL	190 ml
1 cup	250 mL	250 ml
1 quart	1 liter	1 liter
1½ quarts	1.5 liters	1.5 liters
2 quarts	2 liters	2 liters
2½ quarts	2.5 liters	2.5 liters
3 quarts	3 liters	3 liters
4 quarts	4 liters	4 liters

Measurements

INCHES	CENTIMETERS
1	2.5
2	5.0
3	7.5
4	10.0
5	12.5
6	15.0
7	17.5
8	20.5
9	23.0
10	25.5
11	28.0
12	30.5
13	33.0

Temperatures

FAHRENHEIT	CELSIUS
32°	0°
212°	100°
250°	120°
275°	140°
300°	150°
325°	160°
350°	180°
375°	190°
400°	200°
425°	220°
450°	230°
475°	240°
500°	260°

Weight

U.S. UNITS	CANADIAN METRIC	AUSTRALIAN METRIC
1 ounce	30 grams	30 grams
2 ounces	55 grams	60 grams
3 ounces	85 grams	90 grams
4 ounces (¼ pound)	115 grams	125 grams
8 ounces (½ pound)	225 grams	225 grams
16 ounces (1 pound)	455 grams	500 grams
1 pound	455 grams	0.5 kilogram

Note: The recipes in this cookbook have not been developed or tested using metric measures. When converting recipes to metric, some variations in quality may be noted.

index

Recommended intake for a daily diet of 2,000 calories as set by the Food and Drug Administration

Total Fat	Less than 65g
Saturated Fat	Less than 20g
Cholesterol	Less than 300mg
Sodium	Less than 2,400mg
Total Carbohydrate	300g
Dietary Fiber	25g